Web Usability For Dummies®

Usability Design Cycle Checklist

1. **Study User.** Study the current and intended user base. Find out how they are alike and different from overall Web users, current customers, and stakeholders. Find out what they want and expect from your organization. If a version of the site is live, study how it's being used. If appropriate, get feedback on features and usability of competing and comparable sites.

2. **Set Goals.** Set goals for the site. Overall goals should reflect organization's goals, such as getting new customers, reducing costs, etc. Set SMART goals: Specific, Measurable, Achievable, Realistic (this one's the toughest), and Time-bounded. Examples of things to set goals for: number of tech support answer pages viewed, number of PDF files downloaded, and number of sales made.

3. **Design.** Create site navigation, making sure it is appropriate and scalable. Create templates for specific types of pages (section pages, task pages, and content pages). Design home page.

4. **Build.** Fill templates with content and post as Web pages. Adjust file hierarchy or database as needed.

5. **Test.** First get insiders and then real users in front of the product in formal user tests and broader, informal usability tests. Track feature requests and bugs — prioritize bugs and fix the important ones (this is an engineering issue with huge usability impact).

6. **Deliver Product.** Put the changed or new site up live on the Web. Marketing gets users to site. Make sure site shows up in search engine results. Track customer support issues with site, feature requests, and bugs. Keep watch over competitors' Web sites. Start studying the users again as they interact with the site — check that the site is meeting the goals.

7. **Plan for future updates.** Then repeat!

Web Writing Checklist

Principles for writing for the Web:

Short. As short as possible to convey the meaning.

Jargon alert. Avoid jargon; define new terms when used.

Perfect spelling. No spelling or obvious grammatical errors. That means none as in *zero*.

Bullets. Lots of bulleted lists instead of text paragraphs.

Short paragraphs. Paragraphs one to three sentences long with clear topic sentence.

Headers. One heading every few paragraphs.

Inverse pyramid. Key content is at top of page, top of section, and top of paragraph.

Links work. Every link in the text works.

Links stay in site. Links don't go off the site without warning.

PDF equivalent. Key content has a longer, more nicely formatted equivalent in PDF format.

For Dummies: Bestselling Book Series for Beginners

Web Usability For Dummies®

Cheat Sheet

Usability Study Checklist

- Treat the users with respect
- The users can end the study at any time they wish
- Actively listen to the users
- There are no right or wrong answers
- The users have a right to their opinions
- The users have a right to privacy and confidentiality
- The users deserve to be compensated for their time
- The users are a (potential or actual) customer
- The users are not designers, but providers of input that will be used in the design process

Basic Usability Checklist	Advanced Usability Checklist
Acceptable page download time (under 10 seconds at 56K)	Site ranked in search engine results
Site home page appears in search engine results	Specific pages ranked in search engine results
Alternative text for images	Predictable URL for home page
Easy-to-use navigation throughout site	Readable URLs for section pages
Link text is highly descriptive	Readable URLs for content pages
Organized by user goals	Effective error recovery
Top tasks always available	Essential content
Short paths to content	Active personalization
Short paths through tasks	Comprehensive and precise search
Understandable language throughout site	Site adjusts to match user actions
Consistent feedback	Site reliability
Legible text	Contextual help
Links in text use standard colors and formatting	Live help
Prominent display of contact info	Transactions available

Hungry Minds, the Hungry Minds logo, For Dummies, the For Dummies Bestselling Book Series logo and all related trade dress are trademarks or registered trademarks of Hungry Minds, Inc. All other trademarks are the property of their respective owners.

Copyright © 2002 Hungry Minds, Inc.
All rights reserved.
Cheat Sheet $2.95 value. Item 1546-2.
For more information about Hungry Minds,
call 1-800-762-2974.

For Dummies: Bestselling Book Series for Beginners

References for the Rest of Us!®

BESTSELLING BOOK SERIES

Are you intimidated and confused by computers? Do you find that traditional manuals are overloaded with technical details you'll never use? Do your friends and family always call you to fix simple problems on their PCs? Then the For Dummies® computer book series from Hungry Minds, Inc. is for you.

For Dummies books are written for those frustrated computer users who know they aren't really dumb but find that PC hardware, software, and indeed the unique vocabulary of computing make them feel helpless. For Dummies books use a lighthearted approach, a down-to-earth style, and even cartoons and humorous icons to dispel computer novices' fears and build their confidence. Lighthearted but not lightweight, these books are a perfect survival guide for anyone forced to use a computer.

> "I like my copy so much I told friends; now they bought copies."
> — Irene C., Orwell, Ohio

> "Quick, concise, nontechnical, and humorous."
> — Jay A., Elburn, Illinois

> "Thanks, I needed this book. Now I can sleep at night."
> — Robin F., British Columbia, Canada

Already, millions of satisfied readers agree. They have made For Dummies books the #1 introductory level computer book series and have written asking for more. So, if you're looking for the most fun and easy way to learn about computers, look to For Dummies books to give you a helping hand.

Web Usability

FOR

DUMMIES®

by Richard Mander, PhD, and Bud Smith

Best-Selling Books • Digital Downloads • e-Books • Answer Networks • e-Newsletters • Branded Web Sites • e-Learning

New York, NY ♦ Cleveland, OH ♦ Indianapolis, IN

Web Usability For Dummies®

Published by
Hungry Minds, Inc.
909 Third Avenue
New York, NY 10022
www.hungryminds.com
www.dummies.com

Copyright © 2002 Hungry Minds, Inc. All rights reserved. No part of this book, including interior design, cover design, and icons, may be reproduced or transmitted in any form, by any means (electronic, photocopying, recording, or otherwise) without the prior written permission of the publisher.

Library of Congress Control Number: 2001092930

ISBN: 0-7645-1546-2

Printed in the United States of America

10 9 8 7 6 5 4 3 2 1

1B/SZ/RR/QR/IN

Distributed in the United States by Hungry Minds, Inc.

Distributed by CDG Books Canada Inc. for Canada; by Transworld Publishers Limited in the United Kingdom; by IDG Norge Books for Norway; by IDG Sweden Books for Sweden; by IDG Books Australia Publishing Corporation Pty. Ltd. for Australia and New Zealand; by TransQuest Publishers Pte Ltd. for Singapore, Malaysia, Thailand, Indonesia, and Hong Kong; by Gotop Information Inc. for Taiwan; by ICG Muse, Inc. for Japan; by Intersoft for South Africa; by Eyrolles for France; by International Thomson Publishing for Germany, Austria and Switzerland; by Distribuidora Cuspide for Argentina; by LR International for Brazil; by Galileo Libros for Chile; by Ediciones ZETA S.C.R. Ltda. for Peru; by WS Computer Publishing Corporation, Inc., for the Philippines; by Contemporanea de Ediciones for Venezuela; by Express Computer Distributors for the Caribbean and West Indies; by Micronesia Media Distributor, Inc. for Micronesia; by Chips Computadoras S.A. de C.V. for Mexico; by Editorial Norma de Panama S.A. for Panama; by American Bookshops for Finland.

For general information on Hungry Minds' products and services please contact our Customer Care Department within the U.S. at 800-762-2974, outside the U.S. at 317-572-3993 or fax 317-572-4002.

For sales inquiries and reseller information, including discounts, premium and bulk quantity sales, and foreign-language translations, please contact our Customer Care Department at 800-434-3422, fax 317-572-4002, or write to Hungry Minds, Inc., Attn: Customer Care Department, 10475 Crosspoint Boulevard, Indianapolis, IN 46256.

For information on licensing foreign or domestic rights, please contact our Sub-Rights Customer Care Department at 212-884-5000.

For information on using Hungry Minds' products and services in the classroom or for ordering examination copies, please contact our Educational Sales Department at 800-434-2086 or fax 317-572-4005.

For press review copies, author interviews, or other publicity information, please contact our Public Relations Department at 317-572-3168 or fax 317-572-4168.

For authorization to photocopy items for corporate, personal, or educational use, please contact Copyright Clearance Center, 222 Rosewood Drive, Danvers, MA 01923, or fax 978-750-4470.

LIMIT OF LIABILITY/DISCLAIMER OF WARRANTY: THE PUBLISHER AND AUTHOR HAVE USED THEIR BEST EFFORTS IN PREPARING THIS BOOK. THE PUBLISHER AND AUTHOR MAKE NO REPRESENTATIONS OR WARRANTIES WITH RESPECT TO THE ACCURACY OR COMPLETENESS OF THE CONTENTS OF THIS BOOK AND SPECIFICALLY DISCLAIM ANY IMPLIED WARRANTIES OF MERCHANTABILITY OR FITNESS FOR A PARTICULAR PURPOSE. THERE ARE NO WARRANTIES THAT EXTEND BEYOND THE DESCRIPTIONS CONTAINED IN THIS PARAGRAPH. NO WARRANTY MAY BE CREATED OR EXTENDED BY SALES REPRESENTATIVES OR WRITTEN SALES MATERIALS. THE ACCURACY AND COMPLETENESS OF THE INFORMATION PROVIDED HEREIN AND THE OPINIONS STATED HEREIN ARE NOT GUARANTEED OR WARRANTED TO PRODUCE ANY PARTICULAR RESULTS, AND THE ADVICE AND STRATEGIES CONTAINED HEREIN MAY NOT BE SUITABLE FOR EVERY INDIVIDUAL. NEITHER THE PUBLISHER NOR AUTHOR SHALL BE LIABLE FOR ANY LOSS OF PROFIT OR ANY OTHER COMMERCIAL DAMAGES, INCLUDING BUT NOT LIMITED TO SPECIAL, INCIDENTAL, CONSEQUENTIAL, OR OTHER DAMAGES.

Trademarks: Hungry Minds, For Dummies, the Dummies Man logo, A Reference for the Rest of Us!, The Fun and Easy Way, The Dummies Way, Dummies Daily, Hungry Minds a la Carte and related trade dress are registered trademarks or trademarks of Hungry Minds, Inc. in the United States and other countries, and may not be used without written permission. All other trademarks are the property of their respective owners. Hungry Minds, Inc. is not associated with any product or vendor mentioned in this book.

 is a trademark of Hungry Minds, Inc.

About the Authors

Richard Mander: Richard Mander began his working career as a schoolteacher in New Zealand. He later came to Stanford University to study educational psychology and became a Program Manager at Apple Computer involved in both hardware and software projects. Richard is author of numerous papers and holds several patents. Richard has a Bachelor of Arts and a Master of Arts in Education and a Doctor of Philosophy degree in Educational Psychology, with his doctoral thesis on usability issues. He is now principal, with his wife Amanda, of Zanzara, Inc., a leading usability consulting firm whose clients include Apple, IBM, Microsoft, and Sun.

Bud Smith: Bud Smith started in the computer industry as a data entry clerk facing a room full of punch cards and quickly became a programmer and data processing manager. Later work included technical writing, an editorial position at a computer magazine, and work in marketing and Web development for companies such as Apple, Microsoft, AltaVista, and AOL. Bud is the author of the wildly successful *Creating Web Pages For Dummies*, currently in its 5th Edition, with Arthur Bebak, *Internet Marketing For Dummies*, with Frank Catalano, and many other books within and outside of the *For Dummies* series. Bud has a Bachelor of Arts degree in Information Systems Management from the University of San Francisco. He is currently an author and Web marketing consultant in Silicon Valley.

Dedication

This book is dedicated by both authors, with thanks, to the thousands of users who have taken part in our usability studies over the last ten years.

Acknowledgments

Both authors would like to thank Andrea Boucher, our deservedly renowned Project Editor, and Steven Hayes, our tireless Acquisitions Editor, as well as Camille McCue, Technical Editor, Carmen Krikorian, Senior Permissions Editor, and many others who shared the work of editing the book when crunch time came. At Zanzara, Peter Frazier created graphics, and Shelley Thomas got permissions for all the screenshots. Our clients have believed in our process and entrusted us with their products and their customers. Richard would like to thank several of the colleagues who have inspired him and helped him grow professionally: Michael Arent, Lewis Knapp, Eric Zarakov, Kai-Fu Lee, Joy Mountford, David Lundgren, Amanda Mander, Janice Rohn.

Publisher's Acknowledgments

We're proud of this book; please send us your comments through our Hungry Minds Online Registration Form located at www.dummies.com.

Some of the people who helped bring this book to market include the following:

Acquisitions, Editorial, and Media Development

Project Editor: Andrea C. Boucher

Senior Acquisitions Editor: Steven H. Hayes

Technical Editor: Camille McCue

Editorial Manager: Constance Carlisle

Senior Permissions Editor: Carmen Krikorian

Media Development Manager: Laura Carpenter VanWinkle

Media Development Supervisor: Richard Graves

Editorial Assistants: Amanda Foxworth, Jean Rogers

Production

Project Coordinator: Dale White

Layout and Graphics: Jackie Nicholas, Jill Piscitelli, Brian Torwelle, Jeremey Unger

Proofreaders: David Faust, Susan Moritz, Charles Spencer, TECHBOOKS Production Services

Indexer: TECHBOOKS Production Services

General and Administrative

Hungry Minds Technology Publishing Group: Richard Swadley, Senior Vice President and Publisher; Mary Bednarek, Vice President and Publisher, Networking; Joseph Wikert, Vice President and Publisher, Web Development Group; Mary C. Corder, Editorial Director, Dummies Technology; Andy Cummings, Publishing Director, Dummies Technology; Barry Pruett, Publishing Director, Visual/Graphic Design

Hungry Minds Manufacturing: Ivor Parker, Vice President, Manufacturing

Hungry Minds Marketing: John Helmus, Assistant Vice President, Director of Marketing

Hungry Minds Production for Branded Press: Debbie Stailey, Production Director

Hungry Minds Sales: Michael Violano, Vice President, International Sales and Sub Rights

Credits

Image	Source
Figure 2-1	Courtesy of DreamInk Digital Design.
Figure 3-2	Copyright © 1997-2001 by Silicon Valley Confection Company. SVC2, the SVC2 logo, The Chocolate Notebook, Technology You Can Eat, Really Appetizing Morsel, Chocolate Perfection Unit, and Silicon Valley Confection Company are trademarks of Silicon Valley Confection Company. Website design by Rich Yacco, rich@yaccos.com <mailto:rich@yaccos.com>.
Figures 3-3 and 7-1	Courtesy of Sony Electronics, Inc.
Figure 3-4	Courtesy of Jupiter Media Metrix.
Figure 3-5	Copyright © 2001, Western Washington University.
Figure 4-1	Courtesy of Merryvale Vineyards. Merryvale Vineyards, Profile Club, Profile, Silhouette, Starmont, Antigua, Prelude, and Vignette are trademarks of Merryvale.
Figure 4-4	Courtesy of The Seattle Times, www.seattletimes.com.
Figure 4-5	Courtesy of Velosel, Inc.
Chapter 5, "Frames and navigation areas" sidebar figure	Courtesy of RhinoSoft.com. FTP Voyager(r), AllegroSurf™, Serv-U™, and AllegroMail™ are trademarks of RhinoSoft.
Figure 5-2	© Netsurfer Communications, 2001.
Figure 5-4	Courtesy of Harley of Bellingham.
Figures 5-5 and 10-2	© Monterey Bay Aquarium Foundation.
Figures 5-7, 8-3, and 8-7	©2001 Godiva Choclatier, Inc. The figure on horseback and the gold ballotin are registered trademarks.
Figure 5-8	© 1994-2001 CXO Media Inc. All rights reserved.
Figure 6-1	© NetIQ Corporation 2001. "WebTrends" is a registered trademark of NetIQ Corporation. Other product or company names may be the trademarks of their respective owners.
Figures 6-3 and 6-4	Courtesy of City of Bellingham, WA
Figure 6-7	Courtesy of Barnes & Noble, Inc.
Figures 7-3 and 8-5	Courtesy of Rokenbok Toy Company.
Figure 7-5	Courtesy of Google, Inc.
Figures 7-6, 6-5, 9-2, and 9-4	Courtesy of Whatcom Community Foundation.
Figures 8-6 and 9-5	Courtesy of Built-E, Inc. Screenshot taken August 2001.
Figure 9-1	Courtesy of www.zumiez.com. ©2001 Zumiez, Inc. Used with express permission.
Figure 10-1	Courtesy of Northwest Ecosystem Alliance
Figure 10-4	Courtesy of SonoSite, Inc.

Contents at a Glance

Introduction 1

Part I: Introducing Web Usability 9
Chapter 1: Making Your Site Usable 11
Chapter 2: Studying Your Users 29
Chapter 3: Setting Goals for Your Site 49

Part II: Designing Usable Sites 69
Chapter 4: Organizing Your Site 71
Chapter 5: Creating Site Navigation 101
Chapter 6: Taking Navigation to the Next Level 129

Part III: Creating Usable Web Pages 147
Chapter 7: Designing Usable Web Pages 149
Chapter 8: Designing Web Pages by Type 171
Chapter 9: Designing Great Content Pages 195

Part IV: Reaching a Broad Audience 211
Chapter 10: Broadening Your Site's Appeal 213
Chapter 11: Testing, Testing, Testing 237
Chapter 12: More Usability Testing 253

Part V: The Part of Tens 273
Chapter 13: Ten Do's and Don'ts 275
Chapter 14: Top Ten Steps to a Usability Study 283
Chapter 15: Ten Cool Tools for Usability 289
Chapter 16: Ten Resources for Usability Pros 293

Glossary 297

Index 303

Cartoons at a Glance

By Rich Tennant

page 273

page 9

page 211

page 69

page 147

Cartoon Information:
Fax: 978-546-7747
E-Mail: richtennant@the5thwave.com
World Wide Web: www.the5thwave.com

Table of Contents

Introduction 1

About This Book 2
How to Use This Book 3
What's Not in This Book 4
Conventions Used in This Book 4
Foolish Assumptions 5
How This Book Is Organized 6
    Part I: Introducing Web Usability 6
    Part II: Designing Usable Sites 6
    Part III: Designing Usable Web Pages 6
    Part IV: Reaching a Broad Audience 7
    Part V: The Part of Tens 7
Icons Used in This Book 7
Where to Go from Here 8

Part 1: Introducing Web Usability 9

Chapter 1: Making Your Site Usable 11

The Usability Design Cycle 12
    Spinning around the cycle 12
    Getting left in the cycle 14
Usability Walk-Throughs 17
    Pre-checking a site 18
    Walking through a site 19
Walking Through Dummies.com 22
    Dummies.com pre-check 23
    Dummies.com walk-through 25
Checking Yoursite.com 27

Chapter 2: Studying Your Users 29

Identifying the Web User Base 30
    The U.S. is halfway there 30
    Europe and Asia are growing rapidly 32
    Hardware and software trends matter 34
Studying User Needs and Expectations 36
    Studying competing sites 37
    Studying users directly 39
    Executing a simple customer-visits program 40
Using Testing Techniques During Development 46

xiv Web Usability For Dummies

Chapter 3: Setting Goals for Your Site 49

Picking Which User Needs to Meet 50
Setting Business Goals 51
Meeting expectations 53
Reducing costs 56
Increasing revenues 57
Building customer satisfaction 60
Setting Site Goals 61
Tracking Web site metrics 62
Setting and measuring usability goals 64
Setting Goals for Non-Business Sites 66

Part II: Designing Usable Sites *69*

Chapter 4: Organizing Your Site 71

Wayfinding in Old Media 72
Navigating books 72
Navigating newspapers 78
What you can learn from print 81
How Web sites are different 83
Creating New Navigation 84
Navigation Do's and Don'ts 86
Top ten do's for Web navigation 86
Using the Navigation Do scorecard 90
A baker's dozen don'ts for Web navigation 91
Creating the Site Tree 93
Bottom-Up Information Design 95
Whom to get ideas from 96
Getting ideas from stakeholders 97
Getting ideas from users 99

Chapter 5: Creating Site Navigation 101

Charting Your Course 101
Single-Page Sites 104
Goal-setting for the single-page site 104
Navigating the single-page site 106
In the Beginning: Top Navigation Links 108
Plusses of top navigation text links 108
Minuses of top navigation text links 110
When to use top navigation text links 111
Expanding a site with top navigation text links 111
Graphical Top Navigation Bars 113
Plusses of top navigation bars 114
Minuses of top navigation bars 114
When to use a top navigation bar 116
Blending top navigation links and bars 117
Expanding a site with a top navigation bar 117

Table of Contents *xv*

Left Navigation 119
   Plusses of single-level left navigation 121
   Minuses of single-level left navigation 122
   When to use single-level left navigation 125
Expanding a site with single-level left navigation 126

Chapter 6: Taking Navigation to the Next Level 129

Meeting Site Goals with Navigation 129
   User-centered goals 130
   Site metrics 131
   Business goals 134
Adding Levels of Navigation 136
   A site of sites 136
   Navigating the world of Williams-Sonoma 139
   Extron sells online 140
   Navigation examples and site goals 142
Navigating Tasks 142
   Reading an article 143
   Registering 143
   Shopping 144

Part III: Creating Usable Web Pages 147

Chapter 7: Designing Usable Web Pages 149

Web Design and Usability 150
   Color and usability 151
   Readability and usability 154
   Multimedia and usability 156
Helping Users Interact with Web Pages 158
   Helping users find what they need 159
   When users don't find what they need 161
Using the Ideal Page Layout 163
   Popping up Web pages 163
   Keeping pages narrow 166
   Keeping pages short 168

Chapter 8: Designing Web Pages by Type 171

How Design Fits 172
   How design (often) happens 172
   Putting it all together 173
   Identifying Web page types 175
Creating Usable Task Pages 176
   The purpose of task pages 178
   Questions for task pages 179
   Search task pages 180
   Registration task pages 182
   Shopping task pages 184

xvi Web Usability For Dummies

Creating Usable Section & Home Pages 188
    Sectionizing your site 189
    Making your home page not homely 190

Chapter 9: Designing Great Content Pages 195

What Is Great Content? 196
    Who needs great content? 196
    Writing for the Web 197
    Programming your content 200
Creating Usable Content Pages 201
    The purpose of content pages 201
    Questions for content 202
Types of Content Pages 203
    Images in content 203
    Images as content 205
    Adding elements to content pages 206
Special Features for Content Pages 207
    Making printable pages 207
    Making e-mailable pages 208

Part IV: Reaching a Broad Audience 211

Chapter 10: Broadening Your Site's Appeal 213

Dealing with Different Systems 214
    Dealing with different hardware 214
    Dealing with different monitors 216
    Dealing with different software 218
Usability Notes for Multimedia 220
Going Global 223
    About international users 225
    Usability and internationalization 226
Empowering Disabled Users 228
    Site-level changes 229
    Graphics and multimedia 230
Supporting Power Users 230
    Reporters and other press people 231
    Industry analysts and investors 233
    Executives and employees 235

Chapter 11: Testing, Testing, Testing 237

Doing Usability Testing 239
    What a user test is 239
    Figuring out what tasks to test 240
    Anticipating likely results 243
Testing Web Sites 245
    Testing alpha and beta sites 246
    Testing live sites 247

Table of Contents

xvii

Rapid Prototyping 248
    Fat-marker prototypes 249
    Clickable prototypes 249
    Fully interactive prototypes 250
Competitive Site Testing 250

Chapter 12: More Usability Testing 253

Testing Insiders 253
Testing by Reading Site Data 255
    Pageviews and types of Web pages 256
    Example: Zanzara's first site 257
    Traffic flow on Zanzara's first site 259
    Getting more traffic to a page 260
    Finding trouble spots in tasks 262
Using Surveys and Polls 263
Usability and Other Disciplines 265
    How disciplines work together 266
    Hurdles for usability to overcome 267
    Working with other groups 269

Part V: The Part of Tens 273

Chapter 13: Ten Do's and Don'ts 275

Do Have Goals for Your Web Site 275
Do Constantly Check Back with the User 276
Do Manage Your Web Site Like a Real Project 277
Do "Think Different" When Writing for the Web 277
Do Use PDF Files to Preserve Formatting 278
Don't Ignore Download Speeds 278
Don't Eschew Large Graphics and Multimedia 279
Don't Try to Do Too Much Per Revision 279
Don't Listen to the HTML Purists 280
Don't Skip Actual User Tests 280

Chapter 14: Top Ten Steps to a Usability Study ...283

Deciding What You're Going to Test 283
Setting Up Your Testing Room 284
Recruit Your Testers 284
Include Other Team Members in the Study 285
Get Off to a Good Start 285
Take the User Through Tasks 286
Ask for Final Thoughts 286
Get Ready for the Next One 286
Write Up the Results 287
Deliver the News 287

xviii **Web Usability For Dummies**

Chapter 15: Ten Cool Tools for Usability 289
A Good Pair of Ears 289
A Good Laptop 290
A Room (Glass Wall Optional) 290
Solid Writing Skills 290
A Video Camera 291
A Fat Marker 291
A Graphics Editing Tool 291
A Prototyping Tool 292
A Database Program 292
Walkie-Talkies 292

Chapter 16: Ten Resources for Usability Pros 293
The Right Work Experience 294
Jakob Nielsen's Usability Engineering 294
The Right Education 294
Ronald Baecker's Readings in Human-Computer Interaction 295
ACM Interactions magazine 295
The Design Management Journal 295
ACM SIGCHI 296
Donald Norman's The Design of Everyday Things 296
The Usability Professionals Association 296
Henry Petroski's The Pencil 296

Glossary *297*

Index *303*

Introduction

*W*eb usability — using a range of old and new tools and techniques that make Web sites easier to use — is important to a very wide range of people, from business to schools to non-profit organizations to individuals with their own Web sites to each and every Web user. Making Web sites "do their thing" more smoothly, more enjoyably, with less user confusion and mistakes, and with fewer steps between the user's having a need and successfully fulfilling it, matters to everyone reading this book.

Web Usability For Dummies is written for professional and amateur Web site creators and for people who review, approve, direct, or otherwise influence the design and development of Web sites. If you've ever used the Web, you've experienced the frustration of long waits for pages to load, of incomplete, confusing, and hard-to-find information, and of starting a buying process and not being able to complete it or to easily halt it. If you've been involved in Web site development, you've no doubt experienced the angst of helping create something that turns out to be less effective and useful than you'd hoped at the beginning of the project.

Web Usability For Dummies helps you make your Web site much better by showing you how to effectively consult with the ultimate authority on the effectiveness and ease of use of your Web site — your users. We take a two-pronged approach to improving your Web site.

First, we show you how to improve your site with the usability lessons we've learned in our combined 20 years of work in designing and developing Web sites (and other high-tech products) with ongoing input from their intended customers. Our experience can help you avoid making many mistakes that are very commonly found on today's Web sites and immediately get better results from your site.

Second, we show you how to take your own Web site and test it at any stage from conceptual sketch to large, finished product, with potential and actual users — and how to use their feedback to make your site better. As you build various forms of user feedback into your Web site development process, you get better and better at meeting your goals and at making your site something your users will come back to again and again.

Web Usability For Dummies

About This Book

This book isn't designed solely as a book to be read straight through from cover to cover. (Granted, we like having readers pay full attention to our pearls of wisdom, but if you're poring through the index for fun, you've gone too far.) It's also designed as a reference book so that you can dip in and out of it as you run into new topics. You can look for the part that contains the information you want, narrow your search down to a specific chapter, find out what you need to know, and then get back to work.

This book is also not designed to be completely comprehensive. There are a lot of books out there about different topics relating to usability and quite a few usability books, some of which contain more theory or personal opinion than practical information. With this book, you're able to get right to work.

Among other interesting things, this book shows you:

- A new way of looking at the whole cycle of Web site development: the Usability Design Cycle.

- How to do a "walk-through" of a site — how to get a good idea whether your site, or a competing site, is basically doing its job after looking at the site for just a few minutes.

- How to learn more about Web users in general, and specifically about your site's current or intended users, before you start work on your site.

- How to set goals for your site and translate those goals into measurable results that you'll seek to achieve on your site.

- An organized approach to creating a site that's easily navigable — a site that makes it easy for users to find their way around and to get back to their favorite spots.

- How to create clean, attractive pages that "scan" easily and guide the user into taking desired actions.

- New ways to make sure from the get-go that your site will work well for a very wide range of users across current and future computer platforms while allowing you to create a visually interesting site.

- How to take a wide range of audiences into account in your site's design so you can reach worldwide audiences, people who are physically challenged, people who are using a site as an intranet or extranet, and "power users" like the press and analysts who want to get in and out fast.

- Specific tools for interactive functions like e-mailing or printing a page and a comprehensive approach to creating the most highly interactive parts of a site, such as user registration functionality, user profile management, and online shopping.

Introduction   **3**

- All about testing your site, during development and after deployment, with actual users — even how to "sell" their feedback internally so as to get the needed changes made as quickly as possible.

- How to upgrade your knowledge of, and professional credentials in, usability and make yourself an indispensable part of major Web design efforts.

How to Use This Book

If you're new to Web design and the many other areas related to it, usability is a good topic with which to start learning. This book can serve as a primer that shows you a well-thought-out, complete, and practical approach to Web site design that guides you as you begin work on actual sites. Even someone creating his or her first site, or creating a site for personal purposes, can benefit from this book.

If you're an experienced designer, engineer, marketer, manager, or other professional whose job involves creating, upgrading, or maintaining Web sites, this book may serve as a revelation because it answers the crucial question of Web site design: Why? That is, what are the real, underlying reasons for which people create Web sites, especially large, complicated ones; and why are some sites so much better than others? This book shows you how to articulate the goals for your Web site and how to work with users as the ultimate authority on how your site can reach those goals.

For the first time that we're aware of, this book articulates a complete theory for user-centered Web site design: the Usability Design Cycle, illustrated and described in Chapter 1. The Usability Design Cycle is not a particularly easy-to-use bike (pun intended). Instead, it's a cycle that ties together all the many activities involved in Web site design for usability and lets you know where you are in relation to meeting your goals as you work on creating and improving your Web site.

If you're a Web usability professional, or someone who'd like to become one, this book can serve as a crucial aid on the path to becoming a real expert in your field. We give you all the information you need to quickly make a strong contribution to Web site development along with pointers to resources that help you take the next step professionally.

Don't think that the only way to use this book is to read it all the way through, thinking deeply about each topic that we, the authors, bring up. Instead, use this book in conjunction with your work. When you have a question or concern relating to usability, use the table of contents and the index to find the topic that stumps you. Go to that section and read up on the topic.

4 Web Usability For Dummies _____

Usually, you find a set of steps, a bulleted list, a picture, a table, or a description of how to do the task that's troubling you — and often, you find all of the above. Use that section to get yourself back on track and then close the book and go on with your work

What's Not in This Book

This book summarizes the crucial information you need in order to improve the usability of any Web site that you may be working on or responsible for. It doesn't include complete information on a number of related topics you may be interested in.

The history of usability in its many forms over the years, including time and motion studies, human factors research, and other similar topics, is only referred to briefly in Chapter 1. There is already a considerable body of knowledge specifically about Web usability, and there are several books, seminars, and conferences that you'll wish to read or participate in if you want to become an expert in the field.

Web design is a huge topic, and it's usually approached very differently than how we have done it here; most Web design theory starts with the details of what appears on the screen rather than with who your user is and what your goals are. You'll need to understand the graphics-first approach and learn things that aren't in this book in order to become a competent Web designer. A good place to start is a volume that is in some ways the sister book to this one, *Web Design For Dummies*, published by Hungry Minds, Inc.

Business is, of course, an even larger topic, with its own rich history (and sometimes poor history). In this book we encourage you to use your business goals — even non-business sites can have business-like goals — and users' ability to carry out tasks on your site as the two guideposts for creating and improving your Web site. We tell you to articulate your goals before you start on your Web project, but there's a lot of big-picture information about business and organizations, and about how the Web can help (or even hinder) you in carrying out your business or business-like purposes, that we don't cover here.

Conventions Used in This Book

We use several conventions in this book to make it easier for you to scan the pages for just what you need and to remember key points while you're working. Whenever we introduce a new term, we put it in *italics* and define it

Introduction **5**

immediately after. That way you're part of the conversation and not stuck on the outside, wondering what we're talking about.

We use many bulleted lists and steps in this book. These are devices that help you quickly grasp what's important and yet also find those crucial details that can really make a difference in doing things right the first time. Steps let you know when it's important that things be done in a specific order. (Not that rules weren't made to be broken sometimes.)

Web addresses are given in a monospaced font like this: `www.dummies.com`. This is not just an idle example; we actually analyze the usability of the Dummies Web site in Chapter 1.

Sidebars are also set off in their own typeface, with a fancy heading all their own, and are surrounded by a shaded box, much like below.

Foolish Assumptions

We assume that you, as the reader of a book called *Web Usability For Dummies*, are involved in planning, designing, implementing, making money from, or otherwise bringing Web sites to life. We further assume that you want to make your site work better — though you could use this book to make your site work much worse; just read our recommendations and then do the opposite!

You don't need a strong technical background to read this book. Specifically, you don't need to know HTML, Javascript, how to use the graphics program Photoshop, or really any specific technical or creative discipline. If you're involved with Web sites, and care about how users can interact with them better, you're in.

This is a sidebar head

And this is an example of how sidebar text looks. Pretty cool, huh? Try making text look like this on a Web site! (It's hard, but it can be done.) Two-column text is not yet real popular on the Web, but it'll get there. In the meantime, it's real popular with the authors, who can't always fit all of their great ideas into the main flow of the text. And now back to our regularly scheduled programming . . . .

How This Book Is Organized

We began the process for writing this book with a lot of great ideas about how Web sites could be built better and steadily improved after they were created. We struggled with different ways of organizing this information to make it useful to readers of the book — those who would go straight from Page 1 until the end, and others who would dip in and out of the book for reference. Then, as we were writing Chapter 1, we realized that one of the authors (Mander) had the solution in hand all along: the Usability Design Cycle, which Zanzara, his company, uses to show its customers how to organize the Web site design effort for maximum effectiveness.

We then reorganized our plan for the book a bit to fit the Usability Design Cycle. (Our editors didn't exactly love our changing the outline after writing had begun, but in the end they were very supportive, as always.) The result is an organization for the book that not only flows well, but fits how Web work is best done in the real world.

The following sections describe the parts into which we've organized our book:

Part I: Introducing Web Usability

Part I jumps right into Web usability with both feet, showing you the Usability Design Cycle, how to quickly analyze a site, even taking apart the Dummies.com site by our criteria. It then tells you something about Web users, including U.S. users versus those around the world, and how to learn about your user's needs and expectations. Then this part explores how to set goals for your site and how to know whether your site is meeting them.

Part II: Designing Usable Sites

You can create a Web site that's more usable than most simply by following some logical rules and practices when you're designing the site. In this part you get the full benefit of our combined 20 years of experience in creating usable high-tech products, mostly Web sites, but software and hardware as well. This part begins by introducing some of the theoretical background of usability and comparing Web sites to familiar objects such as books and movies. It then shows you how to create Web site navigation that truly supports the user in their desire to get around quickly and knowledgeably.

Part III: Designing Usable Web Pages

Next up is page design — creating individual Web pages that are usable by themselves while fitting in a sensible way into the overall site structure. Finally, we talk about what goes on the pages — Web content that really works — and about how to allow the user to follow the flow of various kinds of information smoothly through a site.

Part IV: Reaching a Broad Audience

This part starts by getting a bit technical, showing you how to create a site that loads fast and that works well on all kinds of computers (from old and cheap to new and fast) and with all kinds of Web connections (from slow and flaky to fast and, well, flaky). It then goes on to demonstrate how to make your site work for users across the world and for users with disabilities, as well as for "power users" who want to get specific information from your site, then get out. We then go into great detail on testing: both user tests, in which you bring users in to try various tasks on your Web site (or prototype), and other kinds of testing such as using Web site reports to identify usability problems.

Part V: The Part of Tens

Ever stay up late to catch a Top 10 list on TV? Or make your own list of reasons to do or not do something? If so, you'll love this part, a collection of lists related to Web usability. You'll find a list of Web usability do's and don'ts, some cool tools you can use, even ten things you can do to move toward becoming a professional usability person. The book then concludes with a glossary, which you can use to define and explain all the new stuff you're discovering, and an index to help you find your way back to all the cool stuff in the book.

Icons Used in This Book

Icons got their start in books and then went forth and multiplied on the computer screens of the world. Now they're back in print, alerting and guiding you through the pages of this book. *For Dummies* books are justly famous for their icons, and we want to hold up our end of the tradition. These icons are much like those used in many computer programs, except there are fewer of them, we use them more consistently than software developers do, and ours are simpler and more readable. Besides that, not much difference.

This icon helps you identify pointed insights that save you work and worry as you create and improve your Web site or work with users on the next round of changes. If scratching your ear with your elbow helps you concentrate on the right thing to do next in your Web site design, a Tip will point that out to you. (Don't hold your breath — or hurt your ear scratching it with your elbow — waiting.)

The Web Design Tip icon shows you tips that relate specifically to how you design — or redesign — your Web site. Ever wonder why some sites seem to work better than others? Web Design Tips show you some of the most important reasons why.

When you see Dummies Man pointing his finger skyward and the words "Technical Stuff," you've found something in the book that you can safely ignore — temporarily, for a while, or forever. Read the areas marked Technical Stuff for an in-depth study of areas in which you're especially interested.

Just as working with users can lead you to do the right things with your site, ignoring them can lead you to do the wrong ones. We point out this and other kinds of potential problems with the Warning label. (And yes, unlike those tags on your mattresses, you are perfectly free to remove these warning labels if you want to — though your book may not look good with eraser fluid all over it.)

There are a few pearls of wisdom in this book so valuable that you'd probably put them on a string and wear them around your neck if you could. The Remember icon highlights things that are especially useful — or that you may need to know again just around the corner.

Where to Go from Here

You can actually reach the authors of this book online. By writing us, you help us improve the book and let us know something about our readers — kind of a usability thing. Of course, we risk insanity in trying to keep up with the potential flood of e-mail, so please go easy on us.

You can give us your feedback on the Zanzara website at www.zanzara.com. We'll also post any changes after the book goes to press there as well. Let us know if we do a good job of integrating the book-related material with the normal business tasks of the Zanzara site.

Part I
Introducing Web Usability

In this part . . .

*W*eb usability is simply knowing your site's users, knowing your goals for your site, and making your site work well for your users so you can meet your goals. We show you how to "walk-through" a site to quickly identify usability problems and come up with strategies for fixing them. We also introduce the Usability Design Cycle to guide your overall site development efforts.

Chapter 1

Making Your Site Usable

In This Chapter

▶ Defining usability

▶ Introducing the Usability Design Cycle

▶ Introducing the Usability Walk-Through

▶ Dummies.com Walk-Through

▶ Checking your own site

*W*eb usability is the art and science of making Web sites easier to use. The usability of a Web site has tremendous impact on its usefulness to site visitors and on its ability to generate the results that you, as someone partly or completely responsible for a Web site, are looking for.

The *art* of Web usability comes in during the design process — some Web site designers and developers seem to create sites that are much easier to use than most, without even trying. Interestingly, the people who create highly usable sites are usually not the same ones who create complex, interesting, but slow-loading and confusing site designs. The first kind of sites are popular with users; the second kind are "cool" and easy to sell to management. Good design balances attractive graphic design, technical requirements, and marketing concerns.

The *science* of Web usability comes from user testing — from sitting users down in front of a computer running your site and watching them try to accomplish various tasks on the site. (Watching someone try to accomplish some task on your site that seems obvious to you — and repeatedly fail — can be truly excruciating.) Some sites get through user testing with only minor tweaks needed to gain acceptable or even exceptional levels of usability. Others require major rethinking and rework to be made at all usable.

In this book, we tackle both the art and the science of usability. Much of this book is about the art of creating usable sites. That means we give you planning and design principles for use in creating an unusually usable Web site. These principles are derived from the authors' experience in watching thousands of users struggle through usability tests of Web sites, as well as a

Part I: Introducing Web Usability

decade of work in areas such as hypertext, Web multimedia, computer software development, integrated hardware/software products, and Web site development. We've distilled these experiences into "how to" rules that you can use to give your sites above-average usability on the first try.

The remainder of this book is about the science of creating usable sites: putting some or all of your site in front of users for informal and formal user testing. The science project continues with assessment of lessons learned and planning to improve the site's usability. It concludes with a new design effort that takes user feedback into account and results in an improved site with exceptional usability.

The Usability Design Cycle

You can use almost any tool, to some extent, for almost any purpose. Try eating a salad with a spoon — it's hard, but if you're hungry, you can get it done. Still, no one would describe the spoon as very usable for salad-eating. So usability is clearly a matter of degree. It's a goal, something you work hard to progress toward, and that you never completely reach.

Like most things that are worth doing, usability is a process, not a separate thing in itself. As we think through the process of making something usable, several questions naturally come up. Capable of being used by whom? Capable of being used for what? And, how will we know when we've attained this mystical quality of usability? The Usability Design Cycle (see Figure 1-1) helps answer all of these questions and more.

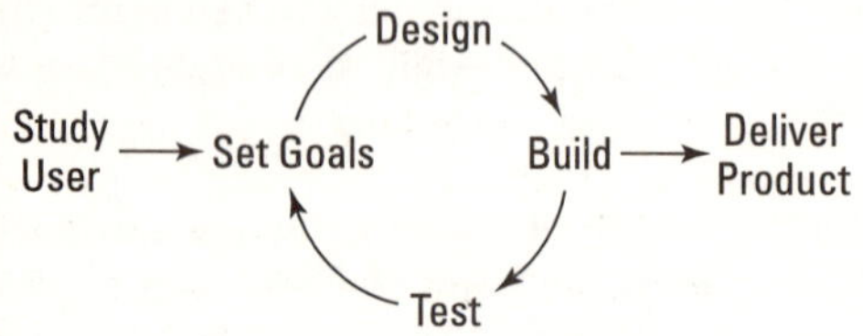

Figure 1-1:
The Usability Design Cycle

Study User → Set Goals → Design → Build → Deliver Product → Test (cycle)

Spinning around the cycle

The Usability Design Cycle was developed by one of the authors (Mander) as a tool for helping answer questions about design for usability. It divides the process of improving usability into a cycle with six repeating steps:

Chapter 1: Making Your Site Usable

1. **Study the user.** You need to know quite a bit about your user to make your Web site something that he or she can get the most out of. Study the kinds of people who are using your site, plus other desired kinds of users that are not using your site yet. Create a few idealized "model" users who you can talk about in discussing various user scenarios.

2. **Set goals.** Your site's goals are a way of expressing what your business, non-profit organization, or you as a person are trying to accomplish by creating and improving your Web site. Set both broad goals, such as "make this the best Web site of its type," and specific, actionable goals, such as "reduce user complaints to 1 percent of unique users per month."

3. **Design.** The design step includes choosing the functionality and content that will appear on the site; deciding how the site will be organized; and creating a look and feel for the site. Design work needs to take into account the users you are trying to empower and the goals you want the site to achieve.

4. **Build.** Building is the actual process of creating the Web pages that users will see and the computer software that makes the site's functionality come to life. Some of the data specifications and computer programming languages used in building your site are HTML, graphics specifications such as GIF and JPEG, JavaScript, C++, Perl, and database programming languages.

5. **Test.** The testing stage includes both functional testing — looking for "bugs" — and usability testing, which determines whether the site can be easily used for its intended purposes. (This process "tests" the patience of both you and your users, but yields otherwise unattainable results.) Functional testing is mostly done before release; usability testing occurs at various times.

6. **Deliver product.** Small changes in the site are often delivered to users quickly, sometimes with little testing; larger changes are delivered only after extensive testing and rework. Major changes to your site are usually delivered with some fanfare, possibly including a press release, a note to site users, and so on. The site continues to be improved as you fix problems, add features, improve existing features, and incorporate new technology.

Each part of the Web site development process shown in the Usability Design Cycle depends on every other part. You have to know your user in order to set realistic goals for your site; you need goals to have something to test the site against; and so on. You can begin the development process at any point in the cycle; and, given that it's a cycle, you're never truly finished.

Getting left in the cycle

The process of Web development has gotten a great deal of attention the last few years, but almost all of that attention has gone to the right side of the Usability Design Cycle: Designing a site, especially the graphical parts of site and page design; building a site, with whole libraries of books published on HTML, JavaScript, and other such technologies; and, to a lesser extent, functional testing (part of "debugging") and the marketing effort around delivering the site as a "finished" product.

This book, by contrast, concentrates on the part that has, until now, been "left" behind: the left-hand side of the Usability Design Cycle. This includes studying your user, which is the foundational effort for usability work. Setting goals, another part of the left-hand side of the cycle, helps you answer the question, "usable for what?"

Design and testing are part of usability, too, but with a different focus than most people are accustomed to: The design emphasis for usability is not so much on the graphical appearance of a site as on the information design and interaction design that guide users through their tasks; usability testing isn't to uncover "bugs" such as a bad link, but to help find out how many ways users can go wrong when they follow a good link!

Table 1-1 breaks the Usability Design Cycle down into some of its component parts, emphasizing the usability-oriented parts of the process. As you look at Table 1-1, think about what areas you need to start working on first in order to quickly improve your planned or existing site. The "Activity" column of the table includes cross-references to the chapters/parts of the book that discuss a particular activity in more detail.

Table 1-1	Highlighting Usability Concerns		
Activity	**Who**	**Overall task**	**Usability role**
1. Study user (Chapter 2)	Sales, marketing, usability	Describe desired users for site, current users of site, non-Web customers.	Create model user descriptions for "thought experiments" identifying usability issues and opportunities.
2. Set goals (Chapter 3)	Executive management, sales, marketing, engineering, usability	Set overall business goals and specific metrics for site	Make sure goals are clear and actionable so as to serve as a yardstick for user testing

Chapter 1: Making Your Site Usable

Activity	Who	Overall task	Usability role
3. Design (Parts II and III)	Information architects, graphic designers, usability	Design navigation for the site, specify major pages and user flow, design look and feel of major types of pages	Make sure navigation and design serve user needs; keep page-loading times low; meet other usability criteria
4. Build	Engineering, HTML	Implement pages in HTML and software code	Check that goals, design targets, usability criteria continue to be met
5. Test (Part IV)	Quality Assurance (QA), usability	Make sure the site works, by removing bugs (QA) and by removing barriers to completion of tasks (usability)	Set up and supervise usability testing, identify problems, recommend and help implement solutions
6. Deliver product	Marketing, engineering	Make sure site gets visitors after launch and that it works under stress	Quickly identify urgent usability problems on delivered site and fix; begin testing for future revisions

Usability is a state of mind as well as a specific set of things to focus on. As you bring usability concerns into the Web site development process, you'll find them affecting the way everyone on the team does his or her job. People writing computer programs for the site try to ensure that they produce results helpful to real people; Quality Assurance(QA) people testing for bugs also point out usability problems that you can address then or later. The result is a much better site for the user, sooner than if you were carrying the usability ball alone.

We'll refer back to the Usability Design Cycle throughout this book to remind you of each important part of the Web site development process while showing you how interdependent each part of the process is. The Usability Design Cycle gives you a framework for understanding any problem that occurs during Web site design, development, use, and improvement.

Part I: Introducing Web Usability

A brief history of usability

A psychologist named James Gibson described a crucial concept for usability: The fact that each tool has an "affordance" that makes it easy to begin using that tool for a certain purpose. A hammer "affords" grasping and banging; a screwdriver just seems to want to be twisted. In computer software design, the equivalent to a tool's affordance is software that's "easy to learn."

The German philosopher Martin Heidegger also had something to say about usability. In his sometimes dense, academic German, he described something usable as being "ready to hand." These highly usable tools become an organic extension of the user, enhancing his or her capabilities with little need for thought about how to use the tool. The software equivalent is being "easy to use."

In software, there can be a large gap between "easy to learn" and "easy to use." Windows is easy to *learn*, but to an experienced user, DOS — in which you enter memorized commands from a prompt — can actually be easier to *use*. The Web itself is easy to learn, but not as easy to use as some other software-based tools.

Good Web design implements both the easy-to-learn and easy-to-use concepts. Adding a 3D look to a button makes it look clickable and easy to learn; providing a set of checkboxes makes a page for managing newsletter subscriptions easy to use.

Frederick Taylor began the process of implementing usability concepts, before they were called that, through his time and motion studies that helped rearrange work for greater efficiency and safety. Human factors work then focused on critical, and dangerous, tasks such as flying a jet at speeds and under forces that tended to induce unconsciousness.

The psychologist Don Norman wrote a classic book called *The Design of Everyday Things*. He extended the concepts of usability from the things we use, well, every day, to the design of software and other complex mechanisms. Henry Petroski wrote a whole book on the evolution of the pencil. And people in related disciplines have contributed as well; every teacher who ever lived has had to make information accessible, and indeed many innovators in usability have been teachers or instructional writers.

Usability is the extension of this and much other work into a truly user-centered discipline in which final answers are derived not from theory, but from user testing. Web usability in particular is a huge challenge because users have so many choices on the Web. If you don't make your Web site both easy to learn and easy to use, users simply go away and do something else. And because a key part of the attraction of the Web is that it's known for ease of use, you can't ask a user to take time to learn how to use your site; only by providing appropriate affordances, and by making the site ready to hand for a number of tasks so it attracts return visits, can you hope to help make your site a success.

The good news, though, is that usability is easier to measure objectively on the Web than in most real-world domains. It's easy to record just what a user clicked, how long they stayed on a Web page, and so on. More advanced Web measurement instruments can even tell us where a user's eyes rested, and for how long.

Web developers are taking advantage of this ease of measurement to rapidly improve the usability of their Web sites, even for complicated functions like online shopping. You risk falling behind competitors quickly if you don't pay attention to usability.

Chapter 1: Making Your Site Usable 17

Usability Walk-Throughs

People tend to work in two different styles: from the top down and from the bottom up. The top-down approach is the Big Picture, the overall plan, like the master blueprint for a large building. The bottom-up approach is getting involved in the actual, hands-on work of creating something, the part where you're using hammer and nails, saw and sawhorse to actually build the great thing that you've planned.

The Usability Design Cycle, described earlier in this chapter, gives us the top-down framework for a Web development effort. A Usability Walk-Through is a way of inspecting a site to get insights into why it does or doesn't work well.

A "walk-through" is any structured discussion of a product that's in development or already in use. We've borrowed the term to mean an informal review of a Web site by a member of the site development team who removes his or her developer hat and puts on a user's or reviewer's hat for a few minutes.

Many usability experts are brought into a project near the end to do something very much like a Usability Walk-Through. This is done to fix any "stoppers" that will make it really hard for users to accomplish things on the site. That's a good idea, as far as it goes, but imagine how much better the site could have been by having usability work done early in the process.

The best way to do a Usability Walk-Through is at the beginning of a Web development project, not at the end. The Usability Walk-Through can then be used to start both a small project and a big one. The small project is to do the "quick fixes" that will quickly improve a site's results. The big project uses the results of the Usability Walk-Through, as well as a review of the site's results, goals, and available resources, to figure out how to rebuild critical parts of a site, or even the whole site, in order to get much better results from it.

The walk-through approach described here skips over a great many important steps that are needed for a thorough approach to usability, but none more so than user testing. The whole idea of a walk-through is to do initial testing in your own head. You can quickly identify crucial issues with your site this way, but you're bound to miss many equally important problems that must be fixed for your site to be fully usable.

Walk through your site to get started, but use the full usability process described in this book, especially informal and formal user testing, to make really impressive improvements in your site's usability.

Pre-checking a site

The first part of doing a walk-through happens before you even look at a site. Before you start surfing through the site — your own site, or someone else's — take a few minutes to think through what the site *should* be like. Given what the company or group does, the features competitors or other comparable sites have, and what you know about the customer or user base, what should you reasonably expect from this site?

The same steps you use for pre-checking existing sites are also very useful for planning new sites. Try using these steps to brainstorm a new site or a new addition to an existing site.

If you're walking through someone else's site, you should be able to brainstorm this "should" list yourself, though it's more fun to look at the site with a friend. If you're doing a walk-through of your own site and you know it too well, involve some people who know it less well than you. They don't have to be totally ignorant of it, as long as they don't know every page with their eyes closed, as you may. (But don't think that actually closing your eyes while using your site will impress people; it will make an impression, but not likely a positive one.)

Follow these steps in pre-checking a site *before* you bring it up on your computer:

- **List the site's target users.** Think through who the users of a site should be. What kinds of customers is the company targeting? What subset of those customers are most likely to be on the Web? Are there any Web-savvy audiences, such as press and analysts, who should be included in the list of targets? List a few top candidates.

- **List the site's goals.** Quickly, and without thinking about it too much, list the major goals you think the site should support. (You can refine the list later.) Typical site goals include finding contact information, finding a job, getting a list of products, and finding out where you can buy each product.

- **List goals by audience.** If you want to get somewhat tricky, separately list the goals for each major audience — press/analyst, prospective customer, user of the product, investor, dealer or reseller, employee, and any other important groups you can think of.

- **Identify possible styles for the site.** Should the site be friendly or official-looking? Should it be relatively dense with information or lighter and more graphical? The style of a site should reflect the company's overall positioning, its customer base, and the specific products or other offerings on the site.

Chapter 1: Making Your Site Usable

- ✔ **List key information assets for the site.** Every site needs some key groupings of information — we call these "information assets" — valuable "nuggets" of text and/or images that users will look for, and enjoy finding, on a site. Such assets include a product list, a list of dealers, a list of open jobs, any desired "chunk" of information.

- ✔ **Describe other content for the site.** What other content might the site have? Describe some fun or interesting things the site could provide. A "related links" list is often a valuable addition. Is there industry news, success stories, or other kinds of information that would be useful for the site?

- ✔ **Describe buying support for the site.** List a set of supporting functionality that the site should provide for people wanting to buy products. (If the site is for a group, focus on how people can join the group, and so on.) Start with the easiest types of support first: Should the site have dealer, vendor, or other type of contact information? Then make it harder: Should this site support online transactions? If so, for which products and services?

- ✔ **Describe registration support for the site.** Decide whether the site needs to be able to register users. If so, should registration be required, optional, or somewhere in-between? (For example, if registration is a high priority, you can make most of a site unavailable to unregistered users who are afflicted with "Join us!" pop-up windows on each visit.) What information should the site be trying to get about users? What will you do with it? Should the site make it easy to manage registration info?

- ✔ **Describe other functionality for the site.** For most sites, buying functionality is crucial. What other functionality can, or should, the site have? For example, a large site should have a search capability; a complicated site should have a Help function; a site for a TV station should have at least a few video clips.

Figure 1-2 shows a checklist for the first part of a Usability Walk-Through. You can also find this checklist on the Web at www.zanzara.com/wufd.

Walking through a site

Actually giving a Web site a Usability Walk-Through is a lot of fun and a great way to help you realize that no site is perfect. However, before you start, take the time to work through the checklist above, as shown in Figure 1-2. Taking a little time up front to figure out what *should* be on a site will much better prepare you to evaluate what *is* on the site.

20 Part I: Introducing Web Usability

TARGET USERS
Customers your company is targeting; Web-savvy customers; press, analysts, others.

GOALS THE SITE WILL FULFILL
Providing contact information, open jobs, product info, how to buy info, community, more.

GOALS BY AUDIENCE
Audience-specific goals: Annual reports for investors, press releases for reporters, more.

STYLES FOR THE SITE
Use company positioning: Friendly? Serious? Authoritative? Leading or challenging?

KEY INFORMATION ASSETS
Lists and/or searchable databases: Maps, contact info, products, salespeople, more.

OTHER CONTENT
Related links, industry news, success stories, more.

BUYING SUPPORT
Sell on the site? Provide where to buy info, how to buy info, pricing, what to buy comparison checklists.

REGISTRATION FOR SITE
Register users? How will the site reflect user preferences and behavior? How much of the site is hidden from unregistered users?

OTHER FUNCTIONALITY
Consider search capability; multimedia additions; site map.

Figure 1-2:
Usability
Walk-
Through
initial
checklist.

Follow these steps to give a site a Usability Walk-Through:

1. **First impression.** Does the site look like what it should look like? Do you know instantly that the site is a bank, bookstore, user group, and so on? Both prominent headings and graphical layout should work together to explicitly and implicitly convey the right impression.

Chapter 1: Making Your Site Usable

2. **List the major areas of the site.** Using the site's main navigation, list the major areas of the site, including top-level categories and categories one level down.

3. **Reverse-engineer the site's goals.** Looking at the list of major areas and the front page, figure out the goals of the site. You should be able to find evidence of goals such as "Help users find a dealer" or "Sell surplus goods online." Compare this to the list of goals you created when thinking about what the site should do.

4. **Drill down to goals by audience.** For a complex site, consider looking further into the site to identify goals for specific audiences, such as current customers, prospective customers, investors, and so on.

5. **Describe the style of the site.** Is the site friendly or formal? Highly structured, accessibly organized, or random? Compare the style of the site to the style you think it should have, given the company's positioning, customer base, and business goals.

6. **Identify key information assets for the site.** Find the key "chunks" of information that make this site worthwhile. For a first pass, identify five to seven of the most prominent information assets. Are they the ones you predicted in advance? How hard are key information assets to find?

7. **Describe the buying process.** Go through the buying process on the site. Do you simply call an 800 number? Go through a dealer locator that puts you in touch with a local dealer for the product? Or can you initiate and complete transactions online? Note how much of the buying process you can complete online, and also note any major difficulties in completing it.

8. **Describe the registration process.** Register as a member of the site. Note what you get asked in the registration process, whether the benefits of registering (if any) are clearly explained to you, whether there is an easily available privacy policy, and how easy it is to update your information after you've entered it. Can you unregister?

9. **Describe any other notable assets or functionality on the site.** Sites can be full of surprises. That all-text industry directory can have a few useful video clips; the stodgy corporate site can turn out to enlighten you on all aspects of a corporate philanthropic effort. Look for surprises and list them.

Figure 1-3 shows a checklist for the second part of a Usability Walk-Through, in which you evaluate a real site. You can also find this checklist on the Web at www.zanzara.com/wufd.

Part I: Introducing Web Usability

FIRST IMPRESSION
If you didn't know, what would you guess this site is for?
What kind of organization put it up?

MAJOR AREAS
List the major areas of the site. Note whether key information assets
are easy to find.

GOALS SITE SEEMS TO MEET
List the goals the site appears to have as you look at it.

GOALS MET FOR SPECIFIC AUDIENCES
List what the site does for specific audiences.

STYLE OF THE SITE
Note whether the site seems serious, fun, competent, authoritative,
friendly, etc. Also note the company's positioning and whether this fits
or conflicts with the site's style.

KEY INFORMATION ASSETS ON THE SITE
Find key information assets (this usually takes some digging around).

BUYING PROCESS
Describe how far you can get in the buying process on the site.

REGISTRATION PROCESS
Describe whether registering is easy or difficult, whether the site
"recognizes" you when you return. Do you really need to make the
user register?

OTHER ASSETS, FUNCTIONALITY
Find anything cool, interesting, or useful on the site not already noted.

Figure 1-3:
Usability
Walk-
Through site
checklist.

Walking Through Dummies.com

We've just described a fairly long and involved process for performing a walk-
through of a Web site — but one that covers a wide range of usability issues.
Rather than just leaving you with a couple of checklists, valuable as they may
be, we're going to take you through a real, live example. To try out the
Usability Walk-Through, we'll analyze a Web site you may already be familiar
with: the Dummies.com site (www.dummies.com).

Chapter 1: Making Your Site Usable   **23**

Dummies.com (see Figure 1-4) is a good example site because it's large and complicated, yet engaged in an overall mission that most people understand: promoting sales of *For Dummies* books. We'll start by listing what we think *should* be on the site; then we'll take you through a tour of what actually *is* on the site. (That's as of this writing, in late 2001; things will certainly change in the future.)

Dummies.com pre-check

Before looking at the Dummies.com site, think through what you would expect the site to do, and what kind of look and feel you would expect it to have. Use Table 1-1 to remind yourself what to look for. Here's what we imagine the site should do:

- ✔ **Users.** Target users for the site should be the general For Dummies audience, which is a very literate but otherwise broad slice of the worldwide public, with a spin toward computer-related titles, because they tie into the Web user demographic. Press (including book reviewers), analysts and other cognoscenti will look at the site for company and brand information as well. (*Cognoscenti* means "those in the know," but we think it really means "those who know they smell.")

- ✔ **Goals.** The site should have as its primary goal helping people find products they want — in this case, *For Dummies* books, and possibly some related products as well. It should also support the needs of investors, press and analysts, and general corporate information-seekers.

- ✔ **Style.** Given that the *For Dummies* line is built around a well-defined, consistent "look and feel" for the books, the Dummies.com site should clearly have a similar look and feel: friendly, approachable, easy to use. The yellow-and-black color scheme of the books should be reflected in the site.

- ✔ **Information assets.** In addition to buying support, described in the next paragraph, the Dummies.com site should have all the standard corporate assets such as stock filings, press releases, job listings, office locations, and contact information.

- ✔ **Other content.** Think big — what other content could reasonably be on the site? Detailed biographies of Dummies executives or employees; links to related assets, such as sites that cover the same topics as Dummies books; and industry news, such as best-selling nonfiction books, can all be included. Don't expect everything you think of to be on the site, but do expect to find a couple of winners from this category on a top-notch site.

- **Buying support.** Any company site should list the company's products — in this case, all the *For Dummies* books and any other products as well. Because there are hundreds of *For Dummies* titles in print, the list needs to be well-organized by category and also support an in-site search engine, to support different styles of finding information. There should also be a way to highlight new and best-selling products. Where-to-buy information is important; online sales from the site would also be valuable, but bookstores (online and real-world) may object to the perceived competition.

- **Registration support.** Providing registration support is optional for this site — you don't need special technical support to read a book, and each book sale is a small transaction, so there isn't an absolute need for end-user registration. Some customers may want to be kept up-to-date on new titles, so a newsletter that users could register for might be a good idea.

- **Other possible functionality.** Possible additional functionality for a book publisher's Web site includes offering free chapters online; Q & A or other events with authors; and clearance sales for damaged or no-longer-viable merchandise. (Stretch your mind: Try to think of a few other possible capabilities for the Dummies.com site before we look at it in the next section.)

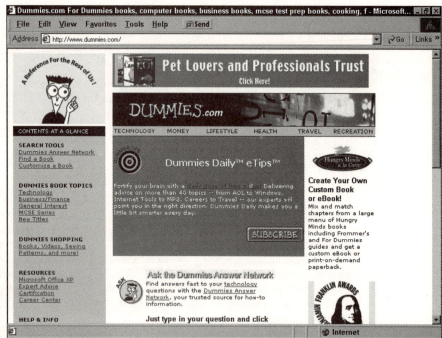

Figure 1-4: Desk-checking Dummies.com

Dummies.com walk-through

Now let's use our walk-through checklist to look at the actual Dummies.com site — a possible career-limiting move for the authors, but an interesting exercise nevertheless. Use Figure 1-3 to prompt you as to what to look for in a typical site, and refer to Figure 1-4 for a screen shot of the site as of this writing. (Bring up the real site if you want to follow through this on the current, live site.). Here's a quick take on the Dummies site:

- **Major site areas.** The site has a number of categories, including major book topic areas: Technology, Money, Lifestyle, Health, Travel, and Recreation. Other areas include the eTips newsletter signup area, the custom book creation area, the Dummies Answer Network, Dummies Shopping, customer support, and advertiser info. Corporate information is *not* included; Hungry Minds, the owners of the Dummies.com brand, have put that info on their company site at `www.hungryminds.com`. (This is a bit hard to find out if you didn't know it before coming to the Dummies site.)

- **The site's goals.** Examining the site, it seems that major goals include: Helping people find the right *For Dummies* books for their interests; getting people to sign up for newsletters; selling related products; and launching newer products such as the Dummies Answer Network. Looking deeper, you see that the site also supports direct sales of books.

- **The site's style.** The style of the site does indeed match the accessible Dummies style, with book graphics, such as Dummies Man, and the books' colors used throughout the site. Navigation from one area of the site, such as a book description, to other areas, such as eBooks, is only through the home page.

- **Key information assets.** Key information assets include the book catalog; the store, which includes related products (sewing patterns for dummies?); the tips database; the certification and career centers; and contact info. Corporate information such as press releases is missing, because it's on the Hungry Minds site.

- **The buying process.** Very briefly, the buying process starts by going to the page for a desired product, clicking a link to order it, adding other products to one's cart the same way, and then clicking a link to complete the transaction over a secure server using a credit card — a process that will be familiar to many Web surfers. (In desk-checking your own site, you would list the steps in the buying process in great detail, because it's crucial to whether your site will meet its goals.)

Part I: Introducing Web Usability

- **The registration process.** Users don't register for the site per se; instead, they register for eTips newsletters. The DummiesDaily.com site, linked to from `www.dummies.com`, allows users to subscribe to or unsubscribe from an impressive number (dozens) of newsletters — unfortunately, not organized in the exact same categories as the books. Figure 1-5 shows the Dummies Daily site.

- **Other notable assets and functionality.** The eBook capability, which allows a user to build his or her own book, is certainly notable. We've already mentioned other outstanding capabilities such as the Dummies Answer Network. Go through the Dummies site and see what you like or dislike.

Overall — and we don't just say this because this is a *For Dummies* book — the Dummies.com site is well-organized, easy to use, and highly capable. The only major concerns about the site that arise in a quick desk check have to do with big-picture organization — the somewhat unclear division of information assets among the Hungry Minds corporate site, the Dummies.com book and tips site, and the Dummies Daily newsletter site.

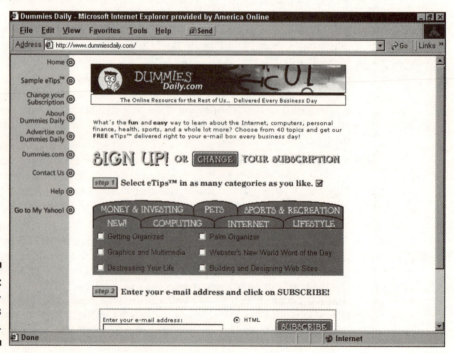

Figure 1-5: Dummies-Daily gives you tips.

Chapter 1: Making Your Site Usable **27**

Checking Yoursite.com

The walk-through process is a great way to get a quick read on the usability of your Web site, without all the time, effort, and coordination needed for formal user testing. Throughout this book, we describe in detail how to improve the usability of every part of your site. But here in this chapter, we focus on the fast and easy walk-through process.

The walk-through process is fun to use on other sites, as described above, but of course the most useful way to try the process is to apply it to your own site. Use the following process to get an initial idea of what you need to do to create a new site, or modify an existing site, that you're responsible for:

- **Think through who the users are.** Use a top-down and a bottom-up process. The top-down part of identifying your users is to create a brief written description of your overall user population — or populations, if you serve multiple audiences. The bottom-up part is to create descriptions of a few "characters," examples of users, giving each a name, age, gender, job, ethnic identity, place of birth and place of residence, degree of computer experience or inexperience — anything you can think of that seems relevant. Then create a personality for each character that fits with the details.

- **Identify goals for your site.** If you're just getting started, these will be big-picture goals, such as "begin selling through the site" or "connect users to existing sales outlets." If you're already rolling, your goals may be more fine-tuned, such as "reduce complaints by 50 percent" or "double sales on the site."

- **Walk through competing and comparable sites.** This is an excellent way to make your site better in every way, especially in usability. That's because it's really hard to be brutally honest about one's own site, but really easy to see the flaws in others' sites. As you analyze sites that compete with yours, or that try to achieve similar goals to your site, you'll learn a lot about the right and wrong way to do things — and then be able to cast a fresh eye on your own site and your plans for it.

- **Walk through your site.** Just as we showed you above for the Dummies.com site, go through your site, using the checklists in this chapter — use the pre-checklist first, then actually look at your site (or site plans, if your site's in development) with the walk-through checklist.

- **Write down your findings.** As you check over your site (or your plans), *write down your findings as you discover them*. For some reason, it's amazingly easy to forget one's impressions of usability difficulties on one's own site. Write down things as you run into them so you don't lose these valuable thoughts. If all you have to review are plans, write down things that sound silly when read from a user's point of view (and you will find such things).

✓ **Create a plan for fixing what you found.** Prioritize your findings. Start discussing them with other people. Identify where you need user testing to get a better read on problems versus where you can "just do it," removing user obstacles without going through a lot of process.

The walk-through process is a great tool in any Web developer's or manager's bag of tricks. It's also a great precursor to the more detailed — and ultimately more powerful — Web usability process we'll describe in the rest of this book.

Chapter 2

Studying Your Users

● ●

In This Chapter

▶ Understanding Web users

▶ Choosing a hardware target

▶ Studying user needs

▶ Carrying out customer visits

▶ Testing while developing

● ●

*A*ctually studying users is what makes Web usability different from other parts of the Web site design process. Finding out more about the audience you're trying to reach with your Web site is one form of studying users. Testing ideas, mockups, and prototypes from your Web site development effort, as well as actual pages from your live Web site, on users — known as *usability testing* — is the other form of studying users. This chapter discusses both techniques.

The characteristics of the audience you're trying to reach should have tremendous implications for the goals, content, and design of your Web site. All too often, though, Web sites are designed and deployed in a vacuum, with members of the Web development team being the only "users" whose opinions impact the final product. No wonder there's often great confusion and frustration on the part of real Web users — who, unfortunately, care a great deal less about your Web site than you do — when they try to use your site.

In this chapter, we give you some basic information about Web users in general because this affects the goals you set for your site and the range of feedback you'll get on your site from the global population of the Web. Then we tell you how to find out more about the specific users who you want to have as users of your Web site, so you can further refine your development effort to better meet their needs.

Also in this chapter, we introduce usability testing and some techniques for quickly getting feedback during the Web site development process, which helps you fine-tune your development effort as you go along. In Part IV, we cover the full range of formal and informal usability testing techniques, which always yield surprises no matter how carefully you listen to users during development.

Identifying the Web User Base

You can rarely get people who aren't already Web users to use your Web site, so it's important to know who's currently on the Web before you set goals for your Web site or begin to develop it. Unfortunately, few people who work with the Web know much about the people using it.

In this section, we introduce you to the overall demographic characteristics of U.S. and worldwide Web users as well as to some specifics about the kind of hardware they're using. This information will help you make intelligent decisions all the way along, from choosing your business goals for the site to the color palette to use when creating Web pages.

The U.S. is halfway there

We'll give demographics for the U.S. Internet market first for a few reasons:

- The U.S. market is the first, the largest, and the richest online market — few can afford to ignore it in the long run
- The most up-to-date, complete, and accurate statistics for consumers in general, and for Internet users in particular, tend to be statistics for the U.S. market
- Other markets' Internet adoption is behind adoption in the U.S., so studying the U.S. Internet market is one way of studying the likely future of other markets

U.S. consumers, including U.S. Internet users, tend to be less sensitive about privacy than consumers in other countries, and privacy laws tend to be weaker in the U.S. than elsewhere. Even as other countries catch up to the U.S. in Internet usage, they may not be as well-characterized statistically due to other nations' privacy concerns and protections.

The most impressive fact about the U.S. Internet market is that over half of the U.S. population is online — the only large country for which this is true. (England is close behind.) Having so many users online means that the online population is fairly representative of the overall market, to a much greater extent than most other countries. It also means that Web-based sales and marketing efforts actually have a chance of reaching most of the people you need to reach if your focus is the U.S. market, while this is not true in most other places.

Table 2-1 shows statistics for the U.S. projected for the year 2003, from Jupiter Media Metrix, the leading online research firm. Some key statistics, and their implications, include:

Chapter 2: Studying Your Users **31**

- ✔ **Total people online**. In 2003, the U.S. online population is projected to be 168 million people — 60 percent of the U.S. population. Growth for the subsequent five-year period is projected to be about 7 percent a year. Better-off, better-educated, and younger people are online at an even higher rate than the overall population. *Implication*: Most companies can reach most of their desired customers online, more so than through any medium except television.

- ✔ **Broadband users**. In 2003, 18 million people, about 26 percent of the U.S. online population, are projected to be using *broadband* Internet access; that is, connections twice as fast or more than a 56K modem connected to a typical phone line. Broadband connections are also always on — you don't have to wait to connect or disconnect, but can go to a Web site as soon as you type in a URL. Having the connection always accessible means that users tend to access the Web more often.

  Growth in broadband usage from 2003 to 2008 is projected to be about 20 percent a year, meaning that it may be about 2008 before 50 percent of the online population is using broadband. *Implication*: Design for an audience with slower, modem-based connections of about 56K; consider limited use of broadband features where it makes sense.

- ✔ **Online retail sales**. In 2003, it's projected that online retail sales will be about $71 billion, less than 2 percent of the staggering $3 trillion-plus total U.S. retail sales picture. Growth from 2003 to 2008 is projected to be about 25 percent a year, but that still means that it will be about the year 2011 before online reaches 10 percent of all retail sales. *Implication*: Most companies will be doing most of their sales offline for decades to come, though some business-to-business sales will move online much faster.

- ✔ **Business versus consumer**. Many business markets, and many niches within the consumer market, will move online much faster than the overall population. However, it's very hard to generalize for all businesspeople or for large groups of consumers. This supports the idea that while it's important to know the overall trends in online usage, it's even more important to study the online usage patterns of your current customer base and desired customers before setting goals for your Web site.

Table 2-1	U.S. Online Population, 2003 (Estimated)		
Statistic	*Number in 2003*	*Percentage in 2003*	*Growth Rate from 2003 to 2008*
Total people online	168 million	60 percent of U.S. population	7 percent per year
Broadband users	18 million	26 percent of U.S. online population	20 percent per year
Online retail sales	$71 billion	About 2 percent of U.S. retail sales	25 percent per year

Consolidation in the U.S. Market

In mid-2001, Jupiter Media Metrix reported that almost 50 percent of the time U.S. users spend online was on sites owned by just three companies: AOL Time Warner, Microsoft, and Yahoo!. That means that all the other companies with Web sites are competing for the remaining half of users' online time. More and more sites that want a lot of Web traffic will have to reach business deals with one or more of the Big Three.

It's important to remember that the U.S. market is at least a few years ahead of most other major markets in online adoption, so if you're doing business in other countries, your online user base will be a lower percentage of the market than in the U.S.

Europe and Asia are growing rapidly

No, the Eurasian landmass isn't getting any larger. What we mean is that European and Asian online markets are growing rapidly, but are still much smaller than the U.S. market in terms of Internet penetration of their overall populations. We look at the statistics for non-U.S. Internet usage in terms of language groups (marketers are interested first in statistics by country, but Web designers have to build or localize their sites for one language at a time, which is why we look at language groups).

Table 2-2 shows statistics for various European and Asian languages projected for the year 2003 from a company called Global Reach (details at www.glreach.com/globstats/index.php3). Key statistics include:

- **Largest markets are English, Spanish, Chinese, and Japanese**. These four markets are each projected to have over 50 million users in 2003. Look to these language groups first to reach very large audiences.

- **Penetration is highest for English, French, German, Italian, Dutch, Japanese, and Korean**. Each of these languages is expected to have over 40 percent Internet penetration in 2003. Look to these language groups first to reach a critical mass of people in a specific market.

- **Reaching everyone is hard**. You would have to translate your Web site into 12 languages to reach every language group of over 6 million people online.

- **Target, target, target**. Highly educated and high-income users in a given language market will move online much faster than the overall population. These elites may also, to varying extents, be able to read content in English as well as their native languages, especially in Europe. While it's very important to know overall trends in the language breakdown of the

Net — actually, we hope the Net doesn't have a language breakdown! — you must study the language usage of your current and intended customers before setting goals for your Web site.

Table 2-2   Worldwide Online Population by Language Group, 2003 (Estimated)

Language	Online in 2003	Total Population in 2003	Percentage Penetration
English	230 million	500 million	46 percent
Spanish	60 million	332 million	18 percent
German	46 million	98 million	47 percent
Portuguese	32 million	170 million	19 percent
French	30 million	72 million	42 percent
Italian	23 million	57 million	40 percent
Russian	15 million	170 million	9 percent
Dutch	10 million	20 million	50 percent
Other European (14 major languages)	74 million	170 million	44 percent
ALL EUROPEAN LANGUAGES	690 million	1,589 million	33 percent
Chinese	160 million	885 million	18 percent
Japanese	58 million	125 million	46 percent
Korean	35 million	75 million	47 percent
Arabic	6 million	130 million	5 percent
Other Asian (3 major languages)	11 million	267 million	4 percent
ALL ASIAN LANGUAGES	270 million	1,482 million	18 percent

Hardware and software trends matter

Imagine a world in which TV broadcasters had to be worried about huge projection screens, tiny portable TVs, black and white sets, color sets, low- and high-resolutions screens, and other complications. Oops — that's the world we live in; it should be pretty easy to imagine.

How do TV broadcasters deal with these complexities? They basically ignore them. Nearly all TV broadcasts are optimized for the majority of the market: 19" to 25", standard-resolution color TV sets. If you use a smaller set, or a black and white set, you miss a lot; if you use a larger, higher-resolution screen, you don't get much advantage, because high-resolution broadcasts are not widely available.

Yet as someone involved in the creation of Web sites, you're told over and over that you should make sure your site works great on Netscape 2.0 — a 10-year-old browser — or on screens with resolutions below 640 x 480, such as TV monitors being used for Web browsing. And oh, remember all those people trying to access your site through a *WAP* phone. (WAP is the acronym for Wide Area Protocol, the standard for accessing the Web through a cell phone and it's tiny screen.)

Fuhgeddaboutit! People accessing the Web with old computers and old software, or with new, small-screen tools like Palm Pilot-type handhelds WAP phones, are well aware that they aren't going to get the best experience from most of the Web sites they visit. They aren't going to be all that angry at you if your site doesn't bend over backward to accommodate them.

Similarly, you don't need to worry about people with huge screens, ultra-fast processors, or T1 connections who might demand more from your site; they're also used to Web sites that aren't optimized for their systems. Design a site that looks and works great for the vast majority of your users; don't worry much about the extremes.

We think that you should be willing to use a technology when 85 percent of your users are able to take advantage of it. Which technologies meet that test? According to statistics quoted on the Web Design Guide by DreamInk (www.dreamink.com/design5.shtml), as shown in Figure 2-1, here are current realities as of late 2001:

> ✔ **4.0 browsers are common.** Microsoft Internet Explorer has about 60 percent of the browser market; Netscape has about 35 percent. 80 percent of users — a number that's growing rapidly — have a 4.0 or greater version of one browser or the other, which means they have reasonably good Javascript support (though differences in support across browsers mean you still have to test Javascripts relentlessly on supported browsers).

Chapter 2: Studying Your Users 35

- ✔ **800 x 600 is the standard.** 85 percent of users have 800 x 600 screen resolution or greater, and this proportion is growing steadily. Over 25 percent have 1024 x 768 resolution. Many widely popular sites depend on 800 x 600 resolution or greater. Design your screens so critical controls and content fit within a 640-pixel width, and then use the right rail for additional content. See Chapter 7 for details.

- ✔ **Count on 256 colors.** Although exact statistics aren't handy, many users run their systems at 256 colors, either because that's all their system supports, because their systems run faster at 256 colors than at greater color depths, or because a game or other program forced the color setting to 256 colors and the user hasn't switched it back.

  What exactly do we mean by *256 colors*? Almost all computer systems can run with their displays showing 256 colors at once. This is enough for word processing, but makes a typical picture look blocky. Most computers can also display thousands of colors at once, making pictures look better, but with slower performance and possibly at lower screen resolution. Because of these tradeoffs, many users run their systems — knowingly or not — with only 256 colors displayed. See Chapter 10 for details.

- ✔ **Use narrowband to reach the broad majority.** As mentioned above, only 26 percent of U.S. users have fast connections; the rest are at 56K or slower. The number of *narrowband* (56K or slower) users, especially in non-U.S. countries, is still growing rapidly; only in the U.S. is there any strong move to broadband, and that's progressing slowly.

- ✔ **Your mileage may vary.** Consider your target market before counting too much on the above statistics. Students and people in less-developed countries often have lesser equipment; people using an intranet within a company often can count on faster connections, when they're not dialing in remotely. However, if you start with the above assumptions as a base, you won't be too far off, and user expectations of how your site will work are dictated by the realities described above.

The touchiest two issues for most users are page download speeds and Javascript. Slow page downloads interrupt the user's ability to smoothly move around the Web, creating great frustration and irritation, some of which will be directed at your site. Javascript causes annoying error messages to appear when it doesn't work right, or when it's not supported at all. See Chapter 7 for details on how to design your pages to work well for the vast majority of your users.

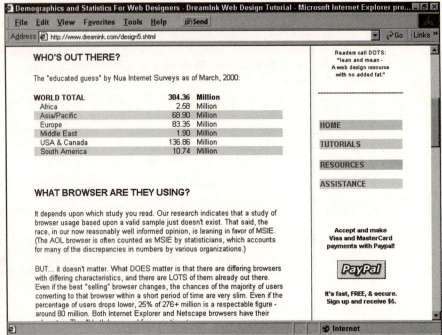

Figure 2-1: The Web Design Guide includes updated statistics.

Studying User Needs and Expectations

Before setting goals, plunging into Web design, testing for usability, and deploying your new or upgraded site, it's really important to understand user needs and expectations. Otherwise you're working in a vacuum.

Understanding user *needs* is difficult, in that to do so you will probably have to go out and talk to some actual users. We'll talk about various ways to do that in a moment.

Understanding user *expectations*, though, is much easier, and equally important. Why so important? Because the most important thing for your company to do is not, as you may expect, meeting customer's needs; it's avoiding looking stupid. If your company does things that make it look stupid, it loses credibility with potential customers, and never has a chance to meet people's needs — they won't trust you enough to let you try.

To avoid looking stupid, you must meet minimal user expectations as to what your site does and how well it works for most users. Unless you are pioneering something really innovative, there's an easy way to find out what your users' minimal expectations are: study the competition. In this case, that means taking a look at competing Web sites before setting goals for your own site.

Chapter 2: Studying Your Users 37

Studying competitors to discover user expectations works well for two reasons. First, your competitors know your mutual users fairly well; they probably have a fairly good understanding of what your shared users expect.

More subtly, and more importantly, your competitors' sites, along with your own, help *set* user expectations. Your customers will think that a credible Web site in the area of, say, online flower sales, must have a level of design complexity and features that roughly matches the average of the top few such sites they're aware of. If your site is obviously not comparable to its competition — if it doesn't meet user expectations — your users won't take your site, or your company, seriously.

Studying competing sites

Doing detailed competitive analysis is a high professional calling (so says one of the authors, Smith, who used to do this for a living); it's part of the job of many marketing people, and is actually a separate job (or a separate, highly paid consulting function) in many companies, especially larger ones. But doing too detailed a competitive analysis can be worse than doing none at all.

You don't want your competitors' efforts to set some kind of a limit on what you *can* do for your users; you want the features on your competitors' sites to help determine the lower limits of what you *must* do for your users. To find out how high the competition has set the bar, it's best to do a quick, rough competitive analysis that concentrates on listing only the major information elements and crucial functional features of competing sites.

Don't worry about the details of how a specific feature works. Just list the major features of the site, and consider making a further note only if a particular feature is very bad or very good.

Here are the major site features you should consider when looking at a competing site:

- **Home page and overall organization.** Does the home page give you quick access to all the major features of the site? Is it well-organized? Does it load quickly?

  A site only has one chance to make a first impression, and the home page is it. Go over the home page several times during any usability update or redesign process.

- **Information assets.** Consider the presence or absence of contact information; company history and description; press releases; investor information, if applicable; and product descriptions. Possible extras include descriptions of the company's industry and pointers to industry resources.

Part I: Introducing Web Usability

✔ **Interaction and community.** Look for opportunities to connect with the company: to get product questions answered, to receive technical support, to reach specific people or at least specific departments within the company. Extras here include the ability to register for an online newsletter and online message boards or live chat, either for product support or for other interaction.

✔ **E-commerce functionality.** Start by looking for basic "how to buy" information. Then check for the ability to buy online. Go through some or all of the buying process and note whether it's highly usable, so-so, poor, or even nonfunctional. (You'd be amazed at how many times e-commerce functionality on a site is very difficult to use.)

✔ **Other areas of note.** Different kinds of sites will have different specific kinds of features. For example, sites for people who share a hobby will have more community and interaction features, and less in the way of e-commerce. Adjust your list of features to include those of particular relevance to your area of business or other focus.

Table 2-3 shows a simplified competitive matrix for the front pages of the Web sites of major automakers. The contrast is striking; the sites range from very spare to very dense, low-tech to high-tech, highly informative to moderately informative to almost completely uninformative. (The term *"ego" graphic* in the table refers to a graphic that looks great when it's downloaded but doesn't provide enough actual information to be worth the wait for many users.) Going through this kind of comparative. exercise with your own and competitors' sites can help keep you from making huge mistakes on your own Web site and can show you large competitive opportunities to take advantage of.

Table 2-3	Comparison of Major Automaker Web Site Front Pages		
Feature	*DaimlerChrysler.com*	*Ford.com*	*GeneralMotors.com*
Loading	Fairly fast, big graphic	Medium speed, lots of little graphics	Very slow, loads Flash and graphics. Site scrolls but nothing at bottom
Languages	German, English	English	English
News or product highlights	N/A	Yes	Yes
Graphics	Large "ego" graphic with one truck and two cars	Smaller graphics and brand logos	Medium-sized "ego" graphic with one car

Chapter 2: Studying Your Users   *39*

Feature	DaimlerChrysler.com	Ford.com	GeneralMotors.com
Corporate info	Text link (German and English)	Links for investors, press, job seekers, environment, charity, more	Links for investors, press, job seekers, environment, more
Product info	Text link (German and English)	Links to vehicles by brand or kind; product selector by model	Links to vehicle shopping, brands, safety, consumer and business offerings
Services info	N/A	List of service offerings and user tips	Some service offerings listed
Buying info	N/A	Dealer locator	Dealer locator
Special features	Nothing that's accessible from front page	Link to racing area, site map, privacy info, FAQs, contact info, more	Link to OnStar info, family info
Overall impression	Much too spare, real waste of space (and user's time). Isn't there one product or piece of news worth highlighting on front page?	Dense but powerful, great use of Web meets difficult information design challenge	Mediocre — uses Flash to no great effect, less info than Ford site but even slower to load

Studying users directly

Finding out what users want is usually a greatly neglected part of the process for any kind of product or service design. However, many large companies have at least built a modest effort to identify user needs into the design cycle. "Have you run it through a focus group?" has become a standard question in executive reviews of development processes.

However, there are actually several related methods for studying users. Each has its plusses and minuses, which we describe in detail below. Here's a quick list of the major ways of finding out from users what they want.

✔ **Secondary market research.** This is digging into published sources such as research reports, census data, even the statistics about Web users given earlier in this chapter, to find out what others say your users want and need.

Part I: Introducing Web Usability

- ✔ **Customer visits.** A customer-visits program is a carefully planned, well-organized effort to visit customers with a pre-planned set of questions or Web site mockups in hand. Customer-visits programs give you a deep understanding of your users and their needs.

- ✔ **Focus groups.** The classic tool for finding user needs, focus groups are a more, well, focused option: They work best when you already know your customers fairly well and are trying to generate specific options for your Web site.

- ✔ **Survey research.** Surveying groups of users about what they want is a great way to make a final decision on the best option when you have a good idea of what the choices are.

All of these methods are useful for both marketing research and for making usability decisions — in fact, for Web site development, marketing and usability needs are sometimes identical. However, we've found that customer visits are the method that's both the least-used and, in many cases, most effective for usability purposes. The other methods are also better known, so we focus here on when to use customer visits and how to get the most out of them.

Executing a simple customer-visits program

A customer-visits program is a set of visits by members of your Web site development team to your customers in their workplaces, homes — wherever they'll be using your Web site.

Visiting customers where they live and work serves some very important purposes. Unlike a focus group or a formal user test, which are performed in your workplace or at a third-party site, customer visits take place where the customer is completely at ease. *You* may be a little uptight at first, but you're not the one who has the needed information here. Customers give you much more detailed information when in their own natural surroundings.

Actually seeing customers' workplaces or home computer setups while talking to them also gives you a vivid mental picture of how your users will be working with your Web site. For example, it shows you convincingly how using your site is only one of many things that your user has going on at any given time.

Having members of the development team involved in visiting and interviewing customers is also an invaluable element of customer visits. Though often reluctant at first, people on the development team generally turn out to be excited about the actual experience of visiting customers *in situ*.

You can make a customer-visits program as simple or elaborate as you wish. It can be preceded by formal study of your user base and can involve visits to dozens of customer sites. However, you'll probably need to find a market

Chapter 2: Studying Your Users

research consultant experienced in customer visit research to get the most out of such an in-depth program. On the other hand, you can easily do a simple customer visit program yourself, with a small team and the expenditure of a moderate amount of time and a small amount of money. We describe how below.

Why study users at all?

Study users up-front to save time and money down the road.

Every time you put a new, or newly updated, version of your Web site out for public consumption, you are, in essence, doing a very large and expensive user test. After all, user and stakeholder feedback from the current version of your Web site will be a significant driver of what goes into the next version. However, when you test features by releasing them on your public site, you lose out on the benefits you'd get by deploying a version that worked well from the start.

Studying users up front, as part of the Web site design process, serves several very important needs. The first benefit, and the easiest to convince others of, is that studying users up front saves a great deal of time and money. Often, you can study users within a period of a few weeks and a budget of a few thousand dollars — then use the information to make improvements to your site that otherwise would have taken another full release cycle to get to. You get the results you want from your Web site — which may include increased sales, more effective PR and marketing, decreased support costs, and more — much sooner by studying users up front.

The second reason is more subtle: by studying users in advance, you make improvements that might never have even been possible through the typical release-then-revise cycle. Usability

people know that many design decisions, once built into a product such as a Web site, are extremely difficult to change. Part of the reason is that the cost of changing something in a finished product is so great that the improvement may not be worth it; another part of the reason is that people on both the product team and in the customer base get attached to the way things are, no matter how suboptimal. Study users in advance to avoid setting bad decisions in concrete within your "finished" Web site.

The third reason is more subtle yet. Undertaking a user research effort during development signals to everyone involved in the project that users are not only important, but are the ultimate authority as to what the end result should look like and how it should work. Researching user needs and desires early on builds support for going to users for feedback again and again throughout the life of the Web site.

A lesson from marketing, however, is that subtle arguments usually don't work. To justify studying users, lead with your best argument: studying users up front saves time and money in the overall development process. If the person you're trying to convince really wants to hear more, talk about how the product may never be as good without testing as it would be with testing because less-than-optimal decisions don't get set in concrete; also talk about how the importance of putting the user first is emphasized by putting user research first in your development process.

42 Part I: Introducing Web Usability

Before you visit customers

Before you actually visit anybody, get ready as follows:

- **Set your goals.** For Web site development, the most suitable goals for customer-visits programs are to identify user needs and to generate ideas for improving your product. Work on user needs if you're near the beginning of the process of creating a new site or doing a major revision to your existing one; generate ideas for improvement if you're doing a modest revision to an existing site or are nearer completion of a project.

- **Create your agenda.** The agenda for a customer visit is a two- to three-page list of the major topics you want to cover, with key questions that you'll ask and things to look out for.

  Figure 2-2 shows a simplified example of an agenda for a customer-visits program for an internal company portal. Use this agenda as a model to create your own agenda for your visit. Keep the agenda simple but try to ask all the questions listed on your agenda on every visit.

- **Devise any mockups or discussion pieces.** You may want to use your current site, work in progress, or competitors' sites as discussion pieces when talking to customers. If you need to have a mockup or printout with you, create it now. Keep your exhibits simple and few; they're jumping-off pieces for discussion, not evidence in a court case.

- **Decide whom to visit.** For a simple customer visits program, choose six to eight customers who represent various types of users. Visit nearby customers where possible, to keep costs down; travel when needed to get the full range of customer types. (It's amazing how so many interesting users turn out to be in Hawaii or Paris.)

- **Select visiting teams.** We recommend putting two or three people on each visiting team, and having each team visit three or four customers. That way you get a wide range of people involved and get a variety of perspectives, yet avoid taking too much time from any one person's schedule. But you can do a simple customer visit program with one "visitor" if that's all you have time and money for.

- **Practice.** Have each visiting team practice by doing a sample customer visit, even if it's within your own workplace. (Each team can even visit the other.) Use your agenda to guide the discussion; show any mockups or other exhibits you have; note anything unexpected that comes up. Mostly, give yourself and your team members a chance to get any stage fright out of the way before your first real visit.

Carrying out visits

When you actually carry out the customer visit, try to immerse yourself as much in the customer's environment as possible. Ask for a tour of the customer's home or workplace. Conduct the actual interview, though, as close as you can to where the customer actually uses your Web site. Ask the customer to set aside two hours, with the understanding that it may go somewhat quicker.

Chapter 2: Studying Your Users 43

WARMUP AND CONTEXT SETTING
Promise the user confidentiality. Ask for examples as you go along;
for instance, if they say they check e-mail, ask to see their e-mail program in action.
• Tell us something about what you do.
• What's a typical day like for you? Walk us through your typical day.
• What tools do you use to do your work?
• Any company systems or tools? Can you show us those?

GENERAL INFORMATION GATHERING FOR PORTAL
Don't use the word "portal"; keep the focus on what the user currently
does, not on the solution you're working on.
• If you want to take time off, how do you do that? Can you show us?
• Tell us about a time you've needed a form from HR. What was it? How did you get it?
• Tell us about other information you need to access from your company.
• Show us any company manuals or documents that you use.
  Show us non-company books and manuals too.
  What do you use that book for? How about that one?

WEB-SPECIFIC INFORMATION GATHERING FOR PORTAL
Again, don't say "portal"; keep the focus on what the user currently does,
not on the solution you're working on. Ask the user what they like and dislike
about each Web site.
• Are there any internal company Web sites you use? Please show us. Likes? Dislikes?
• Are there any internal sites that you can't get to that you wish you could use?
• Show us any vendor sites you use. Any likes or dislikes?
• Show us any customer sites you use. Any likes or dislikes?
• Are there any work-related sites you've bookmarked?
  What made them worth bookmarking?

PORTAL QUESTIONS
Now it's OK to say "portal"; these questions ask about use of portals. Avoid
other jargon, though, such as "customize."
• Show us any portal sites your company currently has. How do you use it? Which parts?
• Do you use any portal sites such as Excite, MyYahoo, MyNetscape, MyAOL?
  Which parts? What do you like or dislike about each?
• Have you done anything to make a site show you the things you're most interested in?

You've really given us a great overview of what you do and the tools you use, thanks!

Figure 2-2:
Here's an
example
agenda for
researching
an internal
company
portal.

Keep the interview relaxed, and constantly remind yourself that the purpose is to find out what the user needs. If members of the interview team are talking very much, you're not giving the customer a chance to speak. And if you ask the customer focused questions, such as exactly what fields should go in a registration form, you've moved into usability testing and away from hearing from them what they really need from your site.

Have one member of your team take detailed notes. Capture a detailed description of what the home or workplace is like, what kind of computer the user has, how he or she tends to use it, and other contextual details. Capture the overall gist of everything the customer discusses, and write down verbatim quotes that sum up important points. Other members of the team should take brief notes on the points they consider most important or surprising.

Decide in advance who's responsible for moving the discussion through the agenda, so all the pre-planned questions get asked. Keep asking the customer what they currently do. Ask "Anything else?," "Anything more?," "Does that make you think of any other things you want?" — questions that keep the customer talking. Time allowing, try to exhaust each topic before moving onto the next.

Always let the customers know, before, during, and especially after the interview, how much you value their opinions and that you appreciate them taking the time to tell you what they think. Avoid, however, making specific commitments about what you're going to do as a result of their comments. Just let them know that their feedback will have a significant impact on your product development efforts.

At the end of the interview, ask the users if they're willing to allow you to take pictures of them at their workplaces. This is a fun way to wrap things up, and the photos will help make the visit "real" when you describe it to others back at your workplace.

What you may hear

If you conduct your interview correctly, you're likely to get a lot of unstructured, unfocused, even rambling information. This will seem odd, because it's unlikely that your interviewee is in politics. But it's actually good, because it's usually in the middle of what starts out as a seemingly pointless digression that customers come up with crucial details about what they really need.

What you're hearing should contain some surprises — it may even be very frustrating, as when customers ask for things a Web site just can't do, or tell you the most important thing is that you add some feature that you just decided to abandon. This kind of frustration is also good; it means that you're not driving the customer through your own concerns, but are actually hearing what they have to say.

Chapter 2: Studying Your Users   45

TIP

> ## When silence is golden
>
> On customer visits, a key mistake interviewers make is to get defensive. The customer may say something on your site is awful; the natural tendency of the interviewer is to then explain why it has to be awful. This tips off the user that you really don't want to hear what they have to say. It's important that everyone on the visit team be thick-skinned and "take his lumps" from the customers' comments. A useful technique is to just nod as the customers speak; they'll gain confidence, and then tell you the truly valuable nuggets of information that you most want to hear.

It's also quite likely that the customer will give you valuable feedback that has nothing to do with your Web site. They may tell you good or bad things about customer service, pricing, plusses and minuses of competitors' offerings, and so on. Provide this feedback, unfiltered, to the appropriate people in your company; they may decide to undertake their own customer-visits program!

Finishing the job: The 4 D's

The experience of carrying out customer visits will make a deep impression on the people on your visiting teams. Now it's time to get the information out of the team members' heads and into the minds of everyone involved with, or supporting, the development effort. You need to go through The 4 D's: Debrief, Discuss, Document, and Disseminate:

- **Debrief.** After each customer visit, have a brief meeting to discuss what was learned. Focus on what the customer said, how and where he/she works, and other parts of "sharing the experience." Do not focus on drawing conclusions. The person who will be creating the final report or presentation, if not present on the visit, should be sure to attend these post-visit meetings. This person should also get copies of the notes from the visit, review them, and ask any questions while the information is still fresh in the visitors' minds.

- **Discuss.** After all the visits are concluded — or halfway through the set of visits, if you want to make mid-course corrections in the agenda, and then again at the end — have a meeting of all involved to discuss what was learned. Here the focus begins to turn to conclusions: not about what to do, but about what patterns you can identify in customer needs. Don't shy away from needs that can't be met in the current revision — or even needs that can't be met by a Web site at all. Just pass such information onto the right person.

- **Document.** One or two people should now work together to create a document describing the results of the customer visit program. Get a good writer plus an experienced person from your industry to do the report. Devote a page or two to describing each visit and summarizing the needs of that customer; pull out verbatim quotes to illustrate important points; and include a picture of the user sitting at his or her computer — this brings home to everyone the real world of your users. When you have all the summaries done, create the beginning of the document: a one-page list of action items for the current project, and a few pages summarizing user needs. Attach your detailed notes from each visit to the end of the report for reference.

✔ **Disseminate.** (*Disseminate* means "spread the word"; don't confuse it with *dissimulate,* which means "lie.") Get the information from the visits out to as many people as possible. Start by distributing the summary document widely — possibly even posting it to an internal Web site — but don't stop there. Create a brief presentation that describes each customer visited and his or her location, key takeaways from that customer, and overall conclusions. Get in front of as many people as possible to share it.

Using Testing Techniques During Development

The details of how to conduct usability testing are given in Part IV; it takes us several chapters to tell you the basics of how to test users and what to do with the results. However, in addition to the full-scale testing efforts described in Part IV, you can also use testing techniques throughout the development process to keep the overall effort on track and reduce the amount of rework you'll have to do — or decide not to do until a future project — after you formally test the usability of your site.

Here are some of the highlights from the usability testing process that you can use during product development:

✔ **Think like a user.** It's very easy, and very natural, during Web site development to get caught up in internal project details like who's doing what work, or whether a specific Javascript program has been tested on all major browser versions. Step back from the details throughout the project and ask yourself what the impact of project work will be on the user. Sometimes, you'll be able to skip work when you realize that it won't really have much user impact.

✔ **Ask "What will this be like for the user?"** When someone tells you about a new idea for the Web site, always ask what it will be like for the user. This will help you better understand what the idea really is, and will also help the person with the idea understand how it will really work when implemented. Sometimes, it will become clear just from the discussion that follows this question that an idea isn't worth pursuing or is too much work to consider implementing in this round of changes.

Chapter 2: Studying Your Users 47

✔ **Find comparable examples on competitors' sites.** As you begin to implement each feature for your site, do a quick search for comparable examples on the sites of competitors or on sites with similar purposes. If none of your competitors have implemented a feature, ask yourself why not. If you do find the feature elsewhere, see if there is anything obvious you can learn about how to implement — or how not to implement — the desired feature.

✔ **Construct "fat marker" mockups.** Use a marking pen to construct a quick mockup of what the feature will look like and how it will fit on a Web page or set of Web pages. Figure 2-3 shows a fat marker mockup for a registration page. By using a fat marker — rather than a pen or pencil — you avoid getting too detailed, and instead focus on the user's overall experience.

✔ **Do little tests.** Create little functional pieces of your site, or single Web pages, and try them out on users. For these informal tests, users can be other members of the development team, coworkers, even friends and family members. Listen carefully to what's said, even if you can't act on all the feedback right away. Doing these little tests as you go, and letting the results guide your development efforts, can save you a great deal of time and difficulty later on.

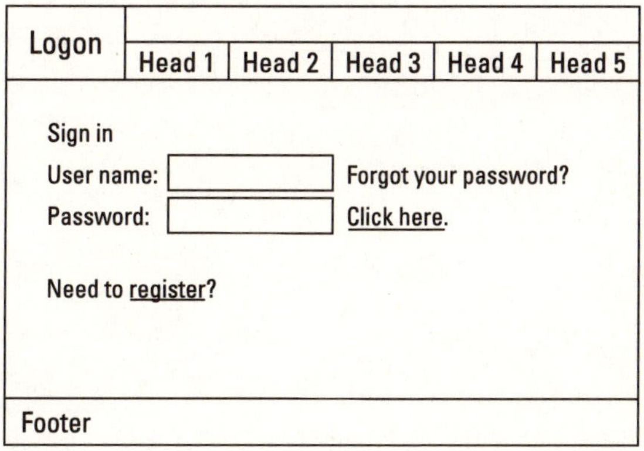

Figure 2-3:
A fat marker mockup helps you get feedback fast.

Logon	Head 1	Head 2	Head 3	Head 4	Head 5

Sign in

User name: [   ]   Forgot your password?

Password: [   ]   Click here.

Need to register?

Footer

48 Part I: Introducing Web Usability

Chapter 3

Setting Goals for Your Site

In This Chapter

▶ Figuring out which user needs you want to meet

▶ Setting your business goals

▶ Meeting user expectations

▶ Reducing costs and increasing revenues

▶ Setting the goals for your site

▶ Using Web site metrics

▶ Setting usability goals

As the old saying goes, "If you don't know where you're going, you're not very likely to get there." Web sites can serve so many purposes that it's easy for Web development projects to create sites that are jacks of all trades, but masters of none. By setting goals for your site, you can meet those key goals while also adequately meeting all the varied demands placed on your Web site.

Setting goals also helps you get adequate funding for your Web site development process. When a company spends hundreds of thousands or millions of dollars developing a Web site, and no one involved feels that the result meets the key goals they have for it — because each person's idea of the goals is different — then it's unlikely that the site will get much further investment. It will just limp along, occasionally updated so as to not become embarrassingly out of date, but never fully developed into a useful tool for the organization. This is like putting out one issue of a magazine, then never putting out a second issue. By setting goals up front and meeting them at implementation time, the Web site development team ensures that the site will play an increasingly useful role over time.

Setting goals is critically important for Web usability. Any time the issue of usability arises, the next logical question is, "usable for what?". By setting goals for the site, you have a ready answer for that question. You can demonstrate the increasing usability of the site as an increasing ability for the site to meet its goals, leading to further development of the site's features and its usability as well.

Is the Web site the business?

The role of a Web site in a business can vary tremendously. The Web site can be the whole business — the only place that sales are made and support is delivered — or the site can simply be "brochureware," an informational site that provides contact information for a business that otherwise exists solely in the real world. Usually, the role of the Web site is something in-between.

In discussing business sites in this book, we mainly focus on sites that are an adjunct to an existing, real-world business because that describes the vast majority of sites. (You can still use this book if you're trying to do most or all of your business on the Web; just ignore the parts about tying in with your real-world business.) Most businesses, regardless of size, need to have at least a brochureware site, and most businesses also need to do everything they can to move some sales, or at least some sales support, to the Web.

Why is this? Despite all the glamour and drama that's been associated with the dot-com boom and bust of the 1990s, there's a very simple business reason to do as much selling and sales support as possible on the Web: It can be your lowest-cost channel for sales and support. Web sales are made directly to the customer, at full price or close to it, and you have few sales costs besides the Web site itself. You can even get customers to pay you to ship your products to them.

If you can set up a sales site relatively cheaply, then drive 10 to 20 percent or more of your sales online within your current advertising and marketing budget, you can grow your top-line revenues and your bottom-line profits substantially with incremental, high-profit online sales.

Similarly, the Web can be used to drive down costs. A brochureware site that provides basic PR and contact information can save you an awful lot of money in printing and mailing costs and 800-number phone charges. Product and "how to buy" information online can help drive sales through all your other sales channels. Answering a technical support question by an online Frequently Asked Questions (FAQ) document instead of by phone may save you $10-20 per question.

Sites for non-business organizations can play a similar wide range of roles. There's a big difference between an information-only site for a long-established university and the site of an online-only university with no real-world classrooms. You can apply businesslike thinking to your Web site to help improve your revenues (or donations) and decrease your costs, no matter what kind of organization you have and how much or little you currently depend on the Web. Then add an extra layer of thought about how to use your Web site to achieve your educational, informational, service, personal, or other goals.

Picking Which User Needs to Meet

Many usability experts and Web designers talk about meeting user needs as if that were the only reason for putting up a Web site. But organizations put up and maintain Web sites, at significant effort and expense, to meet their own goals. If you focus only on the user, you're missing half the picture. Usability practice for business Web sites starts and ends with business goals; helping users means helping them accomplish tasks that contribute to furthering the goals of the business.

Of course, not all business goals are directly profit-oriented or easy to tie to the bottom line. Providing users information about your company's line of business, describing its charitable efforts, even linking to off-site educational resources about your company's industry are part of the "soft" side of doing business and don't drive revenues up directly. They do, however, contribute to other, more general goals of the business.

The trick is for your business to invest most of the available time, energy, and money into things that contribute directly to the core goals of the business, which almost always involve making or saving money. (Though an apple juice company may have disposing of cores as a core goal.)

Some time, energy, and money can go into Web site content and functionality that contribute to broader business goals. No effort should go into things that don't contribute. Ask users what they need from your Web site; then implement the solutions to those needs that contribute to the company's bottom line. Sounds simple, but this kind of decision-making sieve can help weed out Web site ideas that suck up an awful lot of time and money.

Setting Business Goals

Business goals for a site are the first concern we'll take up here because business sites are the major focus of Web site development today, and also because most non-business sites have at least some business-like concerns. So you should read this section no matter what kind of site you're developing, and also read the section on goals for non-business sites at the end of this chapter for further insights.

Setting goals is especially important for business sites. Businesses tend to have the money and personnel to undertake large, expensive site development projects. The lost opportunity when such projects don't operate under clear-cut, agreed-on goals is correspondingly greater.

Business goals for a Web site usually fall into one of a few clear categories. In order of increasing site complexity needed to meet each goal, they are: meeting basic customer or stakeholder expectations; reducing costs; and increasing revenues (see Figure 3-1). Here, we'll explore each of these categories in detail.

In business, "agreed-on goals" doesn't necessarily mean "everyone agrees these are the goals we should follow"; that kind of heartfelt agreement is rare. What it actually means is, "everyone agrees these are the goals we *will* follow." The project's executive sponsor and at least one key person on the site development team should together be responsible for making sure that the goals for the site make sense and that they're followed throughout the development process. Any suggestions for project changes should be approved only after it's shown how they'll improve the project's ability to meet its goals.

Understanding stakeholders

A stakeholder is not an assistant chef at a barbecue, or someone with a bit part in a vampire movie. It's actually someone who, while not necessarily a customer, has some feeling of participation in your business and some ability to influence its success (or to contribute to its failure). Government officials who approve your permit requests or process your tax returns; press people who decide whether to write a story about you based on your press release — or based on a nasty rumor about your company; potential employees who may apply for a job with your company; and bank officers and investors who decide whether to put money into your company are all stakeholders. And all of them can be influenced, for better or for worse, by your Web site.

Web sites are the single best way to begin the relationship with stakeholders on a positive basis. Because stakeholders are generally people who deal with information for a living, most people in the stakeholder role have Web access and are more or less expert Web users. They have generally high expectations for your company's Web site and are very disappointed and frustrated if it fails to meet those expectations. They'll quickly judge your company's overall competence by the quality of your Web site.

Understanding the needs of stakeholders is really fairly simple. Imagine being a press person who has just a few hours to write an overview of the major players in a given industry. You'll quickly understand why the company with the most complete, attractively presented, and easily accessed information on its Web site stands the best chance of getting the lead position in the article — and the company with a bad or non-existent site may get no mention at all.

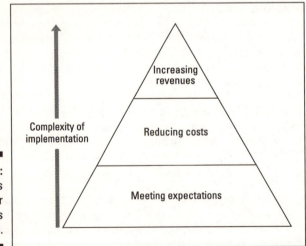

Figure 3-1: Needs pyramid for a business Web site.

Meeting expectations

The simplest Web sites, and those with the least need for formal usability work, are sites that meet basic customer and stakeholder expectations for the Web site of a company like yours. (For a description of "stakeholders" and how your Web site affects them, see the sidebar on "Understanding stakeholders.")

"Meeting expectations" is rarely discussed explicitly as a need driving basic Web site development, but it's becoming increasingly important as the reason any serious business must have a Web site. It's also the reason that many larger business owners feel the need to meet competitive standards for their site's appearance, organization, completeness, and functionality, even when the site doesn't obviously make or save the company much money.

A simple site that works

In today's complex marketplace where there are many ways for potential customers to get their needs met, your business must have certain elements in place before people will even consider dealing with you. Just as in the real world, where you have to dress well and not smell bad, your online presence needs to look good and work as advertised. The details of the basic requirements for your company or other organization vary depending on the type of business you're in, but increasingly, they include at least a basic, competent Web site.

Figure 3-2 shows the attractive, easy-to-navigate front page of the Web site of Silicon Valley Confection Company, a chocolate company in Silicon Valley. You can find the site at www.svc2.com. Its major navigation categories are Home, Chocolate Notebook (the product), Where to Buy, Contact Us, and Press Room. It meets the basic requirements for this kind of site:

- **User needs clearly met.** The Web is still, first and foremost, an informational medium, so users' first purpose in coming to your site is usually to find out more about your products. Their second common desire is to get in touch with you. Silicon Valley Confection Company meets both of these needs by making Chocolate Notebook — a description of their product — and Contact Us two of the five prominent navigation categories on their site.

- **Press and analyst needs clearly met.** Press and analyst needs are addressed by this site in two ways. First of all, press information is readily available, with Press Room as one of the five prominent navigation categories on the site. Secondly, the clever product idea, and equally clever Web site implementation, make it easy to write about the company — as we're doing here!

54 Part I: Introducing Web Usability

✔ **Company needs clearly met.** All companies want to cut costs and increase revenues. By telling you what they sell and where to buy it, Silicon Valley Confection Company is clearly taking steps to increase revenues. And by making this information, plus press information, available on the Web, where cost per user is very low, they've cut costs.

By not actually selling online, Silicon Valley Confection Company has avoided competing with their existing sales channels. Instead, by making Where to Buy a prominent link, they make the Web site support their existing sales channels. This is a good idea for all companies, especially smaller ones, to consider when putting up a site.

✔ **Easy navigation.** The navigation for the Silicon Valley Confection Company site is very clear and direct as well as entertaining in the way it's graphically presented. (Note the text links at the bottom of the page that repeat, in easier-to-read form, the graphical links at the top.)

✔ **Fast-loading.** Silicon Valley Confection Company faced a classic conflict between wanting to create an entertaining page without slowing download time too much. So they made the text parts of the pages load first — you see the navigation bar quickly. All the graphics and text together are about 40K, just small enough to download in about 15 seconds on a typical home modem — and just over the upper limit we recommend for any one Web page in a typical site. (See Chapter 7 for details.)

Figure 3-2: Why not chocolate chips instead of silicon ones?

Chapter 3: Setting Goals for Your Site

Appropriate graphic design is very important for a business site. Silicon Valley Confection Company clearly has a "fun" site, so the look is appropriate. But make sure that several people you trust review your new or revised site before you launch it to make sure the look is appropriate for your business.

Applying competitive pressure

A large part of the burden of cost-justifying a Web site can be easily met if you, and others at your company, understand that creating and maintaining a Web site of quality roughly matching that of your competitors' sites is simply a cost of doing business. And that a site just a little bit better than the competition's may be a big help in creating a perception of your company as a winner.

Usability work is relatively simple in situations where "meeting expectations" simply means providing an attractively laid out informational site with company, product, and contact information. Just put a few users in front of a computer, tell them the name of your company, and ask them to find basic information such as your company's line of business, hours of operation, phone number, major products, and so on. If they encounter barriers to finding such information, fix them and then publish the site. Spend your free time thinking about how you can take your Web site to the next level.

Table 3-1 shows our idea of the information needed to meet basic expectations for very small, small, medium, and large businesses. Note that this table is very general — many businesses need more complete Web sites than we indicate here, and some can get by with less. Check out the Web sites of your direct competitors to help determine what you need to do to meet expectations.

Table 3-1 does not show additional functionality that reduces costs, increases sales, or improves customer satisfaction because those areas are covered in the sections below — but be warned that some of this additional functionality is also becoming part of people's minimal expectations for certain kinds and sizes of companies.

Table 3-1	Site Functionality Needed to Meet Expectations		
Size of Business	*Company Information*	*Product Information*	*Extras*
Very small (fewer than 12 employees)	Name, location, brief history	Basic product description that can be highlighted on front page	Elements from larger sites

(continued)

Table 3-1 *(continued)*

Size of Business	Company Information	Product Information	Extras
Small (dozens of employees)	Press release archive; brief bios of key executives; map to company's headquarters	Detailed product description(s); e-mail links for follow-up; support FAQ	Connection to local sales outlets
Medium (hundreds of employees)	Investor or stockholder information	How to buy information for each product; 800 number; interactive support database	Site search; online sales
Large (thousands of employees)	Detailed stockholder information including live stock quote, annual report, quarterly reports	Major areas of site devoted to different product lines; interactive product advisor; user information management	Printable pages; "e-mail this page"; personalizable site view; multimedia clips of company officers and events

Reducing costs

After meeting basic expectations, reducing costs is the easiest kind of goal to meet with your Web site. In fact, the things you do to meet expectations often reduce costs as well. For instance, providing basic company, contact, and product information on your Web site may reduce phone calls made to your company requesting basic information — thereby saving money on phone help, on calls to your 800 line (if you have one), and on potentially missed calls for more important interactions such as orders. You may also save money on printing brochures, on mailing costs, and so on.

It's usually not worth taking the time to cost-justify these basic cost-reduction efforts because a basic informational Web site is usually a competitive necessity. However, you can do a lot more with your Web site to reduce costs — but before making these additional investments, some cost-justification may be necessary.

The secret to successfully reducing your business costs using the Web is to start not with things you know about or with things you know the Web is good at, but with areas where your business's costs are highest. This may require digging into your company's accounting statements somewhat, though, because many companies don't even know from where the red ink is flowing.

Chapter 3: Setting Goals for Your Site

Find areas where your specific business has high expenses and, for each such area, think through how you can use the Web to significantly cut costs. Pick the easiest — not necessarily the biggest — target first, add the needed functionality to your Web site, document the reduction in expenses, and create a quick, clear, well-documented win. After a successful cost-reduction effort like this, you'll have much less trouble getting support for later Web development work.

The following is a list of some of the areas where you may be able to find high expenses and thereby justify a Web-based cost-reduction effort:

- Printing and mailing costs for direct mail and responses to information requests, if such costs are high for your company
- Opening and routing physical mail, which can be replaced by e-mail contacts
- Telephone answering costs and the "hassle factor" associated with taking, routing, and replying to phone calls
- Post-sales support costs (which may appear as mail handling, telephone answering, and letter writing costs, as well as costs of lost sales from dissatisfied customers)
- Technical support costs (similar to post-sales support costs)

Look for high expenses in these and other areas and consider how to use the Web to reduce costs.

Web usability plays a very strong role in cost-reduction efforts — the easier to find and easier to use you can make specific cost-reducing functionality on your Web site, the more you can reduce costs. The Web design, interaction design, and user testing information in this book are directly applicable to cost-reduction efforts. Cost-reduction efforts are an area where usability can play a leading role.

One good clue to areas for potential cost-reduction is to look at competitors' Web sites — someone at another company may have done your analysis for you. Also, "keeping up with the Joneses" — matching functionality found on competitors' sites — is a strong additional motivator for convincing your company to act.

Increasing revenues

Increasing revenues is often the first thing businesspeople think of when they consider creating or expanding their company Web site — and usually the last thing they achieve. Selling online is the Holy Grail of business Web site development, but getting any reasonable volume of sales online — let alone making a profit in doing so — is very difficult.

The main reason profitable online selling is so difficult is that customer expectations for almost any sales process are very, very high. People really like the personal touch when they're giving your company their money, yet there is nothing more impersonal than the Web; people tend to move to sales channels where there's more hand-holding. Other difficulties include the many hidden costs present in the sales process: giving the customer the opportunity to see and touch the product, providing a person who can answer questions, getting the product from the manufacturer to the customer (often a several-step process), and providing for returns.

Many Web entrepreneurs never quite appreciated the wondrous efficiency of Home Depot, Wal-Mart, or Barnes and Noble until they tried to sell physical goods over the Net. Even products that seem to represent mostly intellectual property, such as newspapers and magazines, research reports, or computer software, turn out to have many issues relating to the physical media that bear the product, such as different sizes, thicknesses, and quality levels of paper, and to the cost of delivery.

Luckily, sales of finished goods are far from the only way for a company to increase its revenues using the Web. Just about every major element commonly found in a business Web site can be considered as a way to increase that company's revenues. And increasingly, not having a decent Web site with solid product information, if not selling capability, is a requirement — you lose credibility and sales if your customers can't find the information they need on your site.

The trick is "proving it" — showing how adding an element to your Web site increases your sales. In many cases, such as providing detailed, attractively laid out product information online, the direct impact on sales can be obvious, yet very difficult to prove.

You can help yourself here, however, by closing the loop as much as possible. When you provide product information, include a "where to buy" link on the Web page that helps the customers find all the ways they can complete the transaction, such as by going to a store, faxing in a form, contacting a salesperson, and more. People who use these kinds of links are much more likely to buy than people who simply peruse an online data sheet, which supports your effort to demonstrate a positive impact on sales. (After the information is up, you can survey customers and ask if they checked out the Web site before buying.) Figure 3-3 shows a page of Sony semiconductor product descriptions with an "Add to Cart" link.

Usability has an immense impact on whether a Web site can help a company increase its revenues. Every barrier that usability advice or usability testing helps remove in a revenue-generating process can lead directly to increased sales. Usability work can help suggest less expensive, yet more effective ways to complete the sales process, online or offline.

Chapter 3: Setting Goals for Your Site 59

Usability work can also lead you to revenue-increasing site features that become "stars" in and of themselves. Dell Computer became famous in the late '90s for making it very easy, even fun, to configure and buy a computer on their Web site. And IBM now has a "call me" feature on many of its Web pages that allows you to ask for help from that page; an IBM representative calls you, and he or she already knows what part of the site you're in. One of the authors (Mander) has had users rave to him about this feature, even when he was trying to get user feedback from them on something else!

Nearly everything in this book is directly applicable to you if you're trying to increase your company's revenues through your Web site. Of particular interest is Part IV, on usability testing, because every Web-supported step in the buying process should be tested and tweaked for maximum usability.

Be cautious: Sales are the very lifeblood of a company, and it's important to make sure the effects of your Web efforts on sales are entirely positive. Make sure to get input from existing sales channels that might see Web sales as a threat.

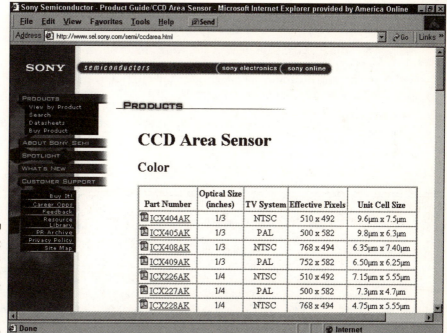

Figure 3-3: Sony makes it easy to buy semiconductors

Building customer satisfaction

Customer satisfaction can be a somewhat nebulous concept, but decades of surveys and other marketing work have show that high customer satisfaction is closely associated with sales success. You can use your Web site to increase customer satisfaction.

All the steps recommended above, when implemented carefully and with close attention to usability, act to increase customer satisfaction. Providing company, contact, and product information, helping users get technical support online, providing a variety of ways to buy a product — including online ordering — are all things that create more satisfied customers. Usability work on each of these features directly reduces customer frustration and increases customer satisfaction.

You can also use the Web to take other steps to increase customer satisfaction. One much-desired goal of many companies is to make their customers feel like a community. You can provide community functions on your Web site such as message boards, conference information, consultant forums, and so on, creating a feeling of community and "locking in" your customers to your company and product line.

The primary goal of your Web site work and of all your company's efforts, the unique element that can make you stand out, is to go beyond cost concerns, selling, and customer satisfaction to building an overall relationship with your customer. In such a relationship, the customer feels that you know and care about him or her as a person. Amazon.com's (`www.amazon.com`) interactive site features, such as putting different books on their front page for each registered customer depending on their buying habits, are a great example of building this kind of relationship online.

Profitable sales through the Web

The most profitable sales you can make through the Web are sales to existing customers, who already know your products and trust your company. Also relatively profitable are sales to customers who already know your company and its products through other means and simply complete the sale on the Web. But it's very difficult to make a profit if you try to drive customers who are doing other things on their computers, and who have never heard of you before, to your site, where you then hope to then convince them to make a purchase. Profitable Web-based sales are nearly always incremental to your existing sales and marketing efforts, not a substitute for them.

Unlike the addition of other Web site functions, which are fairly well understood and thereby can be driven partly or completely by usability concerns, cost-justification and decision-making for increasing customer satisfaction and building customer relationships is very difficult. It may be best to let marketing or executive management drive any customer satisfaction initiatives that can't be justified first as expectation-meeting, cost-reduction, or revenue-increasing measures. Usability work then plays a critical role in making sure that such features are implemented in a way that really does increase, rather than decrease, customer satisfaction.

Setting Site Goals

Business goals are too rarely set or tracked for Web sites, causing all kinds of problems — from sites that don't meet anyone's goals to sites that never get the ongoing funding that might allow them to actually prove their value as a meaningful part of the business. As business gets more accustomed to using the Web as a business tool, business goals will be more commonly set for Web sites.

What many sites are measured on today are site goals, such as pageviews and unique visitors (defined in the next section). Savvy businesses are relating these site goals back to business terms like "expense reduction" and "revenue generation."

In addition to business goals and site goals, usability efforts should target specific usability-related goals, such as response time and task completion. You can make daily use of your Web site a kind of ongoing user test by measuring response time and the completion of specific tasks. Task completion is, to us, the crucial measurement, bridging detailed site goals and overall business goals such as increasing sales.

Web sites: Beauty and the beholder

One of the touchiest issues in Web site development is whether a given Web site is professional looking or amateurish in appearance. Very similar Web sites can look completely unprofessional or very smoothly implemented and reassuring, all due to seemingly minor differences in layout and the usage of graphics and text. And because beauty is in the eye of the beholder, these kinds of issues can be extremely contentious among otherwise competent and well-intentioned people.

Look at competing sites to see how well they address some of these design issues, then get lots of feedback on your site as you design it. Refer to one or more design books — we can heartily recommend *Web Design For Dummies* (Hungry Minds, Inc.), by our friend Lisa Lopuck. Push friends and colleagues for honest feedback. Get a couple of professional opinions. And don't give up until you have a Web site whose appearance is worthy of your business.

Tracking Web site metrics

After you have business goals for your Web site — expressible in either *hard* dollar terms related to expense reduction or revenue growth, or in *soft* terms relating to meeting expectations or increasing customer satisfaction — it's time to take the next step: translating business goals into Web site metrics (measurable quantities) such as *pageviews,* registered users, and so on.

Pageviews refer to the number of times any of the Web site's pages are displayed.

During the dot-com boom, Web site metrics seemed to become business goals in and of themselves. Companies such as the Web portal Excite, or the home page hosting site GeoCities, were valued according to their number of registered users, their monthly pageviews, time spent by users on site, and so on. The assumption was that these metrics would translate into revenues and profits by processes that were not, to put it mildly, well understood.

In fact, in many cases, the processes for converting pageviews, number of registered users, and so on . into profits didn't exist. While pageviews and similar metrics did measure the success of a site in capturing users' attention, sites differed wildly in their potential to convert that attention into dollars — to "monetize" site traffic. (As a comparative example, retail stores try to "monetize" foot traffic, and in fact, most of them do a better job than most Web sites.)

For today's business sites, site metrics are useful proxies for measuring the value of the site to users. However, they are only indirect measures of how well the site supports the goals of the business. Let's examine each of these metrics and how you can use them to track your success in achieving business goals:

- **Hits.** This is not the same thing that Dick Clark plays on American Bandstand or New Year's Rockin' Eve. An outmoded measure, "hit" is sometimes used today to mean "pageview" (below). A hit is, speaking literally, the transfer of one file from a Web server to a user's computer. The problem is, getting the files needed to see a single Web page may involve anywhere from one hit to dozens. Most people who say "hits" today mean "pageviews."
- **Pageviews.** Still the single most popular metric for measuring Web site success. A pageview is the combination of one or many hits needed to make a Web page appear in front of the user. The ability of Web sites to exactly measure pageviews for each page on a site makes it easier to track Web activity than is possible for, say, magazines, newspapers, or even TV shows.

Chapter 3: Setting Goals for Your Site 63

- ✔ **Unique visitors.** The number of separate individuals who visit a Web site during a specific period, usually a month. Jupiter Media Metrix, the most widely respected Web site measurement company, reports every month on the Top 50 Web properties by number of unique visitors. Figure 3-4 shows a monthly Top 50 listing from the middle of 2001.

- ✔ **Registered users.** A registered user is someone who has volunteered information about himself or herself to be stored in a database associated with a site. Many sites ask users to register for various purposes, from the silly to the serious. Silly reasons include wanting to count registered users simply to show the popularity of one's site. Serious reasons include registering users to get their e-mail addresses for later marketing follow-up, or to obtain information that allows the site to be customized to their needs and interests.

- ✔ **Leads generated.** A lead, or prospect, is a simple description of someone whom a company can contact for sales follow-up. (When someone calls you during dinner to sell you something, they're working from a lead.) The information a user provides when registering for a site is usually most of what would be desired for a lead. More sites, we think, should simply ask users if they'd like a salesperson to follow up with them, then route these leads for sales follow-up.

- ✔ **Savings achieved.** Use of specific features of a Web site can be translated into reductions in expenses for the company. For example, use of an online database of technical support questions can be translated into a reduction in phone calls to a technical support hotline, which results in a specific amount of savings per call. Achieving savings is a worthy goal for a Web site, but it takes extra work to show directly that hoped-for savings really did occur.

- ✔ **Revenue generated.** The most impressive metric any Web site can boast of is the dollar volume of sales completed due to the site. Watch your manager's eyes get real big when you stop talking about pageviews and uptime and start talking about revenue generated. This can be a direct measurement of transactions completed on the site or a less direct measurement of sales resulting from leads gained or user follow-up on information from the site. If you really want to show off, calculate the net profitability of part or all of your site based on the amount spent to create and run it versus the gross profit achieved through sales generated by the site.

For usability purposes, you'll want to know how much different parts of a site are used, which you can find out by tracking pageviews. In fact, by matching pageviews to the possible navigation paths through a site, you can deduce how users are moving through the site.

64   Part I: Introducing Web Usability

Figure 3-4: Jupiter Media Metrix counts unique visitors.

You can also contribute to management of the site by making sure that, as part of site design and deployment, regular reporting is enabled for site metrics, especially pageviews. This can be done through reporting software or through engineering work that allows direct measurement of pageviews. Knowing the pageview count for each page of the site will definitely allow you to do a better job of making the site more usable.

For business purposes, which usability is often employed to support, you'll want to use hard measures such as registered users (if you can show a business benefit), leads generated, savings achieved, and revenue generated.

There's no such thing as a free lunch. Generating a steady flow of solid leads from the Web site, for example, will probably require Web or e-mail advertising, careful design of a registration form on the site, and usability testing of the whole process. Work with sales and marketing people to better understand how to set realistic goals for the site that usability can help to meet.

Setting and measuring usability goals

Usability will become a part of normal business processes as it's tied more and more closely to metrics of its own. Here are a few usability-related metrics you should consider tracking for your Web site:

Chapter 3: Setting Goals for Your Site *65*

✔ **Page load time.** As we describe in Chapter 10, page load times are the largest single barrier to efficient use of the Web, and keeping page load times low should be the single biggest concern of usability. Usability should set standards for page load times throughout the site, with stricter standards for frequently used navigation pages, and make sure that load times are checked and reported on an ongoing basis.

✔ **Uptime.** Site uptime is a crucial usability issue; a site that isn't available has no usefulness. In fact, a site that's down actually has "negative usability," because it not only doesn't help the user, but also the failed effort to see the site annoys and disappoints the user, possibly reducing future visits. Uptime should be tracked and reported on as part of over-all tracking of the usability of a site. Site uptime is usually reported as a percentage of the total time in, say, a given week that the site was avail-able to users. Adopt a consistent measurement and track it as part of usability tracking.

✔ **Bad links, Javascript errors, and so on.** Bugs that users experience in a site can be measured, reported, tracked, and reduced over time. Magazine pages don't break; Web pages shouldn't break either, and it should be a matter of urgent concern when they do. Make sure there are mechanisms set up for reporting problems, and treat problems beyond a certain mini-mal frequency as a usability issue.

✔ **Completion of specific tasks.** List all the user tasks on a site (such as finding product information, registering to receive a newsletter, or com-pleting a purchase) and for each task track the number of users who begin it, who get to some midpoint, and who complete the task. Improving user "flow" through specific tasks on the site is a major con-cern of usability, and one we address in detail in Part IV of this book.

Traffic doesn't just happen

One of the enduring dreams of Web site develop-ment is that you can put up a "cool" site, receive hundreds of thousands or even millions of user visits in a short period of time, then sell out and go retire on an island somewhere. For most sites, however, getting traffic is very difficult.

Traffic that comes in from people who are already your customers, or who've already heard of your company in the "real world" and then looked you up online, is more or less "free." But getting lots of new traffic above and beyond these "natural" site visitors is expensive and of dubious net value.

For most sites, set your goals around support-ing people who come to your site because they've heard about your site (or the topic it covers) from an offline resource. Get efficient at meeting the needs of people who already know they want to visit you. Then consider whether and how to seek additional visits from people who are not already regular visitors to your site.

Part I: Introducing Web Usability

Setting Goals for Non-Business Sites

Business sites are hard to set goals for, but many non-business sites have no goals at all. This tends to make them labors of love — and, when the initial passion of putting up a Web site has faded, to lead them to receive intermittent and declining amounts of attention over time.

The answer to neglect for many non-business sites is similar to the answer for businesses: to set goals for the site and work to meet them. These site goals can be tied to goals of the organization or individual responsible for the site. After these steps are taken, management and usability concerns for non-business sites become very similar to those for business sites.

Following are a few notes on the goal-setting and usability measurement processes for non-profit sites, based on the authors' long experience with organizations that, intentionally or unintentionally, failed to turn a profit:

- **Schools and universities.** Schools and universities have many of the same cost-reduction and, in some parts of the organization, money-making goals as businesses. Start with a basic informational site that helps people reach you and cuts down on phone calls and correspondence, then add functionality. Figure 3-5 shows the Web site for Western Washington University as an example.

  Then use roughly the same goal-setting and usability measurement approaches as those described above for a business, with the added satisfaction of knowing at the end of the day that you're serving a worthwhile purpose.

- **Large non-profits.** Non-profit organizations usually have a specific *raison d'etre*, or reason for existence, above and beyond financial survival. The organization's Web site can further these purposes as well as serving basic informational needs for stakeholders and even meeting fundraising goals online. Non-profits need to pay special attention to usability concerns because people have many other possible (and possibly profitable) things to be doing on the Web. Also important is a strong need to support both sophisticated users, such as many board members and large donors, as well as novice users, who may include the people that your organization is trying to help.

- **Small non-profits.** Before anything else, a small non-profit organization should seek to create a simple informational site in order to make it easier for people to find and work with the organization. Many active Web users are interested in donating time or money to non-profit sites, and a decent Web site can help a smaller non-profit get its fair share of this kind of support.

- **Groups and clubs.** Many groups and clubs have Web sites, some quite simple, and some with large message board areas and other special features that would put many business sites to shame. Set straightforward goals for your group or club Web site and use the usability testing techniques described in this book to make sure the site performs as advertised. Consider running a simple e-mail newsletter from your Web site to keep users informed and to reduce costs versus a traditional newsletter that you must print out and mail, often at considerable expense.

- **Hobby sites and personal home pages.** These sites are created by individuals for personal fulfillment, and as such, can have carefully set goals or no goals, and as many or as few usability difficulties as the creator of the site wishes them to have. However, if you wish to improve such a site, the information in this book can be a big help. You can at least make sure that all the people who will be visiting your site have a good experience in doing so.

Figure 3-5: Western Washington University's site is a central contact point.

68 **Part I: Introducing Web Usability**

Part II
Designing Usable Sites

The 5th Wave　　　By Rich Tennant

"Just how accurately should my Web site reflect my place of business?"

In this part . . .

Users are often puzzled by a site's overall layout and by the navigation elements that are intended to help them move around in it. This part shows you how the navigation issue has been solved in other media, such as magazines and books, and how to create navigation that helps your users find information and get things done on your Web site.

Chapter 4

Organizing Your Site

In This Chapter

▶ Wayfinding the old way

▶ What you can learn from print

▶ Creating new navigation

▶ Navigation do's

▶ Navigation don'ts

▶ Creating the Site Tree

*T*here's a reason the first widely popular Web browser was given the name Netscape Navigator: The Web is widely seen as a sea of information, and a tool to help navigate it is clearly a wonderful thing. Luckily, helping users navigate the whole Web isn't your problem; helping them navigate your site is.

Site navigation is the most important usability challenge for most Web sites. Why is this? Well, getting someone to come to your Web site in the first place is a marketing challenge, not a usability challenge (though if marketing is smart, they'll ask for some usability help). And after users find their way to the right page within your Web site, they can generally figure out what to do. (All the same, helping them do so is a worthy challenge that we tackle in the next chapter.) But helping the users get from the front page of the site — or whatever page they linked or bookmarked their way into — to the page they want to be on is nothing except a usability problem, and often a big one.

Why is finding the right page so hard? Because most Web users are intensely focused on the here and now. They're usually trying to accomplish some task, whether that's finding needed information, completing a purchase, changing their registration information, or something else. And they're usually in a hurry. So they don't want to spend time trying to figure out how to get where they're going.

But while your users really don't want to spend time trying to find the right page, they have to do so, or give up. As you no doubt know from your own use of the Web, finding the Web page that you want can be a very difficult task. Giving up can become a very attractive option!

Part II: Designing Usable Sites

You can help your site accomplish the goals for which you create and maintain it by making sure that the things users want to find are easy for them to find, and that the things that you want to encourage users to get to are made constantly available to them.

Wayfinding in Old Media

The problems that people experience in finding their way around in the real world, in human-created environments such as buildings, and in information products such as a magazine or a Web site, are collectively referred to as *wayfinding*. Recent research at Xerox's Palo Alto Research Center — the famous "Xerox PARC" where the modern desktop interface for computers was first fully developed — indicates that people who are looking for information on a Web site use similar techniques as animals hunting for prey, and that this kind of ferreting out (pun intended) of information is part of what makes the Web fun to use.

You actually deal with a number of information systems in your life. Books, newspapers, magazines, maps, and the Yellow Pages are all information systems — and they're all based on static (that is, non-moving) text and images. Because most of a Web site is based on static text and images, it's worth looking at a couple of these text-heavy information systems to see if there are any lessons we can use in Web navigation.

Of course, not all of your site is based on static text and images. For the parts based on tasks, it's worth looking at real-world tasks, which we do in Chapter 8. And if your site makes heavy use of multimedia, you should look at radio, TV, and movies as examples, and we mention this in the section on multimedia in Chapter 10.

Here, we take a quick look at two well-known information media, books and newspapers, to see how they can help you learn about how to make your Web site easier to navigate.

Navigating books

You may not realize it, but a book is actually a cleverly designed information system. Books have evolved over thousands of years into a standard format that makes them pretty easy to use. (Note that even after thousands of years of evolution, books still have usability problems; nothing's perfect, notably including the Web.)

If books had never been invented and were introduced to us tomorrow by aliens from another planet — who may well disguise themselves as encyclopedia salespeople — we could learn a lot about Web design from them (the books, not the alien salespeople). But books aren't just a good example of information design. They're the single most important and most commonly used form in which people find information. Therefore, they have a tremendous influence on what people expect when they go to a Web site. Let's take a close look at books and how they compare to a typical Web site (for this comparison, see Figure 4-1).

Look at the book

Take a close look at the book you hold in your hands. Notice that it fits easily in your hands; the size and shape of different kinds of books have evolved over thousands of years, with publishing as we know it having a 500-year history since Gutenberg printed his first Bible. This book is a "trade paperback," larger and sturdier than the mass-market paperbacks used for most popular fiction. From the size and shape of the book alone, you know that it's probably a nonfiction book. And it is — at least, that's what we, as authors, intended!

The cardboard cover of the book protects the pages inside. It has a coated surface that doesn't show finger marks easily and that will survive coffee spills. The spine binding holds the pages together and allows you to turn them. You can flip through to find something; and once you find it, you may well remember roughly where the page with the desired information on it is physically located, making it easy to get to again. This tie-in of information to specific places on a real-world object is a huge advantage of books and other printed media over the Web.

If you're holding this book in your lap or at arm's length, the text is a size that's pretty easily readable. If you want to, you can put it on a table top and it will lay flat (okay, we're not in hardcover, so you may have to squish the center of the book a little). There's a title on the cover and spine — you can tell which book is which if the book is lying closed on a table or standing on a shelf.

Interestingly, the "title" of a Web site — the Web URL — is always visible as well, up in the address area at the top of a Web page. However, www.yourco.com is pretty geeky and non-informative when compared to a typical book title.

You open the book and typically there's a title page and then a table of contents. In the back there's an index if the book contains information you may want direct access to. In this book, the contents are organized into parts; each relates to a major topic. Within each part are chapters, which break the parts into smaller pieces. Within the chapters are sections. Unlike a novel, this book is designed for reference, and the multiple levels of organization and tools like the table of contents and the index make it easy to find and return to desired information. Web sites, which are generally used for reference rather than read through sequentially, also frequently need multiple levels of organization.

Part II: Designing Usable Sites

Pages within a book can be highly structured or unstructured. Nearly all books have page numbers, but this is relatively new within the history of books; page numbers only appeared a few hundred years ago. A novel has no other page structure except for chapter titles. This book, by contrast, is full of clever little devices to help you quickly home in on needed information, from sub-heads and sub-sub-heads to sidebars and icons. Most Web sites are used for reference, so you should use lots of headings and icons in your Web site too.

As a reader you know how to interact with this book — it follows a set of conventions. Almost all books follow a core set of conventions, such as having a title, a Table of Contents, chapters, and page numbers. Other conventions are particular to certain kinds of books — this book is a nonfiction book (which are often printed as trade paperbacks), as well as a *For Dummies* book, which determines all kinds of things about the cover design, the use of headings, and the use of icons to point out particular kinds of things in the text. A well-designed Web site uses many of the same elements as a nonfiction reference book and uses a set of conventions consistently throughout the site.

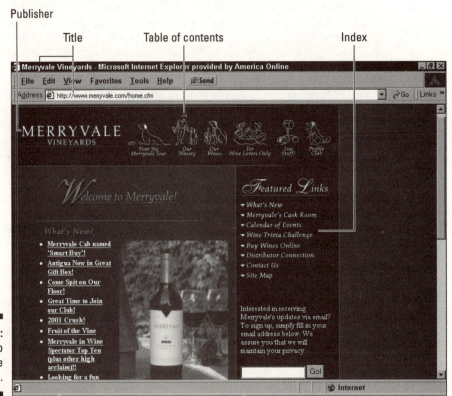

Figure 4-1: How Web sites are like books.

Chapter 4: Organizing Your Site *75*

Books and user expectations

Many of the problems people have with using Web sites come from the fact that Web sites aren't like books, which people are accustomed to using.

Many of the advantages of a book come from its physicality — the fact that it's a real thing that you can hold in your hands. The ability to remember roughly where information is in a book; the way you can quickly flip through some, or even all, its pages to look for something; and the way you can insert a bookmark or sticky note to help you get back to a certain spot in the book are all ways in which books are easier to use.

You can even purposefully damage a book to make it more useful. You can dog-ear a page to make it easy to find again, or write in the book to highlight or add information for your own future interest or reference. At the furthest extreme, you can even tear a page out of a book and take it with you, though neither of the authors can imagine anyone over the age of ten doing such a thing (at least not to *our* book).

Other advantages of books over Web sites come from the relatively simple, but extremely useful, conventions that have evolved to make books more usable. The standard positioning of a title page and a Table of Contents at the front of the book make it very easy to find crucial information. An index is a critical tool for reference books. And page numbers support the use of these other tools.

Unlike books, Web sites have no physical presence; from the user's point of view, the site disappears when the computer is turned off, which would be a pretty neat trick if you could do it with a book. You can't map information in a site to any particular real-world spot or physical place, and you can't put a Post-it note on a specific spot in a Web site. (There is software to allow this, but few people use it.)

You *can* bookmark pages you want to remember, but most people use this to bookmark the front pages of sites, which is a different issue. And you *can* do the equivalent of tearing a page out of a Web site; just print out the page you're looking at. Assuming the Web page is set up well for printing (we tell you how to do this in Chapter 7), you'll have a piece of paper with the content on it that you can refer to. But it's usually impractical to print out a whole Web site for reference in this way. (Each of the authors has taken the time to do this for sites we've worked on; it's a lot of work, often involving several printing tricks, but when you have the site printed out, it's very useful to be able to quickly flip through the site's pages as if it were a book.)

Part II: Designing Usable Sites

How to make your site more like a book

What can you learn from books that may help you in creating an easy-to-navigate Web site? Let's look at some of the highlights of books and whether they make sense in the Web world:

✔ **Title.** Anyone reading a book knows where to find the title, but what's the title of a Web site? The only reliable title for most Web sites is the domain name. Give your site a real title by repeating the name of the site, or the organization it represents, on every page, and use the HTML-based Web page title that shows up in the top of the browser window to put the site's title, plus the current section, on every page. (See Figure 4-2 for an example.)

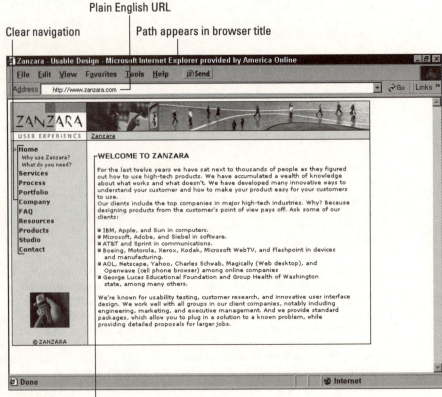

Figure 4-2: It's good to be titled.

Chapter 4: Organizing Your Site

- **Author.** Lest we forget, books have authors! When authors put their names in their books, it indicates a level of personal accountability that's sadly lacking in Web sites. The closest thing to an author of a Web site, from the user's point of view, is the Webmaster. Make sure users can send e-mail to webmaster@yourdomain.com to raise problems or ask questions; also, consider having an "about the Webmaster" page that introduces the person and/or team responsible for the Web site.

- **Copyright info.** Every Web site should be copyrighted; even if you think you don't care about copyright, how'd you like someone to create a "joke" version of your site, making fun of your products and personnel? Without copyright protection, people can legally do this. Show you care by placing a copyright notice on each page. (And respect others' rights by getting permission for any borrowed text or, especially, graphics you put on your own site.)

- **Table of Contents I.** Many books, such as this one, now have a high-level, one-page Table of Contents. The list of major site sections often found in the left navigation pane of a site, or as a set of links at the top or bottom of a page, is the equivalent of this kind of high-level table of contents.

- **Table of Contents II.** Every site should have the equivalent of a detailed Table of Contents, which for a Web site is a *site map*. The site map should go down to the page level or at least to nearly that level of detail. The site map is a critical navigational element, though it's a bit like having a life vest on a sailboat: If the cruise is going well, no one should need it.

Creating a site map is a great exercise for the design team; it makes you think about the structure of your site, what may be missing from it, and what each page should be named. During development, consider creating a new site map every few days to keep structural and organizational issues front and center.

- **Index.** This is a critical component for reference books, and this kind of functionality is even more important for Web sites, in which you can't depend on your spatial sense to remind you where something was. A Site Search function is the equivalent of an Index (though, unlike an index, you can't control the exact phrasing of what a user is able to look up).

- **Beginning, middle, and end.** Books have a beginning, middle, and end, which tell readers a whole bunch of things about what may or may not be important in the book. Web sites can have an implied sequence based on the ordering of major elements in your navigation area. Make sure that any implications that a user may draw about the importance of different things on your Web site is supported by the ordering of the elements in your navigation list.

✔ **Page numbers.** Page numbers don't make sense in a Web site, because there's not much idea of a sequence. But realize that without this key clue used in most other forms of text-heavy media, you need to do a lot of additional things to help users stay oriented. Pay extra attention to ease of navigation in your Web site. And do number pages within an article, or steps within a sequence of steps, as we describe in Chapter 9.

While not having page numbers is hard on users, it can be even harder on the site team during site development. Consider creating a unique identifier for each Web page in your site that incorporates the sections and sub-sections that the page lives in. (Often the URL of a page, which includes the folder and subfolder(s) that the page is in, serves this purpose.) This isn't for the user to see, just something to hide in the HTML code for your own use.

Navigating newspapers

Newspapers are much "newer" than books, merely hundreds rather than thousands of years old. Which is kind of too bad — "Et tu, Brute?" would have made a good headline if only the Romans had newspapers.

The most important thing about newspapers is that they were devised as the cheapest possible way to get lots of information — and advertising — out very quickly to hundreds, thousands, or millions of people. Papers are printed on large sheets, then folded, to save on binding costs. Newsprint, the paper used to make newspapers, is cheap. The ink used for printing newspapers — famous for rubbing off on your fingers — is cheap. The standard style used by each paper makes it cheap to lay out and produce the paper each day. And of course the vast majority of the ink-stained wretches who write newspaper stories were, until recently, paid very little.

Newspapers are even more like Web sites than books are; some specifics are shown in Figure 4-3. Newspapers are divided into different sections, which in a big paper are physically distinct pieces, like the major sections of a Web site. Newspapers are designed to make you look at a lot of pages, just as many Web sites value pageviews. And the most valuable space on a newspaper is on the front page, "above the fold," just as the most valuable space on a Web page is on the top part of the page that's visible when you first link to the page.

Like a Web site, a newspaper is somewhat separate from the specific, always-changing information in it. Newspapers use graphics and layout to create an individual personality for each paper, just as a Web site should have its own "look and feel." Like Web sites, and unlike most books, newspapers use photographs and illustrations to add interest to their content. And like most Web sites, newspaper pages are very densely populated; every square inch is valuable.

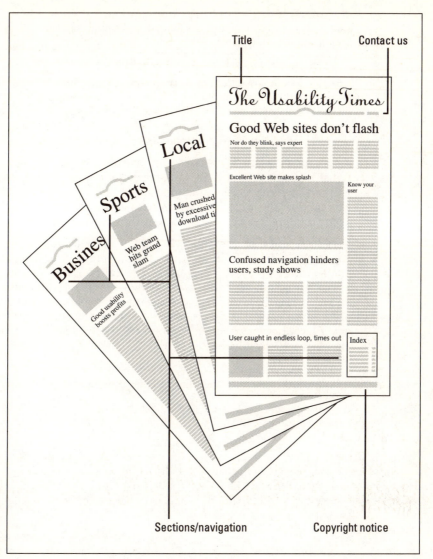

Figure 4-3: Parts is parts.

We look at newspapers again, as well as magazines, when we discuss page design in Part III; but to stay on topic for now, what can we learn from newspapers when it comes to Web site navigation? Here are a few key lessons:

- **Parts is parts.** The physical separation of a large newspaper into parts, or sections, is a very valuable lesson for most Web sites. A typical newspaper reader can tell you at a glance what kind of stories each section contains. You know where you are in the newspaper at all times based on the kind of story you're reading and your knowledge of the paper's parts.

Part II: Designing Usable Sites

Sections on the Web. Web sites are, increasingly, divided into predictable sections, with known content in each area. This kind of "guessability," in which the user knows what to expect within different sections of a site, is a vital advantage for easy site navigation.

✔ **Keep it cheap.** Newspapers were designed to be highly valued, yet have an extremely low production cost. So newspapers spend a lot of money on one-time costs, such as overall design and layout, and amazingly small amounts on recurring costs, such as paper, ink, daily layout, and the salaries of the aforementioned ink-stained wretches.

Keep content cheap. Make it easy and inexpensive to add new informational pages to your site. Spend money up-front on reusable layouts so you can keep the incremental time investment and cost of adding, say, a new product description to your site low. This makes it easier for you to keep your site fresh and up-to-date without incurring high expenses.

✔ **Vary look and feel.** Newspapers subtly vary their look and feel in different sections, and within a section, to create interest and help users recognize where they are. For example, the front page of a newspaper, or of a section, almost never has advertising — yet inside each section, stories are wrapped around huge ads rather shamelessly. Photos are used or not used in different ways across sections; the editorial page almost never has photos, while the sports section nearly always has an action shot featured prominently.

A site is not a library

Too many sites are designed as repositories of information. This isn't a good idea, even if your site *is* a repository of information, because some pieces of information are more valuable than others. Don't bury the most-desired information by putting it at the same level as the less-used stuff.

Typically, a major site has a tremendous amount of stuff on it — usually a great deal of content plus some tasks — and the design of the site is egalitarian, with all functions equally accessible (and therefore equally inaccessible, because everything's buried several levels deep).

This isn't the right thing for users. Most sites follow Pareto's Law: 20 percent of the things on

your site attract 80 percent of the user interest (or some ratio similar to that). You are really, really helping your user if you find out what the top five to seven things are that they want to get to on your site, and then make those things easy to find.

Making everything on a site equally accessible also isn't the right thing for you. Remember, you spend time and money on creating and maintaining your site to serve your own purposes, whether they be commercial, critical, comical — and that's just the C's! — or something else. You should always make it easy for users to do things that serve your purposes. A key function of navigation is to always keep the things that you want users to do accessible.

Chapter 4: Organizing Your Site **81**

Look and feel on your site. You can vary the advertising or marketing presence on your site to make some sections more clearly informational and others more commercial or "salesy." Consider consistently using an eye-catching item such as a photograph on the front page of some sections, and sticking to a more textual approach in others. You can vary the look and feel subtly within each section to let people know what part of your site they're in.

✔ **Use information assets.** From the top down, a newspaper is organized into sections and subsections; from the bottom up it can be considered a container for key information assets such as stories, the comics, editorials, sports scores and standings, the crossword puzzle(s), classified ads, and so on. Most newspaper readers have favorite sections they spend much of their paper-reading time on.

Assets on the Web. Purposefully creating key information assets and usable tools is a sign of inspired Web site design, and creating easy-to-follow paths to those assets is a key element of truly usable navigation schemes. Within a site, you can't give the same sense of a physical "place" as a newspaper does, so you have to find other clues to help your users quickly get to the destinations they want to reach — or that you want them to go to.

✔ **Create a scan plan.** Newspapers are amazingly scannable; headlines, photos, and ads are all arranged to make it interesting and fun to scan through the paper, even if you hardly read a story. (Note that scanning increases your exposure to ads, the economic backbone for the newspaper.) Figure 4-4 shows a Web site for a newspaper that brings the scannability of a printed newspaper to the Web.

Scanning your site. Most Web sites would benefit from being arranged to be scannable like newspapers. The easier and more fun it is to move through your site, the more likely users will be able to complete the tasks they came to your site with — as well as additional tasks you'd like them to take on.

What you can learn from print

So what can you learn from books and newspapers? Isn't the Web going to make them obsolete? Sure, monitors are gradually getting higher in resolution. Someday all your news will be customized, always up to date, and (finally) as easy to read on a computer screen as on paper. We've all heard the arguments — but freezers and microwaves haven't done away with cooking! Don't worry — books and newspapers will be around for a long time yet.

Part II: Designing Usable Sites

Figure 4-4: The Seattle Times provides a real Web newspaper.

Our point in looking at these media is not to say a Web site should be exactly like a book or newspaper; rather, it's to point out that when you read a book or a newspaper, you're interacting with a very refined piece of information design. One day, Web sites will reach this level of design. At the moment there are some "best practice" ways of organizing the contents of your site which we'll pass on to you so you create a great site today without having to wait for the Web to evolve over the next hundred years — whoops, we're on "Internet time" these days, maybe that's more like ten years.

Readers approach newspapers and books with certain expectations. Publishers of books and newspapers who break these conventions run the risk of making their products harder to read — that is, harder to use. To the extent that there are good conventions in Web site design, you need to follow them where possible, because your users will find your site easier to use if it conforms to these emerging standards. We've identified the best of these conventions by watching many users navigate Web sites of all kinds.

The bottom-line take-away from newspapers and books is that the information in them is designed; it isn't an accident that it's the way it is. Here's what these carefully crafted designs share:

✔ You can tell *what it is*. Imagine a book without a title or author, or a newspaper without a front page. Rarely do you pick up a book and not have a pretty good idea of what type of book it is and what it is about.

Chapter 4: Organizing Your Site **83**

- You can tell *where you are* within it. Chapters in books and sections in newspapers all have running page headings so you know where you are. Page numbers help you know where you are within the contents.

- You know *where you can go*. You understand how the information is organized — in most books, you start at the front and progress to the back. Newspapers are also organized roughly in order of the perceived importance of each topic (national and world news, then local, then sports, then entertainment).

- You have *random access* into it. You can open a newspaper and jump right into it; this is also true of some books: encyclopedias, magazines, coffee table books of pictures. Many people have developed their own order for reading a newspaper — for instance, comics, then sports, then editorials, then the front page.

- You can *make it stop*. You can simply shut the book. Bookmark it if you want to. Or just put down the newspaper, it will still be at the point you left it — as long as pets and small children leave it alone — the next time you pick it up.

These features, as illustrated by books and newspapers, are actually key to all information design. We'll get back to these when we talk about how to architect your Web site.

How Web sites are different

You can learn a lot about how to create highly effective navigation for your site by looking at existing media, but Web sites are still very different from any existing medium — in some ways for the better, from a usability point of view, but in some ways for the worse. Here are some of the plusses that Web sites have, for you to take advantage of when creating and upgrading navigation on your site:

- **Clickable.** Web sites have links. *Hyperlinking* — the Web's ability to take you to a new page when you click on a link — is an amazing capability and is really the core of the usefulness of the Web. Helping users deal with this powerful ability is the core challenge of creating Web navigation.

- **Trackable.** You can find out, click by click, what users are clicking within your site; and you can find out, pageview by pageview, what they're looking at. Traditional media are amazingly inept at delivering this information, and it's surprising just how much money changes hands for advertising placements in, for instance, newspapers, when no one knows just how many people see each ad.

- **Customizable.** You can make the content of a Web page dynamic, altering what the users see to fit their interests. Customizable, or self-customizing, Web sites have the potential to be extremely *useful*, because

Part II: Designing Usable Sites

they meet user's needs very well, but are hard to make *usable*, because a site that's constantly changing is so confusing for users. Newspapers are a good example of how to manage change: they use an ironclad "sections" model to contain constantly changing content.

✔ **Flexible.** In looking at print models for navigation, we've only covered part of what the Web can do. A Web site can also support tasks in the same way that computer software does, and it can also deliver multimedia, as do radio and television. We still navigate Web sites using text, so print is the right model to look at for navigation, but within specific areas of your site, a blended approach will be needed to accommodate tasks and multimedia.

✔ **Novel.** The Web is very new. You have many degrees of freedom in how you design, implement, and improve navigation on your site. Traditional media are constrained by the weight of hundreds of years of precedent; it's hard to get support for anything innovative. *USA Today,* the biggest experiment in journalism in decades, faced intense criticism for its short, highly readable stories — which were somewhat Web-like before the Web even existed.

The key challenges of Web navigation, though, are intensely difficult to solve. Here are some of the challenges that make Web navigation very much a work in progress:

✔ **No clue.** Because Web sites are simply images that appear on the computer screen and aren't part of a physical "thing," users don't have any easy way to know where they are in a Web site. It's up to you to help your users find their place, but it's a challenge no matter what you do.

✔ **No loyalty.** Hyperlinks are extremely democratic; they can go anywhere. Even if your site doesn't offer a lot of hyperlinks out, it's very easy for users to type in a new URL or select a bookmark for another site. If your site doesn't meet the user's needs, *right now*, the user will find some other site that can.

✔ **No precedent.** It can be really nice to have a few hundred years of past practice to draw on, and that's lacking on the Web. There are existing models, the best of which we'll introduce later in this chapter, but none of them have yet been proven (or disproven) by years and years of use.

Creating New Navigation

On a typical Web site, navigation is Job One — the one factor you have to work on the hardest as you create a new site, add new functionality, or work to improve the usability of the site.

Chapter 4: Organizing Your Site

If you're creating a new site, you get to create new navigation from scratch. This is a lot of work, but a lot of fun. You can choose the overall organizational approach — along with the supporting clues, reminders, and shortcuts — that help your users get what they need from your site quickly and easily.

If you're adding a new section to an existing site, consistency is the watchword. You should make the new section consistent with the existing site, while also working to make the new section an island of consistency and predictability in a site that may be a bit disorganized overall. If you make one section great, you can then spread that greatness throughout the rest of the site.

If you're revamping an existing site to improve its usability, you have the toughest job of all. You may feel the current navigational scheme for the site is all wrong, but lack the resources to change it (and to retrain your current users) all at once. You need to figure out where, eventually, you want to go, then figure out a relatively smooth, step-by-step path for gradually modifying your existing site into what it should be.

Whether you are creating a new site, adding to an existing site, or solving usability problems with a site, you have to work on three intersecting levels of navigation:

- **Site structure.** Your site has an overall structure made up of sections and, for larger sites, subsections. It's very important to get these "buckets" right. What you're looking for here is consistency and predictability: The site should fit existing models that the user is accustomed to; it should give users a good idea what kind of site they're on; users should be able to predict what's likely to be available on the site (and what's not); and users should be able to predict where to look for a given kind of information on the site.

- **Task design.** Your site needs to support user tasks of various types. (We describe some common tasks and how to support them in Chapter 8.) Users may work across sections to accomplish a task, but it should be very easy to get from one page that supports a specific task to another.

- **Page structure.** Individual Web pages have to serve specific purposes, such as providing information about a product, and also tie back into overall navigation. Ideally, a page should contain information about where it fits in the overall site structure; show whether it's part of a larger task the user may be pursuing; and provide connections to related tasks and information the user may want to find next.

Figure 4-5 shows the home page from the Velosel Corporation Web site, which demonstrates these attributes. As you can see, simultaneously providing valuable information or functionality, tying into user tasks, and linking to related pages requires careful design and layout and can produce a powerful effect.

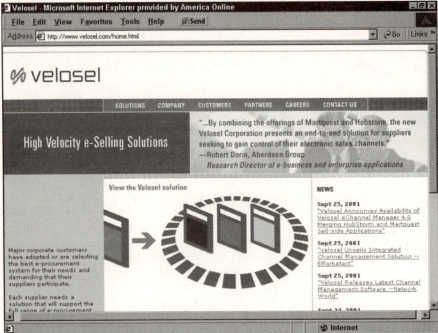

Figure 4-5: Velosel pulls all the pieces together.

Navigation Do's and Don'ts

Over years of creating Web sites — and watching users struggle with our own sites and those of others — we've learned a few things that you should nearly always do, and a few others that you should nearly always not do, in creating site navigation. Follow these rules most of the time, but break them when you have a good reason.

Top ten do's for Web navigation

Use this Top Ten list as a checklist for your Web navigation plan — or to size up your current site for needed improvements:

1. **Put a link to the home page on every page.** Users repeatedly return to the home page of a site when they get lost. By providing a link to your home page on each page, you'll help ensure that your users go to your home page when they're frustrated, and not someone else's!

Use common-sense rules

Some people hate clichés. We love them. Clichés usually reflect a lot of human experience, and a good cliché can help you communicate usability truths faster and more effectively than any 20-page user study. Use these clichés to help guide your Web site navigation efforts:

✔ **The home page of your site gets 20 percent of the pageviews.** This is called the 20% rule — no, not the 80/20 rule, though we like that one, too. The 20% rule says that 20 percent or more of the pageviews that your Web site gets will be on the home page. Users loop through the front page a lot; if they can't quickly find what they want from there, they probably won't stick around to try to find it deep within your site.

✔ **Site visits last 4-5 clicks.** Close cousin to the 20% rule, the 4-5 clicks rule says that a typical visit to a Web site only lasts 4-5 clicks. If users haven't found what they need in just a few clicks, they'll leave your site. (Check your site's records, as we describe in Chapter 12, to find out the actual percentage of home-page pageviews for your site, and how many clicks per visit your site actually gets.)

✔ **People love the words New and Free.** A cardinal rule of marketing is that "New" and "Free" are the two most powerful words in the language. Use them liberally in your Web site. You should always have something new, generally with the word New on it, visible on your front page; and, if your site is used for selling or marketing, you should

consider always having some kind of free offer on your site, again preferably on the front page. ("Free! Get our newsletter." is a good one.)

✔ **"Click here" works.** User interface purists hate the words "Click here" — if text is hyperlinked, it shows up in a different color, and is obviously clickable, so why say "Click here"? Yet research shows that "click here" actually makes more users click. So use phrases like "click here" to encourage users to click.

✔ **People click quickly.** Ever seen an expert TV watcher work a remote control? Channels may get changed in less than a second, just long enough for the person watching to recognize something he or she doesn't want to see. People do the same thing on Web sites — they decide whether to click away, and then do it quickly. Keep your navigation in the top, viewable area so people can quickly find the link they want without having to scroll. (If they don't see the navigation link they want, they may not scroll down and find it but rather may go to another site.)

✔ **Make probabilities work for you.** In most sites, probabilities work against the site's owners, For example, if the selling page is three levels down, the user can just as likely end up at any of several dozen other places on your site except the selling page. Keep putting things you want the user to do in their view and make it more likely that they'll click the "right" things.

2. **Include a persistent navigation area on every page.** You can use a navigation header, footer, sidebar, or some other element, but you should always have a navigation area on every page. This helps reassure users that they can always get back to a known, useful spot, and even reminds them that they're still on your site!

3. **Include Search capability.** If your site is at all large, include a site search capability. This not only helps users who come to your site looking for something, but also users who think they've seen certain kinds of information on your site, but can't remember exactly where. Your users will cleverly remember exact names, or combinations of words, and search for them. Besides, you really do want users to be able to find every single mention of, for example, the hot new 8-cylinder Eliminator — especially if seeing all the info helps them decide to buy one.

4. **Use detailed link text.** Users expect certain kinds of generic labels on your site — Contacts, Jobs, Products. But beneath the top level, use specific, detailed link text. Which would you click: "Automobiles" or "See the hot new 8-cylinder Eliminator"?

5. **Use standard link colors.** The Web standard for link colors is blue for unvisited links, purple for recently visited ones. Don't override these colors! They help your users navigate your site without having to consciously think through where they've already been and where they haven't.

6. **Emphasize text for navigation.** Text loads quickly and is very recognizable to the user; graphics load slowly and take some deciphering. Find ways to give text that cool, graphical look, but use real text rather than graphics wherever you can for your navigation.

7. **Put news on your home page.** Always put news on your site's home page — not just a "What's New" link, but actual information about new events, even site changes. Having updates appear on your front page gives your users a sense of involvement with the site, and a reason to return to your site frequently to check.

8. **Have a What's New area.** Having a What's New area is not, strictly speaking, a navigational necessity, but people who use your site a lot — including internal users, investors, and members of your site team — really, really appreciate this.

9. **Include a site map.** Many users will never use the site map, but some will — and they'll get a lot out of it. Your site map not only shows users what's on your site, but in combination with standard link colors, it shows everywhere users have and haven't been.

A site map helps answer one of the most difficult questions for a Web user to deal with: Is what I'm looking for here? Let's say, for example, that your user wants to see your company's position on global warming — but there isn't one posted on your Web site. By using the site map to quickly find out that this information is absent, your user avoids a great deal of searching and frustration.

Chapter 4: Organizing Your Site **89**

Great content and functionality

Put great content and highly useful tools on your Web site, and it will probably do really well. Navigation *helps* people use Web sites, but it isn't *why* people use Web sites. People use Web sites to find things out and to get things done. If you have valuable information assets, and cool things to do, on your site, people will have a reason to visit. Only then does it even matter if they can find what they came to your site looking for!

10. **Offer shortcuts.** Really good site navigation features well-defined, carefully planned, fully predictable site sections — and "tunnels" connecting users directly to related, highly interesting spots on your site. Hyperlinks are great for this. People love shortcuts in the real world, and on the Web as well.

Figure 4-6 is a Navigation Do scorecard. Use it to quickly size up a site for how well it meets basic navigation needs. Even more fun, use it to compare sites from competing or comparable companies, organizations, or individual users. You'll know who knows where to go — and what to do when they get there.

✓	Requirement	Notes
	1. Link to the home page on every page	
	2. Persistent navigation area on every page	
	3. Search capability	
	4. Detailed link text	
	5. Standard link colors	
	6. Text used for navigation	
	7. News on the home page	
	8. What's New area	
	9. Site map	
	10. Shortcuts	

Figure 4-6:
The Navigation Do scorecard.

Part II: Designing Usable Sites

Using the Navigation Do scorecard

We wanted to give you a taste of how the Navigation Do scorecard works in the real world, so we tried it out on three well-known book-buying sites: Amazon.com (www.amazon.com), Barnes and Noble's site (www.bn.com), and Borders Books and Music's site (www.borders.com). These are major, multi-million-dollar sites that have a lot in common, so you would expect them all to meet most or all of our requirements, which they do for the most part.

Requirement	Amazon.com	Barnes & Noble	Borders	Notes
1. Link to the home page on every page	√	√	√	All have a linked icon in upper-right corner
2. Persistent navigation area on every page	√	√	√	All use the top bar; all but Amazon repeat same links as text at bottom
3. Search capability	√	√	√	On top of the page, every page
4. Detailed link text	√	√	√	Links are to specific books and authors
5. Standard link colors	√	√	X	Borders uses brown for unvisited links, making them all look visited!
6. Text used for navigation	X	X	X	All use graphical bar — which loads slower than the page's text
7. News on the home page	√	√	√	All have new releases and recent book news
8. What's New on the site	X	X	X	This would be hard to do for book sites
9. Site map	√	X	X	Amazon.com's site map is linked from every page
10. Shortcuts to related content	√	√	X	Amazon has several types, Barnes & Noble fewer, Borders almost none

Chapter 4: Organizing Your Site *91*

A baker's dozen don'ts for Web navigation

Users experience serious problems in navigating Web sites all the time. Some of them are the result of site creators not following the do's above, but some are the result of doing specific things that are generally wrong. We'll call them don'ts:

1. **Don't hide the home-page link.** Some sites cleverly put a link to the home page only at the bottom of a (long) Web page, or put it in a graphic that takes users time to decipher visually, or make part of their logo clickable but not all of it. Put an easily clickable link to the home page in the upper-left corner of each page, as well as at the bottom of the page.

2. **Don't put navigation in slow-loading, complex, changing graphics.** Some people think it's important to put the global navigation links in attractive graphics and to vary the navigation graphic depending on what section and subsection the user's in. This means the user has to wait and wait while slightly different navigation graphics load for each new section the user visits. What a way to motivate people to leave your site!

3. **Don't let users search the Web.** (Unless you're Google.) Some sites think it's good to offer a "search the Web" option along with their site search. Why? If you do this, you're confusing the user with extraneous options, and motivating them to leave your site. Believe us, if they want to leave, they know how. And if they want to search the Web, they know how to do that too.

Hunting for information

Web users act like a hunting lion or tiger, constantly looking for desired information or functionality — and rapidly breaking off the hunt if it seems unlikely to be found.

Your users are constantly analyzing the cost of different actions they may take versus the likely benefit. If they click on a link, what are the odds they'll get closer to their goal? If they go to a different site, might they be successful quicker? These kinds of tradeoffs are constantly being made, mostly at a subconscious level, by users as they surf the Web.

This cost/benefit trade-off explains a few things about Web navigation. Familiar-looking navigation schemes let users work their way through your site without having to think much. Using specific link language gives users confidence they're going in the right direction. And bad links (that lead nowhere or result in an error message) and slow-loading pages are anathema; they quickly unbalance the cost/benefit ratio away from staying on your site at all.

Think like a user as you lay out your site. First, create a clear, consistent structure for the site. Then, for each page on your site, think where the user is likely to want to go next. Provide links to those "hot spots." Then test your site on some real users and see if you guessed right!

Part II: Designing Usable Sites _____

4. **Don't use generic link text for specific stuff.** It's okay to use generic link text at the top level or two of navigation, where people expect it: About Us, Products, and Home are all acceptable (though About MyCo and Hot Cars, or whatever product category applies to your company, may be better). But don't use unfathomable terms like Databases, Tools, or Cool Stuff. Give users specifics; if they can't figure out what they're likely to find behind a link, they probably won't click it.

5. **Don't bury the good stuff.** A lot of sites have great assets like, say, a mortgage cost estimator, buried under layers of navigation: Products, Mortgages, Tools, Calculator, and you finally get to the coolest thing on the site. At the least, link to the cool stuff from the home page or major section pages; at best, put the cool things, or some piece of them, front and center.

6. **Don't innovate in site navigation.** Users are busy; they don't have time to learn how to use your site versus others. Make your site navigation boring and predictable (as well as attractive and fast-loading). Exceptions: If you're an artist, and innovation is just what you do, go ahead — on a personal or artistically oriented site, of course. And if you can show a clear usability improvement as a result of innovation, go for it!

7. **Don't design a site to your organization chart.** Web sites are to meet your organization's key needs and to serve users, not to impose every detail of your internal processes on users. Usually, creating a Web site is a joint marketing, PR, customer support, and sales exercise. Don't put categories for organizational departments or other internal stuff on your site unless it meets a clear organizational or user need.

8. **Don't depend on Back.** Many users ignore or don't like to use the Back button in their browser; they depend on you to provide navigation options within your site. Don't provide dead-end pages that the user can't leave except by clicking Back (or typing some other site's URL in the Address field!). Provide links from each page to the key places on your site that they may want to go or that you may want them to visit.

9. **Don't link to spots within a page.** A programmer would call Web site links "overloaded" because they do what are, to the user, three very different things: linking offsite, linking within a site, and linking up and down within a page. For most page styles, stick with linking to other pages in your site; within-page links, except for maybe a Top link at the bottom of a long page, are too confusing to be worthwhile. (Also, if you're linking within your page, it's probably because your pages are too long — we'll deal with that in Part III.)

10. **Don't link offsite.** We don't really mean this, but a flat rule like this is a good place to start. "Don't link offsite without warning the user" is really more like it. Put offsite links in clearly labeled areas with names like "Visit our partners" or "Links we like." Don't surprise the user by putting an

offsite link in the middle of a page that's otherwise exclusively concerned with your own stuff. And don't surprise them even further by popping up a new window without letting them know that's going to happen.

11. **Don't make the user think too much when navigating.** The Web encourages people to click first and ask questions later. If you make users work hard to figure out what to do next, they'll make like a tree and leaf. Make it very obvious what each link will do, and design your site so the actions you want users to take are always prominently offered.

12. **Don't make the user click too much.** Let's say you have five to six top-level categories, two to three levels below each category, and three or four choices at each level. That's about 400 destinations that you can offer within that fairly short tree. And you can always offer shortcuts to key destinations or to pages relevant to the page the user is on. So if you make the user click more than three to four times to get to something they want on your site, you're either making the user work too hard or your site is the size of IBM's.

13. **Don't put it all in.** Every additional thing you put in your site makes it harder for users to find the stuff they really want — or that you really want them to get to. Meet basic user expectations for things like contact information or press releases, meet the four or five top needs you find out from researching your users' needs, meet the four or five top needs you have as an organization, then stop!

Figure 4-7 shows our Navigation Don't scorecard. Use the Navigation Don't scorecard to look at your current or planned site, as well as competing or comparable sites. Figure out how to make your site better than the rest, without adding much to the budget or schedule.

Creating the Site Tree

Most information systems are organized into a hierarchy — like a tree. People are very good at categorizing things; it's one way in which we deal with the complexity of the world. The process of organizing the contents on your site is commonly called *information architecture,* and the job title of those who make a living at it is *information architect.*

Good information architecture leads to good site navigation. That's because good information architecture helps you develop great content and function-ality for your site, and organize it in a logical way. It's easy to create good, usable site navigation when you have great content that fits together into comprehensible groups. User testing then helps you find and fix any remain-ing barriers to top-notch navigation.

✓	Requirement	Notes
	1. Don't hide the home-page link.	
	2. Don't put navigation in slow-loading, complex, changing graphics.	
	3. Don't offer Web-wide search.	
	4. Don't use generic link text for specific stuff.	
	5. Don't bury the good stuff.	
	6. Don't innovate in site navigation.	
	7. Don't design your site to match your organization chart.	
	8. Don't depend on Back.	
	9. Don't link within a page.	
	10. Don't link offsite (without warning).	
	11. Don't make the user think too hard.	
	12. Don't make the user click too much.	
	13. Don't put it all in.	

Figure 4-7: The Navigation Don't scorecard.

When an information architect is not available — or when those responsible for a site don't know what information architecture is — Web designers often get called on to do this work; some are quite good at it, but some aren't. It can be very difficult to get a Web designer who's not very good at information architecture to allow others on the site team to have input into, let alone control of, this function. Usability testing (see Chapter 11) is a great way to separate bad ideas for your site's information design from good ones.

Part of the reason we call someone good at organizing a site's contents an information architect is because building a Web site is a lot like constructing a building. If you've ever worked with a good building architect, you know that they take a lot of things about the users of a building into account before they even start drawing a floor plan. Similarly, when you put your information architect hat on, you need to have a good understanding of your users.

The steps we describe in Part I of this book help you understand your users better. When it comes time to create your site architecture, however, the most important thing is attitude. If you and others on the team are able to think like users, and to realize that the user perspective is most important, you're likely to do a good job. If you focus on your "professional" insights and experiences — if the focus of your efforts becomes impressing management, your peers, or maybe someone giving out Web site awards — you'll lose the user's point of view, and be less likely to succeed. Least Likely to Succeed is not exactly what you're trying for here, so keep your user hat on as much as possible.

Bottom-Up Information Design

After years of working in Web site and product design, during much of which we felt we had more answers than anyone else, we've found that an open, inclusive, bottom-up process is the best way to figure out the top-down information design for your site.

Top-down design is starting from the big picture or the overall structure; bottom-up design is starting with details, like specific content and tasks you want on the site and then trying to arrange these pieces sensibly.

The basic process for bottom-up information design is:

1. **Get ideas for the site.**
2. **Organize the ideas into groups.**
3. **Repeat, getting ideas for the site and its organization from several people.**
4. **Create a rough plan from the features and organization ideas you've received.**
5. **Decide on a site navigation scheme.**
6. **Use the resulting rough plan to get yet more feedback on content, functionality, and organization.**
7. **Implement.**

This is different from a top-down approach, in which you would decide on the categories and sub-categories first, before you were sure you even had anything to go in them!

We'll go into a little detail on each of the early steps; then delve into useful site navigation schemes.

Whom to get ideas from

There are really two groups you need to make happy in creating a Web site: stakeholders and users.

Stakeholders include, but are not limited to, the following:

- ✓ **Management.** Management extends from the senior person on the design team up through the CEO and Board of Directors to other people involved in your organization or effort at a high level.

- ✓ **The site team.** Everyone involved in building the site is a major stakeholder in it.

- ✓ **Employees or group members.** This group is often ignored during development, and then heard from vociferously after *rollout* (the public launch of your site). Employees, or members of the group for which the site is being developed, will be key users of the site — and, whether you like it or not, a major source of feedback on its plusses and minuses.

- ✓ **Partners, suppliers, and customer organizations.** Other companies or organizations that work closely with yours. They're likely to be more polite in their feedback than employees, but they'll definitely have opinions.

- ✓ **Users.** The "silent majority" of users who aren't directly connected to your organization are your most important site stakeholders.

What makes stakeholders important is that you can't avoid hearing what they think about your Web site. The only choice you have is whether you get their opinions early in the site development process, or after the site is ready to launch. (Most site teams are remarkably impervious to outside input during the development process.)

If you solicit stakeholder opinions early in the development process, you basically "co-opt" your stakeholders — you get them on your side. This makes the rest of the development and approval process much easier. Also, you get many great ideas from stakeholders because they're usually pretty good proxies for various kinds of users. (They just can't be the *only* users you get input from.)

Some stakeholders are *really* important because they can veto the rollout of your site. What do you do when the CEO has never seen your site until just before rollout — and then doesn't like it? "Update your resumé" is one good answer. Seriously, you'll either have to fix the site until the CEO can live with it, or begin a crash redesign just after rollout. But if you get the CEO, and other influential stakeholders, involved early, you have every chance of having their support when rollout time comes.

Users, on the other hand, are unlike other stakeholders. Unless you do user testing, they almost never get to "vote" on your site before it's rolled out. But after you launch, user votes are the main ones that count. Get user opinions early in the process, when they can help you, rather than having users try and then ignore your site after it launches, which will hurt.

Only the site team is going to care enough about the site to spend hours and hours working on the site design. (Everyone else will have an opinion, though, if you ask him or her nicely.) Be smart about how you ask for input. Ask people throughout your organization for ideas — but don't wait for everyone's feedback; just grab the good ideas and go. Then, as the site comes together, show your work in progress to key stakeholders. Ask good, leading questions, such as "Anything we should add here?" or "What are some sites you like — and what do they have that we don't?" Remember, stakeholders are users, too.

Getting ideas from stakeholders

Here's a good brainstorming process for stakeholders. Following this process gives everyone a voice and gets a lot of good ideas on the table — or, rather, up on the wall.

1. Sit down with a group of stakeholders at a large table with a lot of large sticky notes.

2. Have everyone start writing down things they want to find on your site, one idea per sticky note. Do this for about ten minutes.

3. Ask one person to take one of his or her ideas and put it on the wall, then ask others, one at a time, to follow. People will naturally tend to group their ideas.

4. Keep putting up sticky notes until all the ideas are up on the wall. If two sticky notes are the same, just put one on top of the other.

5. Ask the group "What's missing?" Ask people what's on other sites they like that you could use here. Add sticky notes with the new ideas.

6. Ask the group "What would you like to be able to do on our site?" Ask people what they can do on other sites that they'd like to be able to do here. Add sticky notes with the new ideas.

7. Ask the group "What do our users need from the site?" This will remind people of any user research you've done so far and of their own experiences with your users. Add sticky notes with the new ideas.

8. Ask people to go up, one at a time, and move sticky notes around into a desired organization. Let them overrule each other during this process. (Note any major changes.)

At the end, the group leader should go up, rearrange things a bit toward the group consensus, then thank everyone. (If things have been too contentious, the leader can do the rearranging after people leave.)

Write up the results! This is a crucial step. Create a list of the major "buckets" of information and functionality and the proposed contents of each "bucket." Figure 4-8 shows an example of such a list.

When you have your site outline, send it around to key stakeholders for input. It will elicit feedback from people who think of additional content and functionality they want on the site.

You almost certainly won't be able to implement all the ideas you get in the first version of your site. That's okay; make clear to the people with whom you're working that prioritization will occur later, and record comments made along the way that will help you choose what to do first.

Information	Possible location on site
Location info: Address, phone number	Contact Us
Location info:	Map
Open hours	In Contact Us area
Bicycles	Products section — one Web page per major line of bikes. (Link to manufacturer on each page.)
Specials	Home page, Specials page
Tune-up clinics schedule	Clinics page
List of managers and e-mail addresses (include Webmaster)	In Contact Us area
List of activities we participate in	Community page

Figure 4-8: Idea list for a bike shop's site.

Chapter 4: Organizing Your Site **99**

Getting ideas from users

The period when you're gathering ideas for the site's contents and organization is a great time to get input from users. After you've gotten stakeholder input, you can effectively use time with one or a few groups of users to put your site plan on track. Try this process, which is similar to the stakeholder process but a little more time-consuming, to give users more of a chance to figure out what they really want:

1. **Get organized.** Take a set of 3 x 5 cards and write a site feature — content or functionality — on each card. Put the feature cards into a pile with some blank cards for additional ideas. Then have a user sit down at a large table and organize the cards into groups of features that belong together. Have each user write down anything he feels is "missing" on a card and put the new feature in the appropriate group.

2. **Get more input.** When the user is done, ask her some leading questions. "Any more features?" "Any features you like on other sites that you'd like to see here?" "What site that's like ours do you like the most — what do you do there?" Have the use put any additional ideas from these discussions on a card and add them to the appropriate group.

3. **Take down names.** Take a photograph of the user's groups of cards, and also write down the groupings — using group names the user suggests (write the group names in big letters on cards). Thank the person, then repeat the process with a half dozen or so potential users.

4. **Brainstorm.** Using the photos, or one-sheet summaries you create, take the users' ideas and put them up on a wall. By yourself, or with one or two other people, try to come up with a grouping that includes all the good ideas you've gotten so far. (There are complex statistical ways to extract this information, but looking at the feedback and thinking about it for a while seems to work just as well.) Keep a list of any site features that haven't made it into a group yet.

5. **Get feedback.** Make a list of worthwhile additions and create a generic user organization from all your input. Sum up the differences between user input and stakeholder ideas in a note, and send it around to people in your organization. Ask them if they have any additional ideas for the site.

100 Part II: Designing Usable Sites

Chapter 5

Creating Site Navigation

In This Chapter

▶ Choosing an approach

▶ One-page sites

▶ Top-level links

▶ Top navigation bars

▶ Left navigation bars

*J*ust as people who know how to read can read any book, people who know how to surf the Web can use any Web site. They shouldn't need to learn a bunch of new vocabulary to add your site to their repertoires.

As you create navigation for your site, there's no reason to reinvent the wheel. Most of your navigation problems can be resolved by choosing the right existing model, implementing your content and functionality within it, testing the result on users, and then fixing any problems.

Web site navigation models have grown in complexity as Web sites do more and more. Some sites are really super-sites, with many minor sites contained within them. Each of these sub-sites has its own purpose and, in some cases, its own look and feel. Other — better — sites are carefully focused, meet a small set of purposes for a well-understood group of users, and have great content and functionality; no "grab bag" here.

The most important step you can take toward making your site work well for users is to pick the right navigation model. This chapter introduces the important approaches already in use and tells you when and how to use each one. If you give this problem just a little bit of thought and work up front, you can create a highly usable site without too much difficulty or rework.

Charting Your Course

Before you pick a site navigation approach, there are a few things you need to do. They're simple but important; if you choose a navigation model poorly,

102 Part II: Designing Usable Sites

you could end up having to halt your project and start over — older, perhaps wiser, but nowhere near meeting the deadline for launching (or re-launching) your site. Follow these steps to keep the stress level under control:

✔ **Surf the Web.** There are a lot of good and bad examples of navigation out there on the Web. Surf around, especially among sites you've visited before, and take some notes about what you like and don't like about how you navigate them. Also search for articles and references on Web navigation. You might not agree with everything you read — we certainly don't agree with all of it — but this research will get you thinking about your own problems and possible solutions.

✔ **Know your users.** As we discuss in Chapter 2, you must know who your users are before you can create a site they'll use well. What other sites do your users frequently visit? Do they tolerate — even enjoy — a certain degree of complexity, or do they want things highly simplified? Refer to your knowledge of your users to make choices during the site design process that will work well when it comes time for testing and deployment.

✔ **Know what you want in your site.** In Chapter 4 we describe how to use index cards to get ideas about site content, functionality, and organization from "insiders" —we call them stakeholders — and potential end users. Read and implement this information if you haven't already; you have to have some idea what's going on your site to get the navigation right.

✔ **Study half a dozen comparables.** Now that you know what your users are like, and what you need to offer users on your site, find five or six competitive or comparable sites that solve the same problems in an attractive and highly functional way. Double-check your list of desired content and functionality against the comparable sites. Look at how these sites handle navigation; identify what works and what doesn't.

✔ **Estimate how many levels of navigation you'll need.** You can have one, two, or more than two major levels of navigation. Within a level you can have additional navigation within a piece of content or a task; we cleverly call this *within-level navigation*. Unless you have a large and experienced team, try to add no more than one level of navigation per project.

For a new site, try to scope the project to fit in a single level of navigation; that is, a set of top-level categories, each holding several Web pages, but no additional navigation within a category. For an existing one-level site, it's a fairly major project to take the site to two levels. Adding within-level navigation to a site that doesn't currently have it can be a project in and of itself.

This chapter shows you the major possible ways to one major level of navigation; the next chapter discusses additional navigation levels and introduces within-level navigation.

How many sites?

After careful consideration, you may decide not to create a usable Web site at all! You may find it better to create two or three smaller usable Web sites.

There are many scenarios in which creating multiple Web sites for a company or organization makes sense. Let's say you have no Web sites at all, and you need a Web site for a product really, really fast. It can be valuable to create the Web site for your product first and fast, and then do your company Web site next and tie the two together.

Targeted Web sites are much simpler to create than one big Web site that does everything. Complex navigation issues become much simpler as huge sites that serve multiple purposes are instead deployed as several simple, single-level sites, each with one purpose. Design becomes fun again as each smaller site takes on its own targeted, focused *raison d'etre* ("reason for being," if French isn't your cup of *thé*).

Of course, making two or more targeted sites work well together creates a new set of issues. Users experience inconsistency and confusion in navigation. Groups of simple sites trade local simplicity — it's easier to get specific things done within a site — for global complexity — complicated tasks, or series of tasks, might require finding and using several different sites.

A good example of using multiple sites to achieve corporate purposes is the For Dummies site at `www.hungryminds.com`. This site is the "child" of the corporate site for Hungry Minds, publisher of the For Dummies series; sibling to the Frommers.com site, another offshoot of Hungry Minds, and parent to dummiesdaily.com, a tips site. The figure shows the relationship of the sites.

Many organizations use a multi-site approach for quick deployment, but later pull all their sites together for greater usability and consistency. These efforts, worthwhile as they are, often take years — yes, that's right, years — which just goes to show how difficult site design for a truly large site can be. So consider deploying several small sites initially — then look forward to several years of job security as you stitch the smaller sites together into the easy-to-use yet powerful megasite that your users deserve.

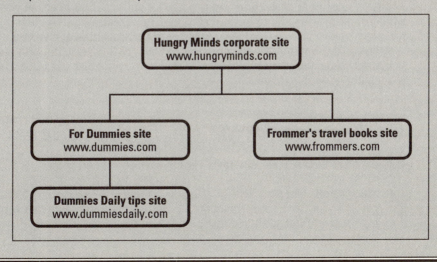

Single-Page Sites

Can you make a good, useful, and attractive single-page site? Definitely. However, we generally recommend that you implement the same content as a single-level site with short pages. If you use the models shown in this chapter, creating a single-level site isn't necessarily that much harder than creating a single-page site, while making a much better impression on your user.

Sometimes, though, all you have the time and energy to do is to create a one-pager that meets the immediate needs of you, your organization, or a specific product or service. If that's the case, never fear: *Web Usability For Dummies* is here!

It's also worth looking at single-page sites as a model to refer to anytime you have to get a bunch of related information up in a hurry — without creating new navigation or going to a great deal of trouble to integrate new content and functionality into your site. A good example is when you need to describe an upcoming or recent event. In a single page you can describe the event, show a couple of pictures from the site, and tell users how to get more information. Just create the one-page "mini-site," link to it from within your existing site — say, as a news item on the front page with a link to the mini-site — and you're off and running.

Single-page sites also work well as "search engine bait." When you put up a Web site, search engine programs called *bots* soon find it, and — if you're lucky — add it to that search engine's index. This cycle takes about three months. Putting up a single-page site gives the bots something to chew on while you create your "real" site.

A single-page site is also a good way to start if you're a bit uncertain about what you want your site to be when it grows up. Creating the single-page site will force you to decide what your key messages are, and will give you a success story to use in driving the creation of your "real" site. It will also give you some initial usability experience as you learn what does and doesn't work within your single-page site.

Goal-setting for the single-page site

A single-page Web site should have a set of simple, related goals:

✔ **Small team.** Aim for a one- or two-person team: the person who needs to get the page up creates the content; then another person helps with layout and HTML coding. Most people can figure out what such a page needs to say — if you can write a memo or a letter, you can lay out a one-page Web site — but need a bit of help to make the page look decent and to get the HTML coding right. Don't get more people involved, or the schedule will stretch out.

✔ **Short schedule.** The main justification for doing a single-page site instead of a more robust, single-level site is that you're in a hurry. So don't let the schedule stretch out on you! Give yourself a few days or, at most, a week to get the page up. Then use the time you've saved by following a compressed schedule to get other things done — or to start working on a more robust site to replace the one-pager.

✔ **Single purpose.** A single-page site should have a single purpose. Good candidates include "give contact information for the company," "describe an event," or "introduce our product." If you have more than one purpose, you'll probably need more than one page.

To keep yourself focused, create a simple project plan for your single-page site. Keep it to one page. You can even put the plan on the Web! (This can help you coordinate efforts among people who work separately and make it easy for management or others to follow your progress.) An example is shown in Figure 5-1.

Under construction?

We discourage "Under Construction" announcements on Web sites; most Web sites are perpetually under construction, and you should always leave things tidy enough to not need an explicit "Under Construction" sign as an excuse for your site's appearance. If you really want to clue people in to coming features on your Web site, put a list of work in progress on a What's New page within the site, and invite user feedback.

However, if you think people might be coming to your site looking for something specific that's on the way, but not quite ready yet, some kind of "it's coming" message is appropriate. For instance, if your company is in the news — for good or ill — but you haven't gotten a response together yet, put a brief note on your site telling people when you'll have more information. This

rationale even applies to the main page of your site: If people expect you to be on the Web, you should at least give them a single-page site with contact information while you work on your "real" Web site.

Another reason to provide a simplified page for a period of time is to make your site searchable. It takes search engines time to find and list your site. You can start the clock running on this lag time by putting up a single page incorporating your organization name and other terms you want people to be able to search for you by. Make the visible part of this placeholder page simple and attractive. That way, when your "real" site is ready, people will be able to find it through search engines. See Chapter 9 for details.

106 Part II: Designing Usable Sites

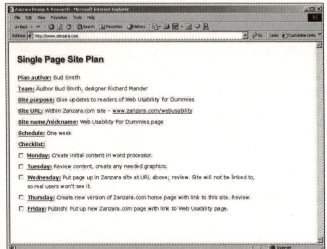

Figure 5-1: A simple plan for a single-page site.

Navigating the single-page site

The amount of information you have on your single-page site dictates what kinds of navigation you need to consider using. Here are the major possibilities for single-page navigation:

- **No navigation.** And we mean **no** navigation: Create a single page that fits within the browser window, and which doesn't scroll up and down. This kind of Web page is usually suited only for an announcement that your site's on the way — which we generally discourage, as explained in the sidebar, "Under construction?"—or for basic contact information.

- **Scrolling navigation only.** In a scrolling-only site, the whole site is one long page, and there are no internal links; the user moves through the page by using the scrollbar (or the keyboard's up and down arrow keys, the page up and page down keys, or the little wheel on top of a wheelie mouse — users are very creative).

  Even on this kind of a site, you might consider one piece of explicit navigation: a Top button at the end of the page to save the user that loooong scroll back to the top.

- **Internal sections.** We both dislike internal links within a Web page, but they have their uses. One such use is for a single-page site that has sections within the page: You can create a single long page with headers, and internal links that take the user up and down to various headers. Each section ends with a "Top" button so the user can go back and start over. Sometimes this is implemented in such a way as to make the sections seem almost like separate pages, and this kind of implementation can be a good placeholder while you create a new version that actually does use separate pages.

Each issue of Netsurfer Digest is published as a single Web page with dozens of stories and external and internal navigation in the left column. Figure 5-2 shows an issue. Nearly the same content is sent out as an HTML-formatted e-mail newsletter to thousands of subscribers.

Single-page site designs tend to be placeholders until you get your "real" site — even if that day is several months in the future. However, it's worth doing a good job: Some users will see your site in this early state, and you may be able to lift pieces of your single-page site for use in a larger site, if they're written and laid out well enough.

For information on how to design Web pages, page navigation, and more, see *Web Design For Dummies* (published by Hungry Minds, Inc.)

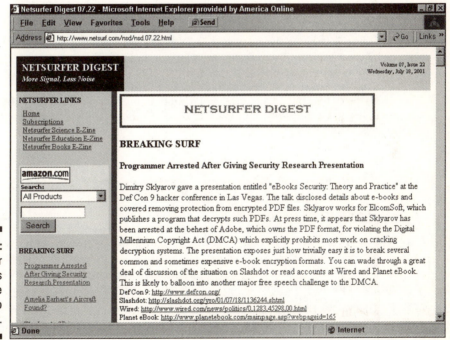

Figure 5-2: Netsurfer Digest uses a single page to good effect.

In the Beginning: Top Navigation Links

Most of the attention in Web design and usability tends to go to big, multi-level sites from large companies and organizations. But creating a usable, attractive, worthwhile single-level Web site is an art form in and of itself. Such a site can handle the needs of most small- to medium-sized companies and organizations, as well as of most individuals who want to create an initial Web presence.

Single-level Web sites have evolved, along with the Web, from ugly but functional aggregations of information to relatively elegant, attractive, and complete Web sites. Even startup companies with millions of dollars of funding, and long-established companies with millions of dollars of revenues, often depend on a site with a single overall level of navigation.

Some single-level sites keep it simple and just have a single page underneath each header; others have multiple pages within some of the levels. In either case, the overall approach is the same.

Early Web sites often featured a single strip of text links across the top as navigation into a site's sections. These links are called *top navigation links*. Figure 5-3 shows the front page of Yahoo!, a famous example of such a site. (Yahoo! spruces the links up a bit with icons, and it has many additional navigation options as well; but if you watch the Yahoo! page load, you can see that the row of text links across the top shows up first.) You can still see strips of text links used as navigation in many Web sites today, either as the sole navigational option for a site or, like Yahoo!, in combination with other options.

Plusses of top navigation text links

The use of a single strip of text links for navigation has several plusses:

- ✔ **Text links load fast.** Text loads first on a typical Web page, so strips of text links appear nearly instantly when someone visits your Web page. This gives users the chance to move where they want to go within your site very quickly, a gratifying feeling for the user.

- ✔ **Strips of links are easy to implement.** Strips of links are very easy to implement — and because they can only support about five to seven sections within a single strip, they practically force you to keep your overall site simple as well.

Chapter 5: Creating Site Navigation *109*

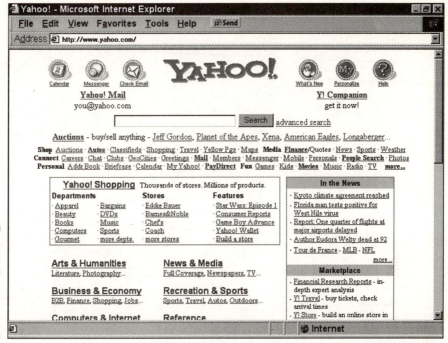

Figure 5-3: Yahoo! uses a strip of text links with graphic icons.

Reproduced with permission of Yahoo! Inc. © 2000 by Yahoo! Inc. YAHOO! and the YAHOO! Logo are trademarks of Yahoo! Inc.

- **Strips of links are easy to code.** The HTML code needed to support strips of links as navigation is so simple that it's almost comprehensible to regular people, while other approaches tend to require HTML code that's unmanageable for anyone who isn't an expert. If you're creating your site yourself and aren't an HTML expert, consider using a strip-of-links approach.

- **Text links can look good.** With adroit use of table cells, background colors, and fonts, you can make your strip of text links look graphical, while keeping the extremely fast loading speed of text. Figure 5-4 shows an example of a site with top navigation links that are formatted to look like a graphical top navigation bar.

- **Strips of links are easy to learn.** Your users have seen many, many sites previously with this kind of navigation, so they recognize it quickly and have no trouble learning how to use it within the context of your site.

Hint: Your users will expect the links to be repeated as a small, simple strip of text links at the bottom of the page.

- **Strips of links take up little space.** A strip of links does take up some vertical space within the page, meaning a bit less of your Web page is visible when the user first arrives; but they take up no horizontal space, giving you the use of the full horizontal width of the page.

Figure 5-4: This top navigation is Harley sophisticated.

Top navigation links must have some plusses — Yahoo! didn't get to be one of the top sites on the Web by doing a bunch of stupid stuff. Using strips of links is a very acceptable, and very simple, approach for implementing basic navigation on a Web site.

Minuses of top navigation text links

In addition to the pluses, there are minuses to using a strip of text links for navigation as well:

- **Text links look old-fashioned.** The Yahoo! front page is sometimes criticized for looking outdated, and other sites that use a strip of text links for navigation run this risk as well.

- **Text links may change format with user preferences.** Text links are subject to user preferences relating to font size, font family, highlighting of visited links and so on. Platform differences between Macintosh, Unix, and Windows also affect the look of text links. Designers hate nothing worse than having their "look" messed up by users or computer makers.

Chapter 5: Creating Site Navigation   111

You may be able to combat the effect of changes in user preferences through careful HTML coding. This requires considerable HTML skill — followed by considerable testing to make sure appearance really is consistent across platforms.

- **Text links may be too simple.** You may have more stuff on your site than a strip of text links can adequately point to. Because horizontal space is limited — as is the user's attention span — the link text has to be short, which can force you to be less descriptive in these links than you'd like.

- **Text links may not be easy to use.** Though text links are easy to learn, they may not be easy to use. Why? For any but the simplest site, additional within-level navigation that may be required to get users around may make your site harder to use than it would be with more robust navigation.

When to use top navigation text links

Top navigation links are a good choice for an initial, simple site. If you're in a hurry to get a new site up, and you don't have a huge amount of content, top navigation links create an easy-to-implement navigation system that contributes to fast-loading pages and that your users will recognize instantly.

Are top navigation links ever a good long-term choice, as well as being good for getting a site up in a hurry? Yes, in some cases. If you are creating a personal site, a small business site, or a site for an organization that will largely be used by "insiders," for shared access to regularly updated information, top navigation links may be a good choice.

However, top navigation links generally aren't a good choice if you're creating a site for a medium-sized or larger business, or one that depends on its Web site for a substantial part of its customer, partner, or stakeholder interaction. Larger business sites need to have a clean, finished, up-to-date look. Most businesspeople are willing to sacrifice some amount of load time efficiency for the better appearance possible with other navigation approaches.

Even if you make another choice for your main site navigation, however, top navigation links may be useful as a supplement to graphical navigation, or for use within a subsite in a larger site.

Expanding a site with top navigation text links

Significantly expanding a site with top navigation links can be harder than expanding a site with other kinds of navigation described later in this chapter.

Part II: Designing Usable Sites

Short or long pages?

There's a huge debate going on right now in Web usability and design: Should pages be designed to be non-scrolling (also known as "short pages"), or scrolling, long pages? And, for non-scrolling Web pages, what screen resolution should you target? The answers you choose have big implications for navigation within your site.

If you've ever used AOL or Compuserve, you've probably noticed that most pages within the service are designed to be non-scrolling. These pages are like TV screen images: They fit comfortably within the bounds of your monitor, even at 800 x 600 resolution. This is really the ultimate in ease-of-learning — you don't need to know how to scroll! Most of the service is designed so you're never scrolling up and down, let alone (shudder) left and right.

A substantial and growing minority of Web pages are now designed to be non-scrolling as well. Overall, we're fans of this approach. We believe that you can achieve extreme ease of use with non-scrolling pages wherever appropriate, such as front pages, navigation pages, and task pages. Content pages should be allowed to scroll when necessary to accommodate large pieces of content.

There are problems with short pages: Highly usable though they are at 800 x 600 resolution, they look odd when displayed in a browser window that's taller and that's recently been used to view long pages. Users who go from a site with long pages to a site with short pages may feel as if they've turned a page in a magazine or newspaper and suddenly found a half-blank page. If the user stays in the site, they get accustomed to short pages, only to be surprised again when they bring up a long page. There's no good answer to this problem, all you can do is stay consistent in your approach within your site.

We'll discuss this topic in excruciating detail in Part III. For now, we'll assume that you aren't putting the equivalent of the front page of USA Today on every page of your site — but that you aren't hacking up all your content to maintain a strict no-scrolling rule either. If you want to go to extremes, we'll show you how in Part III.

The main reason is that top navigation links imply simplicity. If you use a truly simple top navigation scheme — a short row of text links across the top and, maybe, the bottom of each page — users get the impression that you're trying to keep it simple. They expect simple, fast-loading pages without a lot of navigation or complexity. If you add complexity to this kind of site without changing the navigation to a different style, you may befuddle your users.

The Yahoo! site is a great example of the use of top navigation links (though on Yahoo! they're augmented with little icons). Yahoo! also shows some of the problems of building a complex site on this style of navigation. Despite careful and consistent use of *breadcrumbs* — text labels that show the location of a Web page in the site's hierarchy — some areas of the Yahoo! site are hard to access from other parts, and even frequent Yahoo! users are often unaware of much of the functionality available on Yahoo!

Graphical Top Navigation Bars

Top navigation bars, or *nav bars*, are much like top navigation text links; the difference is that the links are embedded in a graphical area called a *clickable image map*. A clickable image map is a graphical area in which different parts of the graphic are linked to different Web addresses; as a Web user, you see them on many, if not most, of the sites you use every day. The Monterey Bay Aquarium site is a good example of a complex site whose primary organization is through a graphical top navigation bar, as shown in Figure 5-5.

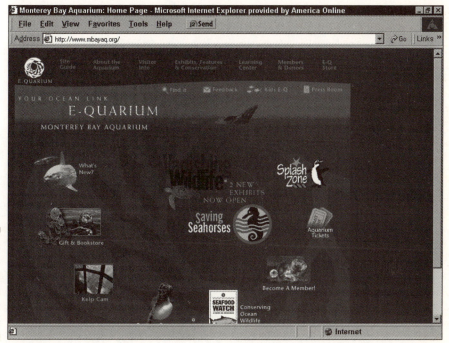

Figure 5-5: The e-quarium uses a top navigation bar.

A clickable image map, as used in graphical top navigation bars, is a combination of two files: a graphics file, usually a GIF file, and a series of coordinates defining which areas in the graphic are clickable and where each clickable area links to. For details about how to create a clickable image map in HTML see *HTML 4 For Dummies*, 3rd Edition (Hungry Minds, Inc.) You may be able to create a clickable image map in a Web page editing program without having to learn the gory details of how the underlying HTML works.

Though creating clickable image maps is kind of complicated, the way they work is simple: you move the mouse pointer over the area you want, wait until the mouse cursor changes to a pointing finger, and click on the area to activate the link. In navigation bars, the clickable image map just about always includes words within the graphic. So the navigation bar works like a set of top navigation text links, but with a much more professional appearance.

Plusses of top navigation bars

Top navigation bars are extremely popular, either as the sole navigation for a site, or in combination with additional levels of navigation and/or other types of navigation. For larger business or organizational sites, either a top navigation bar or a side navigation bar is nearly a requirement if you want your site to have the kind of finished look needed to be taken seriously.

Let's look at why navigation bars are so popular:

- **Most of the plusses of a strip of text links.** Top navigation bars are easy to implement and easy for the user to understand. They take up relatively little space overall, and no precious page width.

- **Very clean look.** Though some sites have goofy-looking ones, most top navigation bars look great. Because the text in the top navigation bar is forever locked into a graphic, it never changes — the designer's choices stay "locked in" forever.

- **Extensible.** Unlike a strip of links, it's relatively easy to extend a top navigation bar to support a second level of navigation, without changing the overall look and feel of the site.

Top navigation bars are as popular as they are for a reason. They can support simple navigational schemes while giving a clean, corporate appearance to your site.

Minuses of top navigation bars

Top navigation bars aren't perfect. They're between top navigation text links and side navigation widgets in complexity — and have some disadvantages compared to either:

- **Slow loading.** Top navigation bars can be relatively large graphics files, taking several seconds to load for users with a slow connection. This can seriously impact the usability of your site, making it hard for users to quickly navigate to where they want to go. Sites that update the navigation bar graphic to reflect what area the user is currently in may inflict this wait on the user several times during a visit.

Chapter 5: Creating Site Navigation 115

A general rule to follow for graphics loading speed over a slow connection is the following: a user on a 56K modem receives data at about 3K per second. So if your graphic is 16K in size, that's about five seconds for the top navigation bar alone — long enough for many users to give up and go do something else.

✔ **Limited room for topics.** The number of topics that can fit in a top navigation bar is limited by the usable horizontal space on a page as well as by your choice of font and the amount of space used for the tab graphic around the text. You have to keep topic labels short in order to fit as many as six or seven items up there. (This is about as many as people can scan in one visual sweep across the top navigation bar anyway.)

Because top navigation bars are, by definition, graphics, you can use some designer's tricks to help you squeeze things in. For example, you can use thin fonts and *kerning* — squeezing together certain pairs of letters that fit well together — to get more characters into the top navigation bar while still keeping its appearance sharp.

✔ **Hard to tell it's a link.** Unlike top navigation links, top navigation bars generally don't telegraph the fact that they're links; the text usually isn't underlined, and it's almost never the same blue as a typical HTML link.

One popular way to combat this problem is to use JavaScript to pop up text that indicates that you're over a link and where the link goes to.

✔ **Can't tell if it's been clicked.** Top navigation bars can be made to change color to reflect the area you're in, but unlike traditional Web links, links you've previously clicked don't take on a different color. This makes it hard for users to either retrace their path or to be sure they're searching new areas after an initial search fails.

✔ **Harder to design.** Many top navigation links have tabs that change colors, pop up slightly, or otherwise change when rolled over and/or selected. Deciding which of these effects to use can be a difficult and time-consuming design decision — and one that may be subject to change as a result of usability testing or even differing opinions among stakeholders.

✔ **Much harder to code.** Unlike top navigation links, top navigation bars are quite hard to code. Clickable image maps are hard to create and harder still to test and debug. Also, to support features such as a different look for selected tabs, many top navigation bars are implemented in Javascript, a "simple" computer language that's about as easy to learn as, well, a computer language.

✔ **Why Javascript is bad for usability.** Javascript is great for the functionality of a site; it allows you to make your site do all kinds of neat things like supporting rollovers, simple animations and more. However, Javascript isn't supported by older browsers, and it's supported inconsistently by newer ones. Though there are some "rock-solid" Javascript routines for simple stuff like basic top navigation bars, try to avoid using Javascript in your site as much as possible; the usability tradeoffs, not to mention the additional complexity of creating, modifying, and testing your site, may not be worth it.

There are ways to reduce the size of graphics that are downloaded each time a user visits your site or different areas within it. For instance, you can keep a large section of your graphic the same, and just download the small part that changes from one part of your site to the next. *Web Design For Dummies* (Hungry Minds, Inc.) is a good source for details on how to efficiently implement the ideas contained in this chapter.

When to use a top navigation bar

Like top navigation links, a top navigation bar is a good choice for an initial, simple site. However, they're slower-loading and harder to implement than top navigation links. The tradeoffs are generally worthwhile if the attractiveness and professional appearance of your site are a top priority for you, if the rest of your site is also well-designed and attractive, and if you have people available to work with you who can create, test, debug, and support this more complicated form of navigation.

Unlike top navigation links, a top navigation bar is also easily extensible to a two-level navigation scheme, and more easily combined with other forms of navigation to create an attractive and useful site. If you plan to have a large and robust site in the long term, a top navigation bar is a good way to start.

If you use long pages in your site, it's useful to include a set of text navigation links at the bottom of each page so users don't have to go to the top of the page to get to navigation again. Some sites accomplish the same thing by repeating the top navigation bar at the bottom of the page; others keep their pages short so that top navigation alone is sufficient.

A war story

One of the authors (Bud Smith) worked at AltaVista, a top search company, in the late 1990s. At the time, the company used a top navigation scheme for its site, and was constantly adding new channels as a result of internal channel development and new channel partnership deals. A new channel he helped develop, the Technology channel, was renamed Tech in order to squeeze its name into the overcrowded top navigation bar. After the Tech channel was added, the addition of further channels was held up for several months, reducing new revenue opportunities, until a site-wide redesign reduced crowding at the top level.

Blending top navigation links and bars

One exciting possibility that can give your site the best of both worlds is a set of top navigation links that are implemented using clever HTML so they look like a top navigation bar.

An example of this is the site of a local Harley Davidson motorcycle dealer in Bellingham, Washington, shown earlier in this chapter. The navigation area looks like a graphical top navigation bar, but is actually a set of top navigation text links. It takes some tricky HTML coding to make this work, but the results can be very much worthwhile.

By implementing a top navigation bar as text with HTML formatting, you get almost all the advantages of top navigation links — fast loading, links that change color when they've been clicked, and relatively easy implementation (some HTML skill needed, but no Javascript programming). The only real disadvantage is graphical — you still can't get quite as sharp a look as with graphical top navigation bars, and you can't support certain tricks like making a button change color when it's selected. To us, the usability advantages of fast page loading and support for color changing of links are often worth the loss of a bit of graphical control.

To create tab-like top navigation text links, use an HTML table with colored cells. You can specify the font and size to a certain extent, but make sure to test your site broadly, as it may be difficult to always override user preferences and platform differences that might otherwise make text too big, small, the wrong font, and so on.

Expanding a site with a top navigation bar

The first kind of expansion you may need to consider for a site with top navigation is, what if you run out of tab space? That is, you may have more top-level options than can fit in a single row of tabs across the top of the page. Typically, the first response to this is to squeeze "one more tab" in by changing fonts, reducing font and tab size, changing tab labels to make them shorter, and so on. But eventually, these tricks run out, and you'll need to add more tabs than you have room for.

The simplest way to do this is to go to a second row of tabs. The problem with a second row of tabs is that you have to do something when the user clicks the "other" row of tabs - the row that's not currently front and center. The content attached to the tab itself moves to the foreground — but what about the tab, which is supposed to be attached to the content? It can't easily stay attached when there's a second row of tabs between the selected tab and the content.

Part II: Designing Usable Sites

The simplest answer, which provides just a so-so user experience, is used in dialog boxes within Microsoft Windows and in Microsoft application programs, as well as on many Web sites: you just slam the top row of tabs down to the bottom, and jam the bottom row of tabs up to the top. The sudden jump of rows of tab buttons up and down is disconcerting to the user, and it makes the overall experience inconsistent, but it solves the problem of keeping the tabs attached to their content.

Figure 5-6 shows a "before and after" example of tabs switching places in the Power Management Properties control panel from a laptop computer. The shading that shows which tab is selected is subtle, which makes the problem of knowing where you are worse. However, the navigation issue of having too many tabs to fit in the space does get resolved, albeit clumsily.

Another way to resolve the problem of "too many tabs" is to go to a left navigation bar rather than a top navigation bar. Although a left navigation bar has its own problems, such as taking away precious content space across the width of the browser window, it does allow you to easily handle several more top-level categories than a top navigation bar. The plusses and minuses of a left navigation bar are described in the next section.

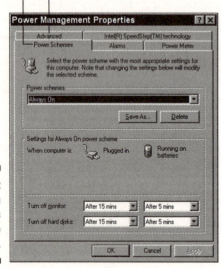
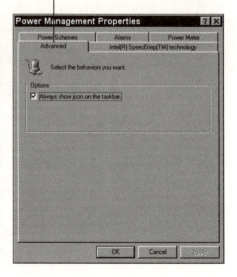

Figure 5-6: Watch Windows tabs jam up and down.

Users see Power Schemes first.
Advanced is in second row.

Clicking Advanced causes the second row of tabs to move forward and pushes the first row back.

Chapter 5: Creating Site Navigation *119*

The case for single-level navigation

From a usability point of view, we can make a pretty strong case for single-level navigation in all but the most complicated sites. For a simple site, this case is easy to make: If you have only seven or eight Web pages, of course you should have only a single level of navigation. But what about when you have anywhere from 12 to 100 pages in your site?

The temptation is to immediately introduce a second level of navigation — sub-navigation under the main set of five to seven buckets. This does help you, as the site developer, know where everything is, and frequent users of your site — employees, management, people on the site development team — will quickly memorize the location of their favorite pages. Voila', you may say, problem solved.

However, navigating a two-level navigation system takes a lot of mentation — yes, "mentation" is in our Oxford English Dictionary, and if you use a lesser dictionary that's your problem. What we mean to say, however, is that navigating a two-level navigation system takes a lot of thought on the part of the user. Users literally have to "think twice" — once for each navigation level — about where the page they want might be. And they will get frustrated when they remember the sub-level a desired page is in, but have to scan through all the top-level categories to find the sub-level they want.

Two-level navigation systems also mean longer download times for each and every page on your system, due to additional navigation graphics (or HTML code if you're clever), and compatibility problems with some users' browsers that don't have full support for Javascript. You also lose precious page space as that second level of navigation pops in and out, up and down, or some other annoying motion.

You can support a lot of navigational complexity in a single level of navigation through carefully considered use of in-page navigation, as we'll describe in the next chapter. And we do agree that a site with as much functionality as, for instance, Yahoo! probably really does need a multi-level navigation system. But if your site's page count is still in the range of dozens of pages, consider keeping the number of levels of major navigation to one.

Left Navigation

Many left navigation schemes are two-level, and we'll discuss some two-level navigation schemes in the next chapter. However, this section describes only single-level left navigation schemes — a highly usable and powerful way to organize sites from the very simple to the moderately complex.

Single-level left navigation schemes are popular, highly usable, and fairly easy to implement — though not as easy to implement as any kind of top navigation scheme. One major problem with implementing any kind of left navigation scheme is the fact that the content of the page has to be "poured" into the area not occupied by the navigation.

Table 5-1 compares the three most common navigation systems — top-level links and top nav bars, discussed earlier in the chapter, and left nav bars, which are described here. As you can see, the tradeoffs are complementary, and there's an overall increase in site complexity from one to the next — though rules are made to be broken, and these rules have been broken many times.

Table 5-1	Comparing Common Navigation Schemes		
Requirement	*Top links*	*Top nav bar*	*Left nav bar*
Common number of categories	3-7	5-8	5-12
Maximum length of category text	Long	Short	Medium
Professional appearance	Somewhat	Yes	Very
Load time	Instant	Moderate	Can be slow
Easy to design	Yes	Somewhat	No
Easy to implement	Yes	Somewhat	No
Extensible to second level	Very difficult	Difficult	Difficult

Also, Web sites that use left navigation are fairly evenly divided between sites that use frames to keep the navigation in the picture when the user scrolls, and sites that let the navigation scroll up and down with other content. This means that users don't know how to expect the navigation to behave when they scroll. It can seem to a user that just as they get used to a site that acts one way, they find themselves on a site that does the opposite.

However, left navigation schemes are still highly usable, and highly popular. A single-level left navigation scheme requires little conscious thought on the user's part and looks attractive and professional. This makes left navigation schemes a favorite among companies with relatively small Web sites that want their site to look somewhat bigger than it really is.

Many venture-capital-funded companies that have an embarrassingly small number of Web pages in their sites use a single-level or simple two-level left navigation scheme to "pump up the volume" on their site and give it the appearance of robustness.

Plusses of single-level left navigation

Single-level left navigation bars are very popular, especially with sites that have more Web design skill in-house than actual content and services on their Web site. Such sites have many plusses:

- **Clean and professional appearance.** Even more than a graphical top nav bar, a left navigation bar makes even a relatively small site look impressive. (You can undermine this by making poor implementation choices though; it only looks good when it's done well.)

- **Extensible to more categories.** Single-level left navigation bars can easily be extended to include more categories — just keep running them down the page.

- **Extensible to more levels.** Single-level left navigation bars can be extended, with some difficulty, to support a second level of navigation, though at the cost of even more precious horizontal space (or at the cost of letting content be obscured when the second level of navigation pops out).

- **Consistent presence.** Any left navigation bar is visible most of the time when you're looking at a page, even if you scroll down somewhat, whereas top navigation links or nav bars disappear entirely from the screen as soon the user scrolls down a bit. Implemented properly, left nav bars can be omnipresent.

- **Lots of links.** Top-level navigation supports five to seven links easily; left navigation bars can support ten to twelve links easily and even more if you and your users are willing to stretch a bit.

Figure 5-7 shows the Corporate Collection of business gift boxes from the site of Godiva Chocolatier, makers of Godiva chocolates. The site features a left navigation bar integrated with several other kinds of functionality and navigation to form a rich, attractive offering — not unlike their chocolates! The left navigation bar is in the middle of the left rail, below the Search box; the navigational and functional elements are kept together to allow the chocolates to be highlighted.

With all these plusses, especially the "big league" look that they bring to a site, left navigation bars are very popular. One of the authors (Bud Smith) once did a survey of new companies funded by Softbank, a large venture capital firm; the vast majority had simple sites with left navigation bars.

Think twice before you try this at home: almost all Softbank-funded companies are, or were, Internet companies, with plenty of talented Web developers on staff who could work around some of the minuses listed in the next section.

Figure 5-7: Godiva keeps navigation compact to give more room to chocolates.

Minuses of single-level left navigation

Left navigation bars have many problems, and it's common to see bad implementations. As you surf the Web looking at examples that might work for your own site, look for examples of the following problems that frequently show up in left-navigation sites:

- **Loss of horizontal space.** As we describe in Part III, page design for the Web is hard — and it only gets harder when you give up a big chunk of horizontal space for left navigation. Every page has to be visually designed to use the limited remaining page width well, and technically designed so as to make updating easy without "*blowing out*" the page — making it an indecipherable mess — by accidentally combining navigation and content HTML. (One of the authors, Bud Smith, has been personally responsible for blowing out the front page of AltaVista for several minutes.)

- **Weak links.** For easy use, the links in the left navigation bar should be easy to understand, which often means longer labels; but to preserve space for content, you really want to make the links short. This conflict is usually resolved in favor of keeping links short, which supports the usability of the page in terms of providing more room for content, but undermines the usability of the navigation in terms of the comprehensibility of navigational labels.

- **Slow loading.** Single-level left navigation bars are slow-loading the first time they're used during a Web session; with repeated pageviews in a site, they usually get cached, and then appear quickly. Adding levels of navigation means adding various submenus and even different versions of the top-level left navigation bar, all of which can slow loading time to a crawl.

This is how caching works: Every Web user has a specific Web cache size set up on his or her computer. Recently used files get stored in the cache and appear very quickly when they're repeatedly called. However, it's common for users to run with caching turned off, with a very small cache, or with multiple windows open, which can cause "cache thrash" as files are stored in and removed from the cache. ISPs such as AOL and Compuserve, as well as smaller providers, also cache files. Don't be surprised if caching helps your site's response time sometimes, but don't count on caching to save your sorry self if your site navigation depends too much on large and frequently changing graphics files.

Web site developers, such as many readers of this book, usually have fast machines with a large hard disk and a large cache setting. They also spend a great deal of time in their own sites. This means that they usually experience their sites with caching operational, speeding performance. Try clearing your cache or turning caching on your Web browser off completely and then accessing your site; you may be surprised at the difference.

- **Harder to design and code.** You have a number of decisions to make with a left navigation bar that you don't have with text links. You have to decide how linked areas act when the user rolls the mouse over them, and how big the clickable "impact area" is around each word. And of course it takes more complex HTML and programming to make it all work right. Also, unlike top navigation of any sort, you have severe constraints on word length, because one long word in a left navigation bar can make it wider and seriously reduce space for content in the rest of the page.

- **Other graphical problems.** Like top navigation bars, left navigation bars are graphics, which causes some usability problems: Users can't tell as easily what is and isn't a link because graphical links don't show up as blue underlined text, and users can't tell where they've been, because graphical links don't change color after use. However, users are accustomed to graphics being used for major navigation, and will recognize what you're doing as long as you're not too creative with your design.

- **Harder to expand.** Expanding a left-nav-based site incrementally is fairly easy; just lengthen the list in the navigation area. But going to a second level of navigation in such a site is difficult and infringes further on the width of the area used for content. Users are accustomed to sites where these problems have been worked out years ago — see the Darwin Magazine site for an example, shown in Figure 5-8 — and aren't going to cut you a lot of slack if your site is hard to use as the result of problems with the left navigation area.

Part II: Designing Usable Sites

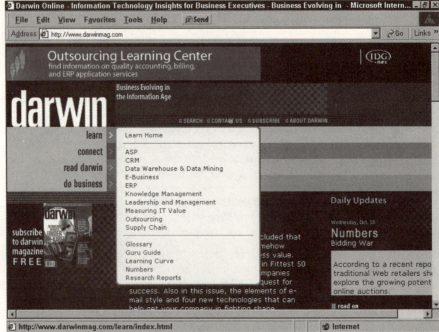

Figure 5-8: Darwin Magazine has a fancy two-level navigation system.

- **Hard to implement.** There's a reason *dot-coms* — that is, companies founded to sell products and services over the Internet — tend to have left navigation schemes, while other companies don't. Dot-coms have — or in many cases, "had" — lots of talented designers and programmers on staff, and little content in their Web sites that might have forced them to make difficult decisions about things like the length of words used in the navigation area. Companies with less Web talent and more pressing business concerns have to think twice about the tradeoffs involved in using a left navigation bar.

Left navigation bars are challenging. Even with just one level of navigation, they're more complex than top navigation links or top nav bars. If you have the talent available to implement and maintain them, they offer a very clean appearance and, with some testing and reworking, the potential for a good user experience.

As with top navigation bars, you can preserve a fairly simple left-nav-bar navigation structure by the artful use of in-page navigation within each "bucket", as described in the next chapter. This kind of blended navigation that preserves easy-to-understand top-level "buckets" is a good approach for medium-sized sites, even if you have up to a hundred Web pages or so in your site.

When to use single-level left navigation

Single-level left navigation is a good choice in many cases, including when:

- **You have more than five to six categories.** If you have just five or six categories in your site, top navigation links or a top navigation bar might be the best choice, especially because it's easier to implement. But if you have more categories, a left navigation bar simplifies things for the user.

- **You have design and implementation talent handy.** Implementing a left navigation bar is tricky, and supporting the complicated pages that result — with content "poured into" the area that isn't taken up by the navigation bar — is trickier still. You need to have sophisticated designers and experienced engineers working with you to create and support these pages.

- **A clean, crisp look is essential.** A small company can make itself seem larger by using an advanced Web page design, and a single-level left navigation qualifies, without being too showy.

Expanding a site with single-level left navigation

Expanding a site with single-level left navigation can quickly go from very easy to very difficult. If you're just adding a couple more categories to the existing left nav, it's a piece of cake — just add the new categories to the list. Unlike horizontal navigation, you don't have a fixed size limit forcing you to reduce the number of categories you use.

Adding additional levels of navigation, however, can be very difficult with single-level left navigation. You either have to add a second level of categories to the left navigation — severely reducing the amount of page width available for content — or integrate another kind of navigation into the site along with left navigation. This basically means opening up all navigation-related questions, and you may find yourself doing any number of things to accommodate your expanding needs. See the next chapter for more details on your choices.

Part II: Designing Usable Sites

Frames and navigation areas

Frames are sometimes used to keep navigation areas onscreen even as the user moves through content. The figure shows the Frazier Healthcare site, a good example of such use of frames. Notice that the top area, with navigation, is not scrollable, but the lower part of the Web page, where the content resides, has a scrollbar. This allows the user to scroll through the content without losing sight of, or access to, the navigation.

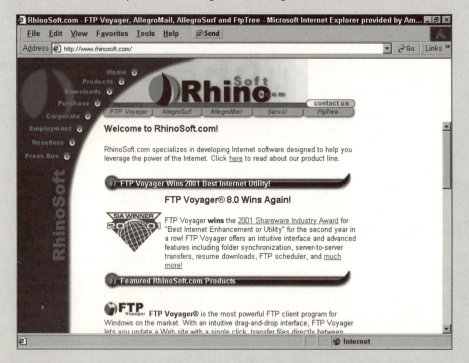

First off, from a usability point of view, using frames to create several independently scrollable areas on a site is a truly bad idea. Yes, there are some clever implementations of this idea on a few sites, but you'll see that major sites almost never do this. Why? It's too confusing for users. If you use independently scrolling frames on your site, it will look amateurish, no matter how hard you work to improve the look and accompanying functionality.

However, using frames to "lock down" a top nav bar or left nav bar, keeping it visible in the browser window, can work out fairly well. It seems to work better with left navigation, which users are used to seeing as stable "background" to a page, than with top navigation, which users expect to see scroll away the minute they touch the scroll bar or the Page Down button. But some sites are using frames to keep the top area — including not only navigation but one or two ads — in the user's view at all times.

Chapter 5: Creating Site Navigation 127

We suggest you design and implement your site without frames of any sort for simplicity of both development and user experience. But if using frames to keep the navigation area in site at all times solves usability problems that your site would otherwise have, by all means consider them. Be ready to take on a substantial design, implementation, and maintenance burden, however, as coding mistakes are easy to make on framed pages. Also, expect to get more user questions and user feedback the more you make the site different from what people are used to.

128 Part II: Designing Usable Sites

Chapter 6

Taking Navigation to the Next Level

In This Chapter

▶ Using navigation to meet your site goals

▶ Adding navigation levels

▶ Taking a look at navigation tasks

Creating basic site navigation, as described in the previous chapter, is difficult. However, there are clear models for it, and when you're done it's pretty easy to tell whether things are working.

For any sites except the simplest, though, there are additional navigational issues that don't necessarily have clear-cut solutions. Setting up the overall structure of your site creates an overall navigational framework. But deciding how to best meet the goals of your site within that framework is a real challenge.

Basic site navigation is about helping the user get where they want to go. More advanced navigation is, for the most part, about you getting the users to where you want them to go. Hopefully, the user wants to go there too, but in creating additional navigation for your site you're mainly seeking to meet your own business goals.

Meeting Site Goals with Navigation

You should choose from among the major types of navigation, described in the previous chapter, based on the number of categories you have in your site and how much complexity you can handle in creating and managing your site. To make further navigation decisions, you need to be clear about your goals for your site.

It's much easier to create the most effective overall navigation for your site if you know, and stay focused on, your site goals. Your goals for your site can be divided into three groups: user-centered goals, which alleviate frustration on the part of the user; site-centered goals, which help make your site more effective in meeting your business goals; and business-centered goals, which contribute directly to your bottom line.

There's considerable overlap between these categories; for instance, if a user can't find a weed-whacker locally, and is able to buy one online, they've alleviated their own frustration as well as helping a power tools company meet its business goals. But it's both possible and useful to keep our categories separate. Let's take a look at the different kinds of goals that are possible for a site and see how navigation can support them.

User-centered goals

The role of navigation in meeting user-centered goals is actually fairly simple: help users find what they're looking for. This is mostly the task of basic site navigation. Because this kind of navigation is user-driven and is so common in Web sites, the basic navigation schemes described in Chapter 5 are well defined and well understood. You can meet user goals with a Web site that fits into one of these well-understood patterns.

User-centered goals for a site center mostly around alleviating user frustration — and what users feel mostly frustrated about is not having enough information. For the vast majority of businesses, the Web is the cheapest and easiest way ever to disseminate information. For the vast majority of Web users, it's a great way to find information.

Typical user-centered goals on a Web site include:

- ✔ **Finding out about the company or organization.** Users like to be able to find out enough about your company or organization to know whether they might need you at some point in the future. People will often surf a site just enough so they feel they know what it's for, and what the organization behind it does. Then they know if they need to give the site and the organization any additional thought in the future.

- ✔ **Finding contact information.** The user needs to call you, send you something, come to your office, or go to a store where your product is sold. The user is visiting your Web site so they can contact you more directly in other ways. The main navigational issue here is to make it as easy as possible for users to find the various kinds of contact information they may need.

Chapter 6: Taking Navigation to the Next Level **131**

✔ **Finding product and service information.** Users like to know what they can get from you. They use this information for immediate buying decisions and to contribute to their overall idea of how to think of your organization in the future. (The look, feel, and navigability of your site as they surf it are affecting their impression of your company as well.)

✔ **Site and business goals.** While your site and business goals are set by you to meet your own needs, they can be user goals as well. For instance, if a user comes to your site knowing he or she really needs to buy a double helical screwdriver, and that's what you sell, your goals and the user's coincide. So don't force users to help you meet your site and business goals; give them the opportunity to do so.

To a significant degree, the benefits to you and your organization of meeting user-centered goals are subtle and hard to track. The concrete benefits tend to center around cost reduction. For instance, it's much cheaper for you to show a Web page 100,000 times than it is to send out 100,000 brochures. And it's cheaper for you to have 100,000 people get a pricing or product support answer on your Web site than it is to take 100,000 phone calls.

However, in real life, the tradeoffs aren't so direct. Not everyone who needs to get info from you will go to your Web site; not everyone who goes to your Web site really needs the info. The costs of people not having information are hard to measure. So when you provide this information online, the benefits can also be hard to measure.

Some companies have such immense costs from meeting user information needs that they can justify significant Web-related expenditures if that moves the cost needle down by a reasonable percentage. For many companies, though, savings are hard to track, and the main motivation for creating a Web site that meets user-centered goals is different: competitive pressure. If a competitor's Web site provides needed information, and yours doesn't, the threat to your business is clear. Also, it's embarrassing to be behind in a "simple" competitive challenge like providing a decent Web site.

Site metrics

Site metrics, and goals based on them, are a strange animal. Site metrics are measurements that only apply to the Web, such as the number of pageviews a Web page gets, the number of unique users a site attracts, how much time users spend on your site, and how many clickthroughs a page, headline, or banner ad receives. Site metrics live in that strange world between what users want from your site and the achievement of the business goals that you need your site to meet.

Part II: Designing Usable Sites

TIP

You don't really want pageviews on your site for their own sake. It costs money to create and serve Web pages. Pageviews that don't ultimately meet some business or organizational goal are a waste of time and money. Don't settle for pageviews as a metric of site success; always make sure the people on your site team can justify their professional existence in terms that make sense to everyone in the company, not in terms of Web jargon. (And see Chapter 12 for more about pageviews.)

Figure 6-1 shows a sample Web site report from WebTrends Log Analyzer (`www.webtrends.com`), a leading product for Web site reporting from NetIQ Corporation. Check out the sample reports on the Webtrends site and see if some of the highlights look familiar from discussions you've had within your Web group.

In creating your site's navigation, meeting site goals is the most fun and interesting part. Meeting site goals, such as pageviews or newsletter registrations, tends to run through the overall navigational scheme of your site. You have to balance the need for a consistent organization with the need to support the pursuit of various tasks that are reflected in whether your site goals are met.

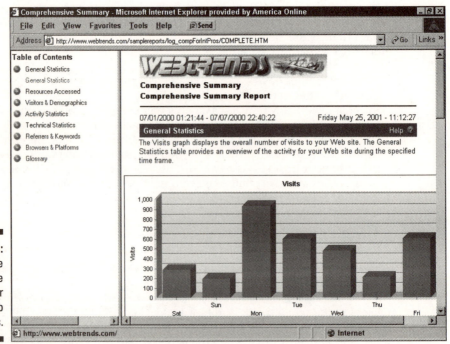

Figure 6-1:
Web site reports are daily fare for Web managers.

Chapter 6: Taking Navigation to the Next Level **133**

Typical site goals include:

- **Pageviews.** A good measure of site activity. This is an impossible number to know exactly, because your pages get cached in many places between your servers and the user's screen; everyone makes do with estimates but throws the numbers around as if they were exact.

- **Unique users.** The number of different people that visit a Web site in a day, week, or month. Even harder to get exactly than pageviews because many people come to your site from multiple machines, whereas in other cases a single machine is the conduit for visits from several people.

- **Clickthroughs for an overall page, for a headline, for an ad, and so on.** How do users leave a page they were looking at? Clickthroughs tell you. Most people in the Internet business have seen a printout or PowerPoint slide of a Web page marked up with the percentage or number of a page's clicks each link on a key Web page has received.

- **Registered users.** Now things are starting to get interesting. If you offer users the ability to customize your site in return for registration, the number of registered users tells you how many people think it's worth customizing your site. If you offer a newsletter, the number of registered users is the number of people you truly have an online relationship with, via e-mail.

- **Newsletter subscribers.** Not everyone who registers for your site will choose to receive your newsletter — if you're polite and give him or her a choice — or you may have more than one newsletter. So the number of newsletter subscribers may be different than the number of registered users.

- **Processes started versus processes completed.** Comparing the number of processes begun — such as registration, purchasing, even reading through a multi-page article — to the number completed is a great usability metric. Find the holes, and solve any user issues they represent, but don't take away users' freedom to opt out if they feel the need to do so.

- **Business goals.** Any site meets some business goals; for example, marketing goals related to letting customers, press, and analysts learn about your company and products. These site features have some impact on reducing your marketing costs as well. If you sell on your site, or solicit donations or offer other financial transactions, you can adopt revenue goals as part of your site goals. Number of transactions, number of customers, total revenue, and revenue per transaction are among the business goals that can be site goals as well.

Site goals such as pageviews and unique users aren't as useless as we imply above, if you assess them correctly. What does "correctly" mean? It means to treat these measurements on a comparative basis — compare days, weeks, and months to each other. The absolute numbers of pageviews and so on aren't very trustworthy, but if you use consistent standards over time, trends in the numbers will be valuable to you.

Just as it's hard to know what the numbers captured in site measurements actually mean, it's equally hard to know what the numbers "should" be. Your competitors and the owners of other sites you would like to compare to aren't going to tell you their numbers, and you wouldn't know just what the numbers meant if they did. Reports from Media Metrix and others will give you a rough idea of what kind of traffic the biggest sites on the Web receive, but don't forget that the numbers Media Metrix reports are different from those sites' server logs, which are different from actual user behavior.

The achievement of your own site goals is relatively easy to measure — the numbers come right from your Web server — but the accuracy and business impact of the numbers is harder to assess. Make sure that you and others in your organization know all you can about how the achievement of site goals is truly affecting your customers and your business.

Business goals

In many organizations, certain departments are where business goals go to die. Human resources, MIS, and other internally-oriented operations can seem like separate planets walled off from the relentless "revenues up — costs down" logic that drives the majority of the organization. Web sites are increasingly marketing and/or sales operations, so they shouldn't be exempt from normal business logic, but they're still often seen to be orbiting just as far out there as the support departments.

Increasingly, however, Web sites will be called on to satisfy typical business metrics to justify their existence. This isn't necessarily difficult to do, just different from standard practice in recent years. (Which saw such oddities as the money-losing online division of a publisher being seen as more valuable than the print group, which is where the profits that paid the online group's bills were made.) In some companies that use business goals to manage their Web sites' plans and budgets, the Web is becoming an ever more integral part of the business, rather than an isolated, special area.

Navigation has a crucial and fascinating role to play in helping a site meet business goals. If people are coming to your site with the intention of buying something, and failing, that's a navigational issue — and a serious business problem. Making people aware of what your site can do, and helping them do it, involves site design, navigation, and business thinking.

Every business — and we include here non-profit organizations, which also have concerns about increasing revenues and reducing costs — is different, so listing business goals is a tricky exercise. However, here are some common ones; if your organization isn't using these goals to help manage its online efforts, it should be:

- **Product support answers viewed.** Wondering how to measure the success of cost-reduction efforts? Here's a good place to start. Your company knows how much it spends on product support. It's well-established that answering support questions online is much cheaper than by phone or mail. (And cheaper still than the cost of losing a customer if you can't help him solve his problem.) So track the number of answers viewed.

- **Product description pages viewed.** Isn't it more effective for people to come to your site and see a product description when they're looking for it than to see a magazine ad they may not even be interested in at that time? Compare the impact of product and service descriptions on your Web site to the impact of paid advertising.

- **Revenue.** This is the one that makes others in your organization sit up and take notice. Revenue is hard to find, and the kind of low-cost, high-profit-margin revenue that can often be derived from the Web is a wonderful addition to your company's income statement. To the extent that work on navigation and other aspects of Web usability increases revenue, expect to get support for your efforts.

- **Cost per sale, revenue per sale, profit per sale.** You can bet that your sales department has these numbers for "real world" sales; it's a good idea to know what they are for Web-based sales, too.

We could go on, but we think the point is made: You can move toward using the same business or organizational metrics to measure your Web site activity that you use for other business activities. The part of your Web presence driven by easing customer frustration or meeting competitive pressures can be justified separately if you wish, but you may be pressured to account for all your Web costs in an overall profit and loss statement for the Web site.

Despite being a shock at first, measuring the success of your online presence — and your usability efforts — by traditional business metrics becomes a huge plus over time. The size of the Web effort is likely to become larger, not smaller, once you describe Web-related efforts in terms that everyone else in the organization can understand.

Figure 6-2 summarizes the major aspects of site goals in a pyramid, with the most commonly addressed (and easiest to meet) goals, those relating to user goals, at the bottom; site goals in the middle; and business goals at the top. The sooner you can do a solid job of meeting user goals with your Web site and move up the pyramid to meeting site and business goals, the better off you'll be.

Part II: Designing Usable Sites

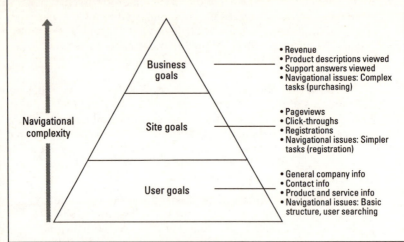

Figure 6-2: Higher goals mean harder navigation.

Adding Levels of Navigation

In Chapter 5 we introduce the major types of navigation for small to medium-sized sites: top navigation links, top nav bars, and left nav bars. Larger sites use these same kinds of navigation, but combine them and add additional levels of navigation to them. The result is sometimes effective, sometimes confusing — and always requires a great deal of work, with large internal staffs commonly working in tandem with expensive external consultants.

Laying out cookie-cutter steps for how to pursue these massive navigation projects is next to impossible, because each one varies depending on the site's needs and how thoroughly the site is being overhauled at any one time. Large sites are usually built like medieval castles, with different parts being created, renovated, improved, or destroyed in an ongoing swirl of activity whose result makes up in complexity what it lacks in consistency.

Instead, we'll discuss the key point of three sites that exemplify some of the navigational principles that apply to large sites. Use these principles as you create and expand your own site into something royalty would be proud of.

A site of sites

The City of Bellingham site (www.cob.org), shown in Figure 6-3, combines top navigation links (in a graphical-looking format) for common user-oriented functions, left navigation for major areas of interest, and links across the bottom of the page — repeating the left navigation links — for a quick transition from the bottom of any page to any major area of the site.

Chapter 6: Taking Navigation to the Next Level 137

Global items

The City of Bellingham site is an example of a common navigational practice in large sites that has filtered down to some smaller sites as well: Providing a kind of toolbar as a separate set of navigational options within a Web site.

In the City of Bellingham site, this toolbar-type navigation includes a set of top text links with six options: COB Home, Departments, Employment, FAQ, Contact Us, and Search. These options are always available no matter where on the City of Bellingham site the user goes, including within a department's sub-site.

The idea behind this set of links, which are persistent throughout the site, is to provide a set of commonly used functions at all times. Notice how the links for this site meet both user and organizational needs: Home, Departments, and Search are navigational options that the user may want to use to do more in the site. Employment and Contact Us help the Web site do a better job of connecting potential employees or users in general to the site. And the FAQ area serves as a kind of Help function to answer user questions.

Many other sites add this additional level to their navigation. It's more or less independent of other choices you make about how to implement navigation. Create the navigation you need for your site; then consider whether adding this kind of list of shortcuts serves your and your users' purposes.

Bellingham has chosen a relatively low-tech approach. The site is almost all HTML tags and text rather than graphical elements. Yet the site is deeper and more complex than many sites that load slower and look worse.

Here's an overview of the major navigational elements of the site:

- **Top navigation links.** The top navigation links are embedded in HTML table cells with background colors that make them look like a graphical nav bar — but instead they're really text links, making them fast-loading and flexible (try resizing the page and watch the size of the links adjust). Bellingham has put common user functions that might be needed at any point in the user's experience across the top — the home page, a list of city departments, jobs, FAQ, contact, and search. See the sidebar, "Global items," for more on this.

- **Departments area.** The Departments link in the top navigation is the big secret of this site. Click it and you get a list of departments, such as the library, fire department, and so on, within city government — and each department's name is a clickable link to a separate Web site. (This is what makes the City of Bellingham site a "site of sites.") Most of the separate sites have the same header area as the main site, but the left navigation area and the corresponding links on the bottom are distinctive. See Figure 6-4 for an example.

Part II: Designing Usable Sites

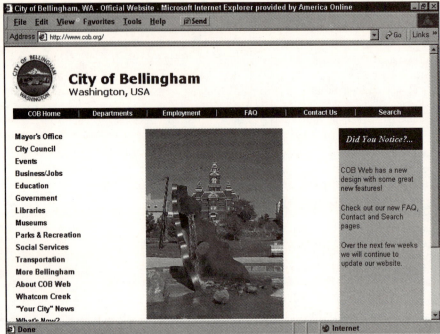

Figure 6-3: The City of Bellingham has put together a good site.

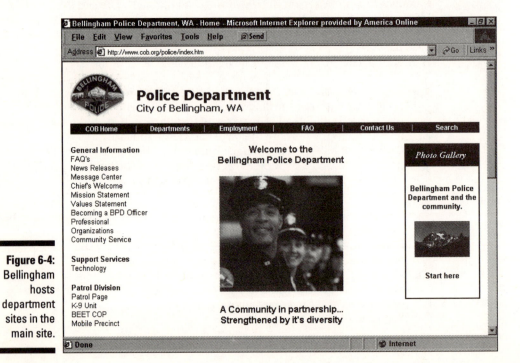

Figure 6-4: Bellingham hosts department sites in the main site.

Chapter 6: Taking Navigation to the Next Level

- **Left navigation "bar."** In both the main site and the department sub-sites, the left navigation links are not fully a "navigation bar" because they're not graphical — like the top navigation area, they're true HTML links. These links are the main navigational element allowing users to access the various major elements of city government.

- **Bottom navigation links.** The bottom navigation links simply repeat the left navigation links — this is useful, but in most sites bottom links repeat the top navigation bar, so having the bottom links repeat the left navigation might be confusing. It is efficient, however, as a way for users to quickly jump forward after scrolling to the bottom of a long page.

The City of Bellingham has done an admirable job of creating a simple template for use by dozens of departments. The pages are almost all text and links, making them very accessible to users with slow computers or slow connections — an important consideration for a government site, which really should be accessible to everyone. This kind of approach would make a great framework to use in testing the overall structure of a large site, but probably is too sparse in appearance and too lacking in feedback to be entirely suitable for company sites and other sites where a more "designed" look is important.

Be sure to title your pages. The City of Bellingham site doesn't give a title at the top of each page to indicate what that page is about and remind the user what they clicked to get there. Have a title of short to moderate length at the top of every page in your site. Ideally, the title should be at the top of the Web page — where a report or other document would have its title — and also in the top of the browser window.

Navigating the world of Williams-Sonoma

The Williams-Sonoma company is famous for its cooking-related products. Williams-Sonoma sells not only cooking products but a lifestyle, practical yet elegant. As with other sites that sell a way of living as well as actual goods, the Williams-Sonoma site therefore has to look very good and work very well in order to effectively support the company's efforts.

The Williams-Sonoma site (www.williams-sonoma.com) is not really very "webby" — it's more like a well-constructed catalog that happens to be both interactive and online. By using the familiar catalog model, the site can offer a graphically sophisticated appearance and interface without appearing to be "techy" or intimidating.

Part II: Designing Usable Sites

Despite its rich appearance, the elements of the Williams-Sonoma site are similar to those in the City of Bellingham, with the major additions of graphical pizzazz, registration, and shopping:

- **Top navigation bar.** The Williams-Sonoma site has a true, graphical top navigation bar, allowing for a very "designed" look in this major element that's consistent across the site. (On the home page, the top navigation bar's elements appear on the left side of the screen.) The navigation bar always has the major "buckets" that mirror the tasks users can complete on the site: Shopping (regular shopping and "quick shop"), getting gift ideas, and finding recipes.

- **Category sub-sites.** Like the City of Bellingham site, the Williams-Sonoma site gives each department its own subsite with dozens of products. The top graphic and top navigation are kept consistent, but the rest of the content and functionality change within each area.

- **Bottom links.** The bottom links serve two major purposes: They support common Web site features such as company information and privacy information, but they also tie into the company's other "points of presence" — its catalog and its real-world stories. The company information is therefore a bit buried compared to a typical corporate site, but it's easy enough for users who are looking for it to find the link they need.

The Williams-Sonoma site shows how attractive "dress" can be applied to a simple skeleton structure. While a lot of work goes into maintaining the images, descriptions, and prices of the many products sold on the site, the navigational categories stay the same. You'll probably need some graphically talented employees or consultants to get a look anything like this good on your site, but the results may be worth the effort.

Extron sells online

Extron Electronics is a global manufacturer of electronics components such as computer-video interfaces and cable. Its site, which you can find at www.extron.com, doesn't provide a lot of introductory information; you'd pretty much have to know that you needed these kinds of products before you could make much use of the Extron site. But for someone who's ready to buy, this site is a deep and extensive resource.

Product information on this site is as complete as on any site we've seen. Clearly, Extron saves a great deal of money on printing and distributing brochures by using the Web, and supports a good deal of its sales activity through its site. The site's primary audience is Extron's dealers, but its secondary audience is end customers; dealers can point their customers to the Extron site for detailed information.

Chapter 6: Taking Navigation to the Next Level   *141*

The Extron site includes product information as well as news, access for consultants and dealers, and features — not exactly as widely interesting as the Williams-Sonoma site, but an attempt to achieve broad appeal within Extron's very specialized target market.

Here's a look at the major elements of this complex site:

- **Top navigation bar.** The top navigation bar includes only four major areas: Products, Technologies, Company, and Download. Icons on the upper right side allow access to common functions (Home, Login, and Contact Us). By keeping the number of top-level categories so few, Extron forces its largest category, Products, to support very deep in-category navigation.

- **Product descriptions.** The Extron site gives you information about choosing a product, but you have to know something about electronics to make a useful choice, which reflects the fact that Extron sells only through dealers and not to end users. End customers use the site to research products which they then order from their dealer.

  The product areas feature a *step wizard* — a combination of graphics, Javascript, and HTML that helps the user move steadily through a multi-step process for selecting the right product. You can see an example of a Step wizard in the Godiva site shown in Chapter 5.

  When the user picks a product to learn about or buy, he or she can get a tremendous amount of information about it — a photo of the front and back of the product, a description, features, specs, a diagram and a drawing, for example. Much of the information is available in Web page format, a printable Web page, or a PDF file. Some is also available in languages other than English.

- **Shortcuts.** Another product-related feature, the shortcuts pull-down within the Products section, gives direct access to products by name — using specific product names such as AAP 102 and System 4LDxi. Confusing to the novice, but a real power tool for experienced customers.

- **Left navigation.** The left navigation includes a clickable interface with + and – symbols that allow the user to expand or contract an outline list of Extron products. This left navigation interface is basically the same as the Microsoft Windows file access interface, taking advantage of what the user already knows to support the user in drilling down deep into a hierarchy of products.

- **No bottom navigation.** Unlike the great majority of robust business sites, the Extron site doesn't provide additional navigation on the bottom of the page. Instead, it keeps pages short, so you're never that far from the known navigation on the top and left.

The Extron site provides just about everything needed by experienced buyers. The Step wizard "walks" less experienced customers through the product line. This Extron's intense focus on its core audience allows the site to be an effective tool for helping the company sell its products. Navigation in this site is very effective and straightforward, considering the amount of information presented here.

Navigation examples and site goals

The sites we've just examined as navigational examples also demonstrate a focus on different kinds of goals, as we describe earlier in this chapter:

- ✔ **City of Bellingham and user goals.** The City of Bellingham site is focused almost exclusively on user goals — helping users find contact and other information about city government. There's very little here that supports site goals, such as registering for the site or a newsletter, or business goals, such as making money or cutting costs. The site is just about providing needed information to users.

- ✔ **Williams-Sonoma and site goals.** The Williams-Sonoma site clearly lends itself to tracking by site goals. Users can sign in, generating registered users for the site, and shop, generating pageviews for specific products. While the user can buy on the site as well, the site's links to the Williams-Sonoma catalog and stores show that business doesn't begin and end at the site.

- ✔ **Extron Electronics and business goals.** The Extron Electronics site cuts out all the fluff and brings the site visitor right into the products pages. This site is clearly all about cutting costs (for brochure printing and distribution) and increasing sales through dealers. Most dealers could not provide such extensive product info on all the products they sell. Instead they can point customers to the Extron site.

As you set goals for your own site, keep in mind what it can take to do a good job of meeting site and business goals. Make sure you've covered your bases in terms of satisfying the user's goals on your site before moving up the chain to the more advanced site goal and business goal level.

Navigating Tasks

In using your site, your users are constantly accomplishing small tasks: reading an article, learning about a product or service, registering in order to get some benefit, or making a purchase. Accomplishing these tasks is easy on some sites and maddeningly difficult on others. To do a good job in creating usable navigation, you need to switch back and forth frequently from the "big picture" view of what's on your site, and where, to the "mole's eye" view of a user trying to get a task accomplished quickly.

Reading an article

There are a lot of frustrations possible even in a simple task like reading an article online. For example, The Seattle Times newspaper site is an excellent site, but its articles vary wildly in how many pages they're split into. It's very common on The Seattle Times site to read to the bottom of a long page and find there are still one, two, or more additional pages in the article. Unlike in the printed newspaper, it's difficult to "preview" the article to know what you're getting into before you start.

You can make reading an article easy through simple navigational techniques. Start by splitting the article into chunks that are each one screen in length — the user can read these chunks without scrolling. Then use a graphic with hyperlinks at the top and bottom of each page to let the user move back and forth smoothly through the article.

The philanthropy article on the Whatcom County site (www.philanthropycatalog.org) shown in Figure 6-5 is a good example of making an article easy to get through. (However, the article was "chunked" into screen views that are one page each only if you have a 1024 x 768 monitor, rather than the very common 800 x 600 resolution monitor setting.)

The user's current page location in the article is shown right up at the top — "1 of 3," in this case. Users can quickly determine how many clicks they need to make to read the article and guesstimate how long it will take them to do so.

You should also link to a printable version of each article on your Web page. The printable version can be a carefully formatted Web page — this can be tricky, because printers can surprise you — or an Adobe PDF (Portable Document Format) file, which allows for few surprises on printing. Use a single long Web page if the text is the important part, a PDF file if appearances and page breaks are crucial.

In creating navigation for your site, look hard at "small" tasks like reading an article. Provide context to help the users make quick decisions about how to spend their time. Help the user navigate forward and backward without having to think much about it.

Registering

To users, registering is actually one of the scarier tasks on many Web sites. Registration processes can be long, intrusive, confusing, and error-prone. Sites often fail to make clear the benefits of registering — for the user or for the site — and don't communicate in advance what kind of information will be asked of the user or what will be done with it.

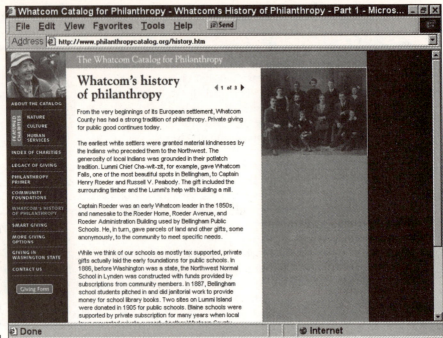

Figure 6-5: Whatcom County tells you where you're going.

The About.com site's newsletter registration area is a great example of a registration process that avoids these pitfalls. Newsletter sign-up from within the Birding area (at http://birding.about.com) is shown in Figure 6-6. The purpose of the registration process is clearly stated: Get newsletters. Only a few personal information fields are requested, and only one of those, the e-mail address, is required. Unlike other sites, About.com doesn't make intrusive requests for "nice to know," but unnecessary, fields like your ZIP code, income, and more.

Be sure to give users clear benefit statements about what they'll get from registering, and keep the process as simple as humanly possible. You can get your marketing information through online and offline surveys; don't burden your registration process with questions that don't directly help the user do business with you.

Shopping

Shopping, unlike registering, at least has a consistently clear value proposition: Buy! But because shopping involves money, it's a process about which users get nervous.

Chapter 6: Taking Navigation to the Next Level

Figure 6-6: About's Birding newsletter sign-up doesn't try anything cheep.

© By Chrstine Tarski (www.birding.about.com) licensed to About.com, Inc. Used by permission of About.com, Inc. which can be found on the Web at www.about.com. All rights reserved.

Shopping cart technology has benefited from of tremendous amounts of work, but it's still in its early stages of development. Users going into a shopping process have a large number of concerns about issues such as privacy, flexibility, shipping, gift wrapping, security and more. They'll bounce in and out of the shopping process as they pursue information about the process itself and about their options. Not quite as simple as the "ka-ching!" sound made by an old-fashioned cash register!

The online site of the huge bookstore chain Barnes & Noble, after making many mistakes in its online efforts against amazon.com, now matches its better-known cyber-rival in many areas of the user experience. (We wonder if Barnes & Noble will ever be able to match the rich array of reviewer and customer comments about books and other products found on amazon.com.) For an example of the highly usable book-buying process on barnesandnoble.com, check out the Out of Print area within the Barnes & Noble Web site, shown in Figure 6-7.

Search options for this process are highly flexible. If you find a book you like, you then go into the standard Barnes & Noble buying process. The steps you follow to buy are presented in an overall context that's easy to understand. It's easy to link off from within the process at any time to view the policies that Barnes & Noble follows for online shopping. There's an overall navigational "flow" in the desired direction, forward; but it's easy to swim out of the main current when needed.

Part II: Designing Usable Sites

Figure 6-7: Look for a rare book-buying experience.

Building a shopping experience like that on amazon.com or barnesandnoble.com doesn't guarantee you the same kind of revenues as these sites. These sites have spent millions of dollars building trust with huge numbers of consumers. Many people won't buy from you until they feel they have a long-term relationship. It may take users months and years of visiting your site to escalate from looking only online, to occasional small purchases, to the kind of frequent, larger purchases you're hoping for. Keep your expectations low when you make your initial venture into online sales.

Before implementing online shopping, carefully study competitive and comparable sites that support it. List all the elements of the buying process and make sure your process meets all the same needs as the other sites — or carefully justify why it doesn't. With this approach, you're likely to remember all the important parts of the online shopping process.

Part III
Creating Usable Web Pages

In this part . . .

Savvy Web site creators use page templates to help them solve usability problems once — in the template — and then propagate the right answers through dozens or even hundreds of pages in their site. In this part we identify the major problems users face in making the most of your Web pages and show you how to solve them on all of the pages of your site.

Chapter 7

Designing Usable Web Pages

In This Chapter

▶ Getting your page design right

▶ Helping your users to interact

▶ Finding the ideal page layout

▶ Being short and to the point

*W*eb page design has been a fast-evolving craft. Until recently, important elements of the Web experience — such as the technical underpinnings of the Internet, Web programming languages such as HTML and JavaScript, and users' needs and expectations — were all changing so fast that designers had to struggle just to keep up, as well as to take advantage of the latest and greatest new opportunities.

Now the Web world is settling down. Large Web projects take years — and designers can be relatively confident that the standards they write to will be relatively unchanged during that timeframe. It's now possible to take a fresh look at Web page design based on usability concerns — on the work that's been done so far in usability, on the way users interact with today's Web pages, and on what's likely to be important to users three to five years down the road.

We think it's possible to design Web pages in a somewhat different way than is most commonly done today, a new approach that will enhance the consistency and usability of Web pages within a site and, eventually, across the Web. The next section explains how to build Web pages for usability from the ground up.

Web Design and Usability

Web design means different things to different people. Most people involved with the Web think that Web design is the art of creating attractive Web pages. We think this is fundamentally wrong, on a couple of fronts:

- **Web design is not just an art.** For the most part, Web pages are containers of information. So creating them is not simply an art — it's also a craft, something done for a purpose.

- **Web design is not about Web pages.** Web pages are not ends in themselves. If you could accomplish a goal on the Web without creating an additional Web page, you would do so. If, to accomplish your goals, you needed to create a thousand Web pages, you would do that instead. The point is that Web design is about accomplishing your goals; the number of Web pages you need to create — or, in some cases, delete — to get to your goal is secondary.

By contrast, we would like to define Web design as follows:

> ▶ *Web design is the art and craft of creating useful Web sites.* ◀

Let's take a look at each piece of this definition:

- **Web design is an art and a craft.** We explained above that Web pages are containers of information. Because our purpose in Web design is only partly to create something attractive, Web design is both an art and a craft.

- **Web design is about Web sites.** Web design includes not just the look of a page — that's graphic design — but the overall design and structure of the site, the way information is arranged in the site, and the way users complete tasks within the site. These are information architecture, site design, and task design issues, not just page design issues. So true Web design is about creating Web sites.

- **Web design is about creating things that are useful.** Saying that sites are of necessity "useful" may seem kind of limiting. After all, many sites are created for entertainment purposes, for sheer fun, to shock, or to share. However, the Web is at its core an educational medium (which is part of the reason a "hard sell" approach seems so out of place on the Web). Even when being entertained, or when buying and selling, Web users are most often seeking to learn as well. And the kinds of sites that demand serious usability attention are most often sites that are trying to help the user accomplish something. So we'll keep "useful" as a core part of our definition of what Web design is.

Chapter 7: Designing Usable Web Pages

So now that we've defined Web design — at least within the context of a book about Web usability — how does that affect the issues relating to page design that usually engage most of the attention of Web designers? We have a different take on many of these issues than most of the Web design books you'll see out there. To us, it all comes back to usability. As attractive as the result may be, if design choices don't result in a usable Web site, they aren't good design choices.

What does that mean, specifically? We discuss what usable Web navigation is in previous chapters. Now we'll show how usability impacts some of the other issues affecting Web designers.

Color and usability

Usability concerns have already significantly affected the debate about a key Web design issue: color.

Artistically oriented Web designers would like to have millions of colors to work with, just as magazine designers do. However, the need to create Web sites that work for all users have led most Web designers to accept the need for a much more limited palette: specifically, 216 colors, the *Web-safe color palette*. Why 216 colors? Many users run at 256 colors, and some of those 256 colors are different on Macs and PCs. Only 216 colors are present on both the PC and Mac 256-color palettes. You can read a discussion of the Web-safe color palette and how to use it effectively in many books on Web design, notably including *Web Design For Dummies* (published by Hungry Minds, Inc.)

The 216-color restriction means that color images don't fulfill quite the same role on the Web that they do in print. In the print world, if you work really, really hard, you can create and — with skill and luck — successfully print an image that looks a whole heck of a lot like something in the real world. (Sometimes even better than anything real.) You can't do this on the Web. From a purist's point of view, Web images are horrible. Here's why:

 ✓ **216 colors are not enough.** You can't accurately reproduce most real images in 216 colors. Real-world images have subtle shadings that might require a hundred shades of color just to capture the highlighted area where light strikes an apple, or a forehead, or a car bumper. Using 216 colors means you're going to have obvious color banding within the body of an image, and jagged edges wherever colors change sharply. Shadowing, which is important for suggesting the shape objects have in the real, three-dimensional world, is impaired by the very small number of grays found in the 216-color palette.

152 **Part III: Creating Usable Web Pages** _____

- ✔ **Things in real life don't glow.** Every image displayed on your computer screen is lit from within. Unless you live on a different planet, it's unlikely that most of the objects and people you encounter in normal life are lit from within. Images on the Web don't look real. Printed images, on the other hand, are illuminated by reflected light, just like real-world objects. (Printed images are a bit on the shiny side though!)

- ✔ **Web images are tiny and ugly.** The larger and higher quality a Web image, the longer it takes to load. This is not true in real life or in magazines, where even the largest and highest-quality images appear as fast as you can flip a page. Web images, already unreal, are made more so by the size and quality tradeoffs needed to make them appear fairly quickly.

- ✔ **Web images still take time to load.** No matter how much you downsize (and thereby uglify) your images, they still show up on the user's screen more slowly than the text of the Web page they're in. So your users are irritated by the image — and the wait it makes them endure — even before it's rendered completely.

We could go on, but we think the point is made. Images on the Web have severe usability problems.

What are the implications of the poor quality of Web images for the overall usability of your site? We think there are several — and that they've been largely ignored up until now:

- ✔ **Many Web images are never seen.** Users are really good at watching a page load (text and text-based hyperlinks first), finding what they need in the text, and clicking away before images appear. (Think about how quick you've gotten at closing pop-up ad windows before the ad renders.) Many Web images simply never get displayed.

- ✔ **Web images remind more than show.** Web images of real objects aren't good enough to show things very well. They function more to remind users of things they've seen in real life, in (better) pictures, or even on television. You can't show much detail in a Web image — the image reminds people of other, better images and real-life objects they've seen.

- ✔ **Web images can't sell well.** A Web image generally can't do a good job of selling something compared to a printed image or, even better, seeing the object for real. If the user already has a really good idea of what something looks like, or if the way something looks really doesn't matter in selling it, then maybe the Web image will be enough. But Web images are often more annoying than illuminating when you try to use them to close a sale.

- ✔ **Web images are spice, not substance.** Web images are best used to spice up text and to add graphic interest to the overall page layout. They can't deliver a great deal of actual useful information themselves. If a picture is worth a thousand words, a Web image is only worth a hundred words or so.

Chapter 7: Designing Usable Web Pages

✔ **Large images should be paired with small ones.** It is worth offering users large images to let them get more detail, but not as a first step, and not without warning. Use small images as "eye candy" to brighten up a page and to remind users what the real thing looks like. Then link them to larger images that users can access if they have a fast connection or are willing to wait for the image to download over a slow connection. (Images with a large file size are referred to as "high-weight" images; in some cases, the weight is worth the wait!)

✔ **You need to offer users alternatives to Web images.** Let's say you want to sell sweaters using the Web. You need to consider that the user may not be able to get a good enough idea of what the sweater looks like from a Web image to make a good purchase decision. Offer alternatives: a text description that refers to fabrics and the design of the sweater using terms the user is already familiar with; a downloadable PDF file or multimedia slide show with high-quality images; a real-world place they can go to see the sweater and complete the purchase; a liberal return policy so the user can buy online, then return the item easily if dissatisfied or just surprised. And target your Web sales efforts at existing customers who already know darn well (no pun intended) what your sweaters look like.

The Vaio Notebooks area of the Sony site, shown in Figure 7-1, uses small "reminder" graphics as navigational elements, and a large, relatively high-quality image to convey as much as possible of the look of the Vaio online.

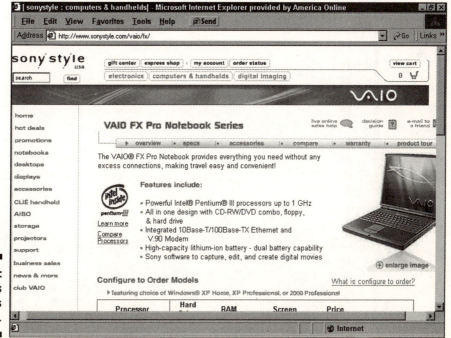

Figure 7-1: Sony makes notebooks for pros.

Part III: Creating Usable Web Pages

 From a usability point of view, you should be wary of depending too much on images. Try turning off the display of graphics in your Web browser, then do a usability walk-through of your site, as described in Chapter 1. If you can't accomplish all, or almost all, of the site's tasks without looking at graphics, then you should consider redesigning the site to reduce its dependence on images.

Readability and usability

A computer screen is not nearly as easy to read as a printed page. A typical printed page varies in resolution between about 600 dots per inch (on a good laser printer) and thousands of dots per inch (on a well-printed magazine page). A computer monitor tends to display about 70 dots per inch, at low resolution, or about 100 dots per inch at high resolution — far less than even a laser-printed page. Figure 7-2 shows a close-up view of several characters from a computer screen, with obvious "jaggies" — which are nearly invisible in similar printed characters.

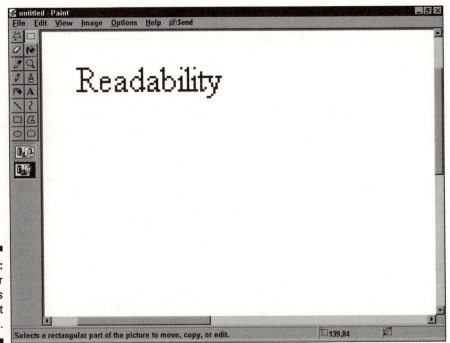

Figure 7-2: Computer monitors display text with jaggies.

What's a user to do?

From a usability point of view, the best thing for a user to do is to get a high-resolution monitor, say one capable of 1280 x 1024 resolution, then run it at a lower resolution, such as 800 x 600. This makes text and graphics sharper because the display system is throwing more picture elements (pixels) at each piece of the page image. Unfortunately, no one does this — they get high-resolution monitors and run them at the highest possible resolution, at least until their eyes give out and they have to go get trifocals. One of the authors (Smith) even hooks up a large monitor to his laptop and uses both screens separately, each at high resolution, in an extended desktop that displays the most information possible — but with the most eyestrain possible — at once.

The low resolution of computer screens causes a number of problems for the user, which are, briefly:

- **Low resolution equals small amounts of information.** A user looking at a typical Web page on an 800 x 600 screen sees only a hundred or so words at most — far fewer than on a printed page of the same size. In order to take in a meaningful amount of information, the user has to scroll or move through a bunch of different pages.

- **Higher resolution equals small icons and graphics.** A user looking at a higher-resolution monitor, say 1024 x 768 or (shudder) 1280 x 1024, is looking at tiny icons and text characters, often squinting to make them out. Some users even wear three-part, trifocal glasses with the top adjusted for long-distance viewing, the bottom for reading printed text, and the middle for deciphering what's on their computer monitor.

- **Reading online is tiring and, ultimately, frustrating.** Users get tired when they try to read large amounts of text online. The need to scroll or click to read the next page doesn't help; it's not nearly as natural a motion as turning a page. Users get irritated when they want to read more but find themselves having trouble continuing due to their eyes being tired.

- **Readers scan rather than read online.** Because reading online is difficult, readers don't do it more than they have to. Even more than in a magazine, they scan rather than read — focusing on headlines, underlined link text, bold words, even *mouseover text* (text that appears when you move the mouse over a graphic), anything except reading large blocks of text word for word.

As with problems with Web display of color, problems with Web display of text have significant usability implications. This is sad because the Web is the cheapest way yet to deliver huge amounts of text to users. In Chapter 9 we describe various things you can do to make text work better online. However, the best single thing you can do is to follow some silly-sounding advice: "Use fewer words." If you can restrict yourself to making your major points, and make those economically, your users will be far better off. Previews, excerpts, summaries, and bulleted lists all work better online than large blocks of text.

Multimedia and usability

In the early days of the PC revolution, computer users would sneer at television, confidently predicting that PCs would soon outclass television in every possible way — choice, picture quality, special features, and more. The arrival of the Web in the early '90s seemed to provide the last missing piece ready to make the triumph of PCs over TV possible.

Is the Web really that bad?

In this chapter we point out serious usability problems for Web use of text, graphics, and multimedia — pretty much all the content on the Web. Is the Web really that bad?

Yes and no. Yes, in that the quality of the Web as a media delivery mechanism is lower than existing alternatives. A newspaper, the cheapest form of print that most people encounter regularly, has much better resolution and readability than a typical computer monitor. And a cheap TV or ordinary car radio is a much better way to experience multimedia than even the best multimedia Web site. We really do believe that most substantial Web sites should be redesigned — we mean done over, from the ground up — to take into account, and do a better job of working around, the poor quality of Web text, graphics, and multimedia.

But no, the Web is not bad at all in that it gives users choices. The user is constantly in control on the Web. The Web lets users choose to visit sites that use text, graphics, and multimedia in every form and in every combination, an unprecedented array of choices.

The main problem on today's Web is that so many sites were designed as if text were highly readable, graphic images were nearly perfect, and multimedia worked smoothly and well. This causes problems for users who have to deal with the difficulties we describe in this chapter. Over time, the quality of text, graphics, and multimedia on the Web will steadily get better — and the user's position as general manager of his or her own experience will only improve.

You need to make careful choices in creating, testing, and modifying Web sites that work well on the Web as it exists today. By doing so you can create sites that are much more usable, and therefore allow their users to be much more productive and effective, than the competition. At the same time, don't think that the Web will always take a back seat to other media. It will compete with and, eventually, exceed other media in many ways that reflect quality as well as quantity.

Chapter 7: Designing Usable Web Pages 157

Unfortunately, most PC-delivered video makes a typical TV image look like a masterpiece. Tiny, low-resolution, jerky images that skip annoyingly — when they don't break down and stop completely, or even hang up the entire computer — are standard fare for Web video.

PC-delivered audio fares somewhat better. Streaming audio delivers music and, especially, speech at nearly acceptable quality. Unfortunately, many users don't have any kind of sound output, and others don't like to play back sound because the noise bothers other people and they lack headphones to keep the sound to themselves. However, for users with sound built into their PC and either headphones or privacy, PC audio is a viable option.

Video and audio create even greater problems for developers than text and graphics. Video and audio files are expensive to create, produce, and serve. It's hard to prove the return on investment you achieve for the extra effort (hint: it's no accident that TV is so popular and therefore so expensive to advertise on). And users have developed the expectation that multimedia will be constantly updated, probably because they have ongoing experience with TV and radio, which offer new stuff all the time. (Well, there are reruns on TV and oldies — oops, I mean "classic rock" and "old school" — stations on radio, but you get the point.)

What does this mean for usability and multimedia? You should use multimedia very sparingly, because it's either of low quality (video) or low accessibility to most users (audio), while being expensive to offer. You can build sites around multimedia, but expect them to have a narrow, if — hopefully — intense appeal. Use this book to help remove any and all usability barriers and make sure nothing gets in the way of the users who do find multimedia worthwhile.

For mainstream sites, offer multimedia experiences as an option, and make sure that no important information is delivered by multimedia only. Realize that every time you offer multimedia on your site you'll cause usability problems for many of your users due to their slow connections, lack of needed playback software, lack of audio hardware or headphones, and on and on. Some of them will contact you about their problems, often making their concerns clear in a rather heated fashion, so be ready.

Figure 7-3 shows a toy site that uses multimedia appropriately — as an added-value extra that's attractive and interesting, but far from the main point of the site.

For mainstream sites, postpone the use of multimedia until the site works well overall, then deploy it initially as an experiment under careful cost and usability controls.

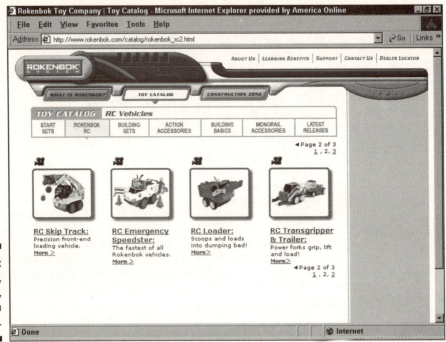

Figure 7-3: Multimedia, done right, is not a fright.

Helping Users Interact with Web Pages

We've shown that the Web is a bit rough around the edges as a tool for presenting large quantities of text, images that need to be rendered at high resolution, or high-quality multimedia. Yet users continue to be very enthusiastic about the Web. What are users doing online?

For the most part, users are trying to get things done. They generally aren't looking for recreation; other media are better for that. They're looking to accomplish tasks. At any given point in an online session they have a goal, or several goals, they're trying to achieve.

So when users reach a Web page on your site, they usually don't read the text all the way through, and they don't look at the pictures right away. They scan the page looking for something that will help them reach their goal. That may be information, the beginning of a task, or navigation (which leads to information and task sequences).

Users typically start looking at the top left-hand corner of the screen. They scan downward and to the right. They're looking for an indicator that the information, or the navigational link that leads to the information, is there.

Chapter 7: Designing Usable Web Pages **159**

Users act differently depending on whether they find what they're looking for. If they find the desired information they act on it by memorizing it, by cutting and pasting text on the computer, by writing a note on paper, or by taking some immediate action such as filling in a form on your Web site or picking up the phone and making a call.

Helping users find what they need

There are several things you can do in designing your Web pages to help users get tasks accomplished:

- **Make every page part of achieving at least one goal.** Every page should answer some user need that you want to fulfill on your site. Navigating is a user need, too, so it's okay to have pages that are used for navigation. But you should keep navigation pages (such as the home page, section pages, or a site map) few and far between compared to content or task pages that provide information or help your user get something done.

- **Put the important part of the content "above the fold."** The easiest way to put the *important* part of Web content "above the fold" — visible in the first screenful of information that the user sees, without scrolling — is to put *all* of the content "above the fold." This isn't yet a popular solution in Web design. If you can't bring yourself to design pages that don't need to be scrolled downward, then make sure that the area above the fold clearly communicates what's on the page. For example, put only one lengthy product description on a page, and use the header and so on to make the user understand that they don't have to scroll to see if there are more products farther down the same page.

- **Highlight what's on the page.** Especially in the "above the fold" area, use headings, Web page titles, items in bulleted lists, even link text (which is highlighted in a different color and underlined) to help users quickly identify what's on the page. That way they know right away if they've reached their destination or whether they need to keep looking.

- **Put top tasks "front and center."** Figure out the most important tasks your user is trying to accomplish on your site, or in a given part of your site, and make sure those tasks are easy to find, placed above the fold, and highlighted with headings or links.

- **Use recognizable terms.** A user who needs to know who to call about a product that doesn't work is going to be looking for any of several terms. "Support" is vague; "product support" is better; "replacements and repairs" may be better yet. Don't use vague, category-type terms; use specific words and phrases that relate to your products, your services, and your customers or users. Test these terms on actual users to see if they're truly recognizable.

Figure 7-4 shows a page from the old version of the Zanzara Web site that accomplishes these goals, as follows:

- **Make every page achieve at least one goal.** This page lists Zanzara's services — what the company sells. It's prominently mentioned in the navigation and always easy to find.

- **Put important content above the fold.** The Zanzara site fits a quote, a brief overview, and a bulleted, linked list of services above the fold (with the monitor at 800 x 600 resolution). Users can read or scan the visible part of the page and know, without scrolling, whether they need to keep reading or go to another page.

- **Highlight what's on the page.** It's a long page, but the core content is summed up in the bulleted list, visible above the fold. Note that the bulleted text is in bold as well, to further compel the user's attention.

- **Put top tasks front and center.** The Zanzara site has all its services listed in the first pageview - not quite at the top, but plainly visible.

- **Use recognizable terms.** The Zanzara site uses terms that are, for the most part, recognizable to the target audience — "application design" may be a bit on the vague side for some users. When a new or unclear term is used, it's either explained in the same sentence or a link is provided that gives more detail.

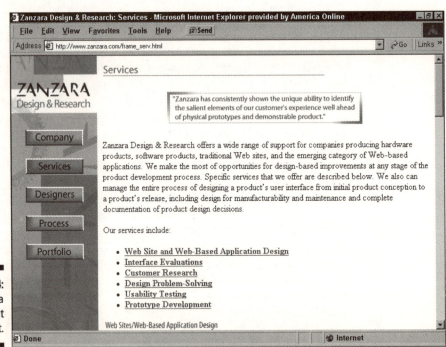

Figure 7-4: The Zanzara site does it right.

Chapter 7: Designing Usable Web Pages   161

You can see the old Zanzara site at www.zanzara.com/old.

Many other sites accomplish these goals as well — does yours?

As we mention in Chapter 3, users who successfully accomplish tasks on your site are more likely to keep using your site, both during their current Web session and in the future. This gives you many more chances to accomplish your site goals and business goals through your site.

When users don't find what they need

When users wait for the main content of a screen to fill in and don't see what they need, they really have only eight choices. None of them is really very good, so you should always try to meet user needs with your Web pages. Here's what your users can do when their needs aren't met:

- **Scroll downward.** Users don't scroll downward if they can help it. They will usually scroll to complete a form because that's helping them accomplish a task. They will often scroll to keep reading a story — they know what's coming, and they know that they want to see it. But they often won't scroll to see more items in a list or just to see what more may be on the page. Users figure you've put the important stuff at the top; if they don't see what they need above the fold, they're likely to bail out.

- **Click a link in the content.** This is a somewhat desperate act — to accomplish it, users have to half-read, half-scan your content looking for what they want. Most link text is vague, so when users click it, they know they run a significant chance of being disappointed. And because links in the content aren't part of your overall site navigation, and may even lead off your site, it's easy for users to get lost this way.

- **Drag the mouse around looking for the cursor to change to a hand.** Users move the mouse around, using their cursor like a metal detector to try to find a relevant link.

- **Click navigation, such as an item in a navigation bar.** This is another desperate act; the user has already looked at your navigation to find what she wants and followed it to the current page that's let her down. Going back into navigation means she's trying again where she failed before.

- **Click the Back button.** The Back button gives the user the chance to try again on a previously seen screen — but again, the user already took their best shot on that previous Web page and failed, so hitting Back is likely to lead to more frustration.

- **Click Search (if present).** Users search e the site for what they're looking for. This is an acknowledgement by users that they're unlikely to find what they're looking for by using the site's navigation.

162 Part III: Creating Usable Web Pages

✔ **Leave your site.** Users can type in a different URL or choose a bookmark or Favorite to go somewhere else on the Web. This leaves them frustrated as to their specific goal and with a bad feeling about your site in general.

✔ **Exit the Web.** Users who are really disgusted — or who have just run out of time to look at Web pages — will leave the Web entirely.

How can you help users avoid taking these actions? Up front, you can design your site, and each page on your site, to support the user in finding the tasks they may want to accomplish, or that you may want them to accomplish, and helping them get each task done as quickly and easily as possible.

You can also add features that help users find what they want if the usual methods fail. Site search capabilities and site maps are great for this. Such capabilities need to be highly functional, easy to use, and complete, or they may cause more problems than they solve. But if you meet the users' needs with search capabilities and a site map, they're much more likely to experience success.

You also help users by letting them be sure, if such is the case, that what they want isn't on your site. Let's say a user wants a product that your company doesn't carry. If users can easily see a list of all your products, look there and notice that there's no match to what they're looking for, they'll know fairly quickly that they can stop looking — which is an answer to their task in and of itself.

Speed thrills

Research on users shows that you have only a few tenths of a second to put up a new screen if you want the user to perceive system response as instantaneous. This is possible with desktop software, but not with the Web.

If you get a new screen image up within one second, the user notices the delay, but it doesn't bother them. A Web page that uses previously viewed graphics, now stored in the system's cache, and with the only new element in the page being new text might possibly appear in as little as a second. But this is the exception rather than the rule.

If a new screen image appears in less than ten seconds, the user is bothered by the delay, but stays focused on the current task. If all is going well, a ten-second window gives you up to 30K of content to play with, assuming the user is connecting with a 56K modem. Fair enough. Use every trick you can to keep pages under 30K.

If the screen image takes longer than ten seconds to appear, you've basically lost the user's attention. A few delays like this and the user is likely to lose interest completely and start doing something else entirely.

Chapter 7: Designing Usable Web Pages   *163*

Using the Ideal Page Layout

So now you know how to help users find what they need — and what they may do if they don't find what they need. What kind of page layout is going to help you support them?

Let's set up some ground rules for the ideal page layout:

- **Downloads in less than ten seconds.** As we explain in the sidebar "Speed thrills," if pages take longer than 10 seconds to download, users tend to give up on waiting and either click away or start doing something else while the page is downloading. For a typical home user on a 56 Kbps modem, a ten second limit gives you a 30 Kb budget for the page. Somewhat less is better.

- **Never requires scrolling left and right or resizing the window.** Users should never have to scroll horizontally — left to right. If they have their browser window set to a narrow width and come to your site and find unusually wide pages, they'll have to scroll or resize their window. Keep your pages narrow.

- **Rarely requires scrolling up and down.** Users frequently refuse to scroll. (Popular Web sites can sell ad space "above the fold" for big bucks; space "below the fold" is nearly worthless.) Continuous flows of text, and some kinds of lists, need to flow below the fold; navigational pages, task pages, and most content pages should stay above the fold.

- **Prints "as is."** Users love to print Web pages. (So much for the "paperless office.") You should make your page layouts narrow enough that they print without causing the printer to cut off the right edge. That's pretty darn narrow. Details appear later in this chapter.

Following these rules is a lot of trouble, but following them brings big benefits. Below, we take a closer look at each rule and how to follow it — and when you may really need to break it.

Popping up Web pages

Many Web page designers take concerns about page-loading time seriously enough that they keep their pages under 25K or so. When accessed over a 56K modem, their pages slowly appear on the screen, text and text-based links flowing in quickly, slowly followed by navigation (usually embedded in graphics), graphic images, and ads. Such a page is well-balanced, in an odd sense: It contains enough text, graphics, and code so that each element works together to produce an unpleasant, but not quite actually painful, user experience. Users on corporate networks or with home cable or ISDN connections see these pages somewhat faster, but network congestion and other factors slow them down somewhat as well.

But a really well-designed Web page that's displaying mostly text content should "pop" up onto the screen. When a graphic is being displayed, it should be large enough to really do what it needs to do: The rest of the screen can pop up, making it easy for users to surf on if they need to or they can wait for the entire graphic to appear if that's what's needed.

But how can you create a page layout that "pops" onto the screen? It takes work, testing, rework, and more testing. But there are a few keys to making really fast-appearing pages:

- **Keep pages small in "page weight."** Pages that are relatively narrow (and therefore highly printable) and short (and therefore don't require scrolling) are much easier to make "pop" up. There are simply fewer elements in the page that might contribute to making it oversized.

  If the only thing that makes your page require scrolling is text flowing down the page, you may still be able to maintain "pop"-ability. But if you have navigation, complicated tables, and graphics that extend below the fold, forget it.

- **Don't make the system "think" too much.** Complicated tables, complex Javascript programs, and too many separate elements in the page take up valuable time while the system either "thinks" — executes code — or does a bunch of little HTTP (HyperText Transfer Protocol) file accesses to grab all the different parts of the page. Some badly designed pages even begin to load, then grab an oversized graphic, shift all the page elements to accommodate it — making the page lurch alarmingly in front of the user, who had probably begun reading the text — then continue loading. What a terrible user experience! Keep your page layouts simple. (You can still get fancy on specific pages if needed, but don't bog down your whole Web site by using complicated layouts throughout.) Figure 7-5 shows the front page of Google, a Web search engine famed for its speed and simplicity. The Google front page pops up — except for the Google graphic, but you don't need that to do work — and doesn't require scrolling vertically or horizontally.

- **Keep navigation simple.** If you build lots of different levels, fancy graphics, and Javascript into your site's navigation, you've added a big burden to every page in your system. Each of the authors regularly sees Web pages that take over five seconds, over a 56K modem, just to load the identifying graphical area at the top of the page and the navigation elements, making the user watch a complex but pointless ballet of small graphics loading in seemingly random order. Don't impose this response-time "tax" throughout your Web site.

Chapter 7: Designing Usable Web Pages   *165*

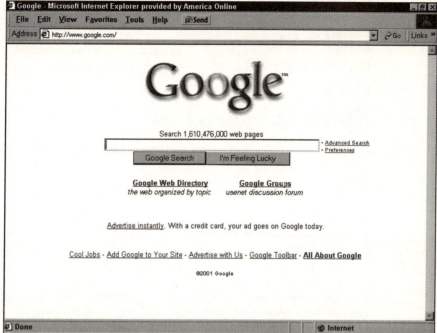

Figure 7-5: You can create pages that pop up onscreen fast.

- ✔ **Don't use banner ads in page layouts.** Don't build *banner ads* — the wide, narrow ads that appear at the top of so many Web pages — into your Web pages as a default element. Ads are always graphical, sometimes even animated, making them large; and they're often served by external servers that get overloaded and respond slowly. If you must serve ads, use buttons, text links and other lower-impact placements in preference to banner ads in most of your site and avoid dependence on ad servers wherever possible. (Your staff or consulting engineers may be able to create a much faster ad system that can cycle a few carefully chosen ads for you efficiently, and they may enjoy the challenge of doing so.)

- ✔ **Do some serious engineering.** Really good engineers can do really cool things like simplify Javascripts, make sure your content is all on fast servers that are on fast connections to the Internet, replace server-side code with lighter client-side programs, and combine dozens of elements in a Web page into pre-set pages that get transmitted to the user in two or three content grabs. If you make fast page loading a serious goal, you'll find lots of help from fellow team members and from outside consultants and companies that specialize in fast Web response.

✓ **Test, test, test.** Get your engineers and debugging people to understand that having a fast, responsive site is a must, and then test page response times under various conditions. Get the basic templates underlying all your pages small and fast. Have employees, debuggers, and "real" users test your site's performance one page at a time.

Keeping pages narrow

You really need to keep your Web pages narrow. If you do, three good things happen:

✓ Users never need to scroll sideways to view your pages.

✓ Users never need to resize their windows to be wider when they leave a site with narrower pages and come to your site.

✓ Users who print pages from your site get something they can really use, without the right edge of the Web page being cut off in printing.

If you — or the graphic designer(s) you're working with — are really good, you can make your pages resizeable horizontally as well as sufficiently narrow when needed. On such a page, the content self-adjusts to fit well in almost any width of page that the user chooses.

Such resizability is a worthy goal, but we'll settle for seeing you create pages with a fixed width that are sufficiently narrow. You can more easily get a look you really like this way — and prevent the user from resizing the page to the point that it's too wide to print well. Besides, those resizeable pages sometimes shift their overall layout alarmingly while all the pieces are loading. Fixed-width pages can be more easily designed so as not to do that.

So just how wide can you go in your Web page design and maintain "printability"? The answer is roughly 670 pixels. This is 84 percent of the width of an 800 x 600 pixel screen — the most common size in use today. Figure 7-6 shows a 670-pixel width on a 1024 x 768 screen.

Staying to a page width of 670 pixels solves a whole raft of problems for you:

✓ **Printability.** The original reason for keeping your pages 670 pixels wide is that it makes them easily printable. Any compromise you make in keeping to this width will make your pages print with the right margin cut off, an irritating — and possibly serious — problem for your users.

✓ **No need to scroll sideways.** Users won't have to scroll horizontally, unless they're running at 640 x 480 resolution, with a width of 670 pixels. It's really unacceptable to ask users to scroll horizontally, yet some sites demand it of their users running at 800 x 600 resolution. See the sidebar, "Page width for the rest of us," for how to help users running at 640 x 480.

Page width for the rest of us

You can accommodate your users running at 640 x 480 by making the right rail different, possibly optional or supplemental content, as is done on the Whatcom philanthropy site in Figure 7-6.

Eighty percent or more of users have an 800 x 600 screen or larger. Unfortunately, close to 20 percent of users don't. Many computer users, especially those with older portables, run at 640 x 480 resolution. And people who use WebTV, AOLTV, Pocket PCs and other platforms with small or low-resolution screens can't even see 640 pixels. (See the sidebar, "I want my WebTV"). How to accommodate them?

Here's a compromise to please everyone: Use a 670-pixel page width, but use the rightmost 130 pixels or so as a separate column, or "right rail," with related links, advertisements, or other content that's distinct from the main content area in the middle of the screen. That way, users with lower-resolution screens who have to scroll to see the right edge can deal with the main content area first, then scroll over to the right and inspect what's in the right column. (By using a 130-pixel right rail, you keep your main content visible even to WebTV and AOLTV users, who can only see 544 pixels of width at a time.)

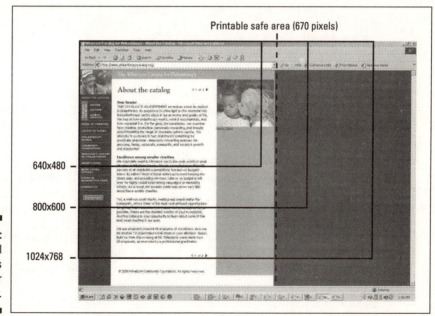

Figure 7-6: A 670-pixel width works for printability.

Part III: Creating Usable Web Pages

✔ **No resizing.** Users will often come to your site with their browser window set to a narrow width — because it's the default width of their browser window, because they've just been on another site that was set up to be narrow, or because they like it that way. Many users multitask heavily, with several browser windows and other windows open at once, and narrow browser windows are great for doing so. By keeping to a 670-pixel width, you avoid making them resize their browser window.

✔ **No special features.** Many sites that are originally designed for higher-end system requirements — a wide monitor and wide browser window setting, a fast connection, Flash graphics support and so on — end up having to create separate versions or special features to accommodate "the rest of us." You then have to go back and solve the design problem you were trying to avoid by setting your system requirements higher in the first place. Better to design your site to meet the widest possible range of user needs from the start.

Keeping pages short

Almost all of us involved in creating Web sites have been guilty of creating long Web pages — pages that require the user to scroll vertically. And most of us will continue to be guilty of doing so — there are just too many advantages to creating long Web pages to entirely give them up. However, there is a balanced approach that can give you and the user most of the best of short pages and long pages within your site.

We recommend that you keep pages short (about 400 pixels tall, to fit within an 800 x 600-pixel screen and the browser header and footer) wherever possible. Then use long pages, two to four times as high, for a few kinds of content.

The argument for short pages

It's fairly easy to make the argument for keeping pages less than 400 pixels tall:

✔ **That's how big the screen is!** Most users have 800 x 600 screens that only allow about 400 pixels of height, after the top and bottom parts of the browser window and the Windows toolbar are accounted for . No one would ever think of putting on a TV show that required users to scroll to see the whole image, so not respecting this limit wherever possible seems silly.

✔ **Users sometimes don't realize they have to scroll.** As more Web sites avoid making users scroll, users may not notice that *your* site requires scrolling to see the entire page. Entire online services such as America Online and CompuServe are avoiding scrolling throughout most of their services, and many sites on the open Web are avoiding scrolling mostly or entirely as well. So, as we've seen happen many times in usability testing, users often don't realize they need to scroll.

Chapter 7: Designing Usable Web Pages **169**

✔ **Users just don't scroll.** Even users who realize they need to scroll often just don't do it. As more sites eschew scrolling, users are even less inclined to bother with doing so — and think you're causing them grief by making scrolling part of your site.

Using occasional long pages

The argument for short screens is not quite as clear-cut as the argument for narrow ones. One caveat: many users have 1024 x 768 or even higher-resolution monitors. When a user has been looking at long Web pages in a tall browser window, a short screen — optimized to avoid scrolling by users with smaller screens — looks odd.

Another problem is that it can be a tremendous amount of trouble to put long blocks of text, or mixed text and graphics, into a whole bunch of little windows. And it can sometimes be more tedious to the user to navigate through several screens than to scroll through one longish screen.

Here's how we suggest you resolve this conundrum:

✔ **Pick a height limit.** Pick a basic page height limit — preferably 400 pixels, to accommodate users on 800 x 600-pixel screens.

✔ **Keep navigation small.** You have to keep navigation, especially left navigation, small — preferably within the 400-pixel limit for an 800 x 600 screen. That way, all users have the entire main navigation area in view when they come to a new page, and you allow Web pages that lack a lot of content beyond navigation to fit the limit overall.

✔ **Design navigation pages to fit within your limit.** The front page of your site and internal pages that are mainly navigational should always fit within the height limit you're designing to.

✔ **Keep task pages within your limit — or within one long page.** If you have a multi-step task for the user to accomplish, keep each page that's part of the task within your height limit. That way the user can navigate through with a Next or arrow button without having to scroll. But if you have a task that can fit in a slightly long page, consider keeping it to a single, long page to reduce navigation. Make sure to communicate to the user that they have to scroll to complete the task. Screens intended for printing should be designed with the height of the printed page in mind, rather than the height of the onscreen page.

✔ **Keep content pages to two to four times your height limit.** Content pages, especially those with long flows of text, naturally bring the reader's eye down the page. Let these pages go long, but keep them to two to four times your height limit — otherwise, your user will simply get lost within the vertical expanse of the page. Using height limits improves the manageability of your site while making the user scroll only when absolutely needed.

Avoid making the user scroll and also hit Next or arrow buttons within a given task. Combining long pages and Next or arrow buttons is really confusing for users — they can't always see the Next or arrow buttons, because they're scrolling up or down within a page, and they can't easily get back to the place where they entered a given piece of information.

I want my WebTV

WebTV allows users to connect to the Internet for e-mail and Websurfing using their television as a viewing device. (And a remote control and infrared keyboard for input.) AOLTV is a competing solution from AOL. These devices have only been moderately successful —about 1 million users compared to hundreds of millions of PC-using Websurfers — but the users they do have are vocal. And some hotel chains are now rolling out TV-based Net access, which may rapidly increase the number of people who see your Web site via TV at least some of the time. Why should you care? Because TV is a really bad device for displaying Web pages. Although there is little "browser junk" at the top and bottom of a WebTV display, there are still only 544 pixels of width and 376 pixels of height available for display. WebTV also does a number of weird things when displaying your site, like enlarging the fonts used to display text. Seeing your carefully designed Web site displayed on WebTV is likely to make you first laugh, then cry.

WebTV-type devices are still few enough that you can basically ignore them in your designs — there's really no sense in damaging the user experience for 99 percent of your users in order to make life better for 1 percent. If you find yourself fielding a lot of complaints from WebTV users about your site, though, you may find yourself needing to accommodate them. How best to do so?

We recommend that, if user needs require it, you create a separate, simplified version of your site that works well on WebTV. (It's a bit of a nightmare to maintain two versions of your site, but it's more of a nightmare to "dumb down" what your PC users see so your site works well on WebTV and its cousins.) See the WebTV site at `www.webtv.com` for details on how to do this.

Chapter 8
Designing Web Pages by Type

In This Chapter

▶ Working design into your plan
▶ Identifying types of Web pages
▶ Creating usable task pages
▶ Getting shopping pages right
▶ Creating a usable home page

The typical Web site design project starts from the bottom up. A varied group of people sits in a room and starts talking about what the home page of the site should look like. The conversation veers between various separate, yet intertwined, topics — negative experiences with existing Web sites; design principles people have encountered in books, magazines, or on the Web; ideas for features and content the site should have; and strong opinions in all directions about the way the site should, or shouldn't, look.

You need to make this kind of discussion happen somewhat differently in order to end up with a highly usable Web site. A varied group of people should indeed discuss your site plans — but they should be talking about what information and functionality the site should contain, not how it should look or details of navigation. It is, indeed, important to bring in people's experiences — but the people listened to most should be actual users, not insiders working in the company or organization who are responsible for the site. And it's important for someone to design the home page — but that "someone" should be a professional designer (or designers) who gives mockups and prototypes to the group for feedback. And the home page should be designed last, not first, because it has to represent the most important content and functionality available from the Web site. You generally don't know what that's going to be until late in the project.

In fact, the best Web designers almost never design a Web page — they design a Web site. The most important graphic design work an expert Web designer does is of a site's navigation system and of templates for major types of pages. The home page, because it has unique requirements, is one of the few Web pages on the site that gets individually designed. (Key task pages also may merit this kind of individual attention.) This chapter discusses the design requirements and choices for most of the major Web page types; content pages, which have many special requirements, are discussed in the next chapter.

How Design Fits

Web designers traditionally come from a graphic design background. Yet their job often extends beyond graphic design into information design, business modeling, and user psychology. As Web sites get more complex, several different kinds of tasks need to be blended to create a usable and effective site. Here are some rules we follow that make design work well with other functions and roles:

- ✔ Don't start designing your site until you know your user and the goals of the site.
- ✔ Design the site's navigational structure first.
- ✔ Design page templates before designing individual pages.
- ✔ Put design effort where it will have the most impact: Task pages first, then section front and home pages, and content pages last.
- ✔ Design the appearance of the home page last.

What we often see happening in site design is nearly the opposite of these recommendations — home pages get designed first, individual Web pages throughout the site are designed one at a time, navigation is an afterthought, and task pages receive less attention than other pages. If you can resist the pull of what has become traditional practice and start with goals, then get navigation right, design templates before pages, and focus on task pages first, your site is much more likely to be usable and effective.

How design (often) happens

Many designers and Web site consultants do, in a way, follow the principles we've outlined, but they do so at a subconscious level and aren't willing or even able to discuss their underlying assumptions and approaches with you. Typically, such designers simply have a certain approach they use to site navigation and to the design of different kinds of pages.

A given designer's habitual design approach is not particularly responsive to the specific needs your organization and users may have; it tends to be consistent across the projects a designer does whether that's appropriate for each job or not. If you are talking to a designer who's doing a project with you and the designer seems to be ignoring you, this is probably why — the very decisions you want to discuss have, in the designer's mind, already been made. Top-notch designers, on the other hand, ask you a lot of questions about your business and your users and customers before her or she gets down to actual design work.

So you need to have a clear understanding of what you're trying to accomplish with your Web site before working with a designer, and limit the designer's role to accomplishing specific tasks within the project, such as designing the look and feel of the site's navigation and templates for content, task, and section pages. Then let the designer go to town on multiple versions of the home page from which you and others on your team can choose.

If you are a designer and you enjoy the goal-related and organizationally related parts of the overall Web site design task, you can take the opportunity this gives you to move up the decision tree and become more involved in site strategy and overall usability. You can continue to do the core graphical design work as well, informed by your new perspective, or bring in others to do that. Or you can continue to work primarily on the look and feel of the site, with the understanding that those elements need to serve the goals of the site and be modified by feedback from user testing.

Putting it all together

The Usability Design Cycle, introduced in Chapter 1, sums up the overall process of site design for usability: Study the user; set goals; design the site; build the site; test the product; continue to design, build, and test until the site is ready; then deliver the product.

The Usability Design Cycle puts the beginner at the beginning, middle, and end of the design process. Figure 8-1 shows where the user is formally involved in the design for usability process.

Putting the user in design, too

Figure 8-1 shows the user involved in several steps of the Usability Design Cycle, but not in the Design phase. Participatory design puts the user in the design phase as well. You can think of it as "customer-centered design," the description one of the authors (Mander) uses in explaining it to people who aren't design experts.

Participatory design is a fairly new approach, and there's ongoing debate about what specific practices it does and doesn't include. However, after you've implemented the usability ideas in this book, and if you're then interested in bringing the user into the process even further make the effort to learn more about participatory design. One good place is at the Web site of the Computer Professionals for Social Responsibility, www.cpsr.org.

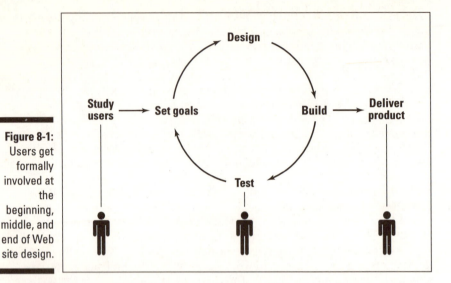

Figure 8-1: Users get formally involved at the beginning, middle, and end of Web site design.

Looping through the Usability Design Cycle

When we've shown customers the Usability Design Cycle, their eyes go straight to one feature of it: The perpetual loop in the middle. Where we see an admirable commitment to getting the job done right, our customers tend to see slipping schedules and mounting consulting bills. However, we usually only repeat the middle part of the loop — set goals, design, build, test — once during a project. After "delivering," however, we go right back to the beginning of the cycle and study the user again. Only this time we study how they interact with the new product.

How can you keep the development loop in your projects from turning into an endless spiral in which nothing ever gets delivered? The same way we do: by using software development-style discipline in our Web site development process. The main features of this approach are to develop, and rigorously maintain, a feature list and a bug list.

For a given project to create or update a site, you work on adding features until about two-thirds of the project time has elapsed. Then you quickly wrap up your feature work and start finding and, as we colorfully put it, "killing" bugs. Any features that didn't get done during the development period — or were completed but can't be made to work correctly during debugging — are left out of the current release and put on a new feature list to be worked on in the next release.

This kind of discipline is rare in Web site development — but so are fully featured sites that work properly, and these two rarities are not unrelated. A careful approach to site development leads to a better, more stable, and more usable site than an undisciplined one.

The Usability Design Cycle, while a wonderful invention that we are very proud of, may be a little discouraging if you're creating a new site from scratch and don't have much time. The loop in the middle, with its endless repetition, may seem particularly troublesome. And there isn't much detail in the "Design" part of the cycle, which is the subject of this part of the book.

So let's flatten out the Usability Design Cycle and give details where that part of the cycle is placed. Figure 8-2 shows the steps for design for usability with the Design step "exploded" to a higher level of detail.

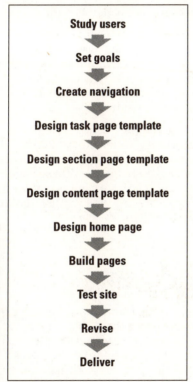

Figure 8-2: The Usability Design Cycle with detailed steps for the Design piece.

The rest of this chapter spells out usability considerations for the major kinds of pages found in most Web sites, except content pages, which are covered in the next chapter.

Identifying Web page types

You may not have even thought much about the fact that there are different types of Web pages. Yet the categorization of Web pages into types, and the

176   Part III: Creating Usable Web Pages

shared design elements of those types (in a well-put-together site), give an inherent structure to a Web site that users find pleasing and empowering.

The major types of Web pages you are likely to have in your Web site are:

- **Content pages.** Content pages make up most of the pages in a typical Web site. A content page is a page that holds text or graphical content such as an article, a press release, a story, a product description, a technical support tip, even a large image. To sum up, content pages hold information, and because the main purpose of most Web sites is to convey information, content pages make up the bulk of most Web sites. We describe content pages in excruciating detail in the next chapter.

- **Task pages.** Task pages go beyond conveying information to help the user accomplish something concrete. Task pages get information from the user and give them something of value in return. Pages that help the user complete a purchase are the most obvious example of task pages, but search, user registration, and software downloading are other examples of tasks. We describe task pages below.

- **The home page and section front pages.** Section front pages and a site's home page are navigational and organizational pages. Some sites have only one such page — the home page — but larger sites also have a section front page for each major section of the site. These pages are only a fraction of the pages in a site, but they're very important for helping users quickly find what they need. We describe section front pages and the home page later in this chapter.

Creating Usable Task Pages

Task pages are Web pages that support the user in carrying out a specific task. While almost anything that users do on the Web can be thought of as a task, we use the term "task pages" to refer to interactions that result in the user entering data, often including data that begins or completes a selling transaction. Here's a measuring stick: If a process is designed so that you enter data or download data, then it's almost certainly an example of what we mean by a task.

For Web sites that support tasks, task pages are the most important pages on the site. Task pages are the ones that contribute directly to saving significant amounts of money or to bringing in revenue. And it's only by testing and improving task pages that you can make the tasks on your site highly effective.

Figure 8-3 shows an example Web page from within the Godiva Chocolatier shopping process, a well-designed task. Showing customers the rich — pun intended — variety of products that Godiva sells shifts smoothly into selling one or more of any given item. The familiar shopping cart-type metaphor, here labeled a "shopping bag" to remind the user of a chocolate shop, makes it easy to pick up a product and then continue browsing around the site.

As someone involved in Web site creation, you probably have a fairly good intuitive understanding of content pages. This is because, like anyone else literate, you've been trained how to interact with and use printed content pages since birth. Dr. Suess's *Go, Dog, Go* was only the start of your experience with content pages.

You almost certainly never saw, let alone used, a task page in your life before you started to use the Web less than ten years ago. So you have no deep or intuitive understanding of how one should work. (Which is okay — we don't have that kind of deep or intuitive understanding either, though we're trying to develop it.)

As a really new kind of thing, task pages deserve more academic and usability attention than they've received to date. Among other interesting characteristics, they cause users a lot of excitement and anxiety. Excitement because users have the prospect of getting something done; anxiety because they have the very real possibility of making a serious mistake, something that just isn't possible when reading a magazine or book.

Figure 8-3: Buying Godiva chocolates can be a fun task.

There are many types of task pages, but overall, task pages have much more in common with one another than do content pages. Task pages on your site should be designed to be very similar to the best existing task pages on popular Web sites because that's what users are used to, and users only have room in their minds for one or two successful models of task pages. (Amazon.com's ordering process, which flows smoothly from product descriptions to reading reviews to ordering, and which includes a user-friendly one-click buying process, is the best-known example of an excellent model for tasks.)

Using tasks pages from existing sites as a model makes the pages seem familiar, which makes them seem safe, alleviating user anxiety — which may be the most important single criterion in designing task pages.

The purpose of task pages

Task pages generally support one of a few kinds of tasks. Important tasks include:

- **Searching.** Searching your site is a simple example of a task. (Simple from a conceptual level — an awful lot of deep thought, testing, and engineering work have gone into making searching work well.) Unlike most tasks, searching doesn't directly affect business goals, but it can greatly improve the usability of a site.

- **Downloading and installing software.** Many organizations have a need to get software into the hands of users, whether to fix bugs in existing software — which saves the organization money — or to sell upgraded or new software, which brings in revenue.

- **Registering for a newsletter, site personalization, or other benefit.** All tasks where the user creates a self-description or profile that's then stored for future use can be referred to simply as "registration."

- **Making a purchase.** Some tasks support all of the purchase process, some only part of it — finding a local dealer, for example, or specifying an order that's then faxed or mailed in. But all of these purchase-related activities can be thought of as special cases of the overall process of making a purchase.

There are many engineering issues relating to the storage and transmission of data, checking and clearing credit card transactions, and so on that are related to various tasks. However, our focus here is only on usability issues as they affect the design of task pages. If you get the task flow right and design Web pages for usability, both graphical design — the look of the Web pages involved — and engineering work will be in support of the right kind of solution instead of a mistaken one. We discuss how everyone on the team can best work together under this new approach in Chapter 12.

Chapter 8: Designing Web Pages by Type *179*

Generating revenue

Creating tasks involves real engineering work and quality assurance testing as well as Web page design, task design, and usability testing. It takes significant investments and many different kinds of resources to implement task support on a Web site, so the decision to support tasks on your Web site is a major one that must be supported by all levels of your organization. You may also need to get the support of outsiders who may be affected, such as dealers who have existing relationships with your customers. Getting this support can require you to compromise on the exact workings of your solution and is likely to be a major organizational task in and of itself.

The benefits, however, of supporting tasks on your site can be great. For example, as use of the Web grows, a company that doesn't support a Web purchase option is not offering a complete buying solution to its customers and potential customers. In some cases, not implementing Web purchasing support leaves a company vulnerable to new, Web-only competition or to inroads from existing competitors who implement Web-based selling first.

Carefully scope the costs and benefits of implementing major task support on your site. Get the needed support from inside and outside your organization. Then take advantage of the usability information in this chapter to quickly achieve success in meeting your goals.

Questions for task pages

In designing a task page template, ask yourself the following questions:

- **Where's the navigation?** Task page templates should support the user in completing the task, from start to finish. You should consider *removing* general navigation options and *adding* specific options for task-related issues such as looking up privacy or warranty information.

- **Wide or narrow pages?** Users may wish to print specific task-related pages, so narrow pages are recommended, as described in the previous chapter. It may be distracting to ask the user to go to a printable version of a page from within a task, so it's best to simply make the normal pages printable they are.

- **Borrowed content or Web-specific content?** Please don't borrow language or process for Web-based tasks from existing printed forms or documents, except for specific legal language such as disclaimers or warranties. Create Web-specific task flow and create new language that supports the informal feel of the Web while using as few words as possible.

180 Part III: Creating Usable Web Pages _____

✔ **Long or short pages?** In task pages, you're encouraging the user to complete the task. This means you want to minimize both the need to scroll and the number of steps in the process, which means simplifying every part of the process as much as possible. Try to create short pages — or, at the least, put everything users generally need to complete a step above the fold, and put legal language or detailed explanations appear below the fold. (See Chapter 7 for more details.)

Search task pages

For any site but the smallest, site search is an important capability. We recommend you consider offering site search if you have more than 25 pages in your Web site (because that's the most we can imagine going through if we wanted to manually search every page for something). Site search functions as a kind of accelerated — or last-ditch — navigation capability.

You can get site search capabilities from a number of free, low-cost, or relatively expensive sources. The leaders in offering site search are AltaVista and Inktomi; AltaVista offers its excellent search for free to smaller sites. You can learn more at www.altavista.com or at www.searchenginewatch.com.

What we're concerned with here, though, is not the engine behind your search capability, but making the search capability usable. Here's how we recommend you do so:

✔ **Offer search on the home page.** Ideally, Search is a "global" tool — something available from any page on your site. Try to work it into your navigation so it's always "at hand" for the user. At the very least, offer a search box, or a link to search, from your home page and from section pages, which have a navigational role and therefore need search. Offering a search box on every page is, in our humble opinion, a bit much.

✔ **Make sure every page is searchable.** You may have to index each new page manually or create a list of keywords by which the page can be searched. Make sure that you enter not just obvious keywords, such as the product name mentioned in a press release, but also less obvious ones — conceptual terms relating to the page, names of competing products or services to your offering that's mentioned on a page, even misspelled variants of the names of products or people that are mentioned on a page.

✔ **Test your search capability relentlessly.** There are few things that make a site look worse than for it to offer a search capability that doesn't work well. Unfortunately, users don't understand how search works, and they expect a lot from it. (Users may think to themselves, "If Google can search the whole Web, why can't your search function even search your site?") Test every page on your site to make sure it shows up near the top of the list when you search using terms related to it. Make sure that any new page you put on the site is put into the index of your search engine at the time you put it up — new pages are among the pages users are most likely to look for using search.

✔ **Make searched-for items prominent.** Watch what users search for and make these items easier to find. If users are searching for something that isn't present, try to put it on the site, or make it plain that it isn't there. For instance, if users are repeatedly searching your site for the name of your executives, consider putting executive biographies on the site — and linking to them from the home page.

✔ **Create a search page with frequently searched items listed.** You can create a "Search Me" page that includes not only search, but also frequently viewed pages, recent additions to the site, and frequently asked questions. This kind of "out of the box" thinking — going beyond what others offer by offering everything you can think of to meet the user's needs — will earn your users' trust.

Figure 8-4 shows the search results for the term Javascript within the Sun site, a site that has done a good job of integrating search. Use examples of search areas that you find on sites like your own as a guide to what to do — and what to avoid.

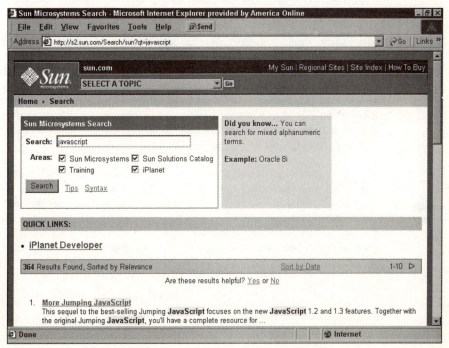

Figure 8-4: Shining the Sun on search.

Reprinted by permission of Sun Microsystems, Inc. Copyright (c) 2001 Sun Microsystems, Inc. All rights reserved.

For most sites we recommend that you not offer overall Web search. Many sites offer Web search in addition to site search, but we really don't see the point — Web search simply takes people off your site, rather than helping them fulfill their purpose in coming to your site in the first place. Also, just about every Web user already knows about and uses one or more search sites and is more or less familiar with what to expect from his or her favorite(s). There isn't much sense in giving your users a Web search capability that's likely to act somewhat differently than what they're used to.

Registration task pages

Registration is potentially highly valuable, both for you in meeting your site and business goals and for your user in getting benefits from your site. But many Web users have had bad experiences with registration as well. Given that your users are likely to be carrying some baggage with them related to registration, it's important that you do things right if you're going to offer registration capability.

The most important thing to do in making registration work well on your site is having a very clear understanding of what you're asking the user for and what you're offering in return. Users consider registration to be a tremendous hassle, based on the time and hassle it takes and their often-negative past experiences. So make your registration process simple — and advertise it as such up front.

More important, though, make sure that what you're offering the user is worth registering for — then keep the overhead of the registration process proportional to the benefit. For example, an online newsletter is a nice thing to get, if you're very interested in the topic that it covers. But all users need to tell you to get your newsletter is their e-mail address; asking for much more than that is out of proportion to the benefit the user is getting. Figure 8-5 shows a site that makes the limited amount of information that the user has to give very clear.

Also be aware of a hidden downside of registration: the anxiety it can cause users. When a site offers registration, users worry that they're missing out if they don't register — and that they may be subjecting themselves to a burdensome signup process or to unwanted phone calls, physical mail, or e-mail (spam) if they do. Your registration process and its results must be of significant value to both you and your user to make it worth having on your site at all.

Chapter 8: Designing Web Pages by Type   183

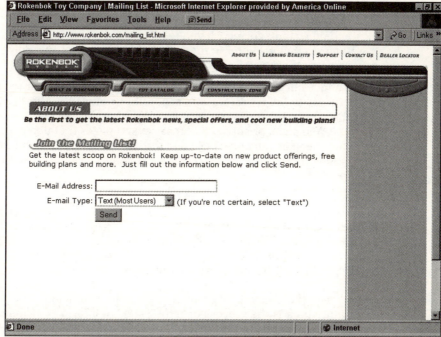

Figure 8-5: Rokenbok gives you a lot (of newsletter) for a little (data).

Follow these rules to make registration pleasant and valuable:

- **Make your privacy policy clear.** Over and over again we hear concerns from users about what will be done with the information that they give to a Web site. Set user-friendly privacy policies and make them very clear to users before you ask for information. Don't be afraid to over-communicate; for instance, put a summary of your privacy policy up front, then a prominent link to a more detailed description of it on each of the Web pages in your registration task.

- **Ask for as little information as possible.** Some people in your company would like to get as much information from every registrant as possible, but there are problems with this. First of all, registration information is not from a statistically valid sample, so it doesn't tell you much at all about your customers or Web site users. Second, asking more questions gets you fewer registrants, diminishing the value of the whole process. Relentlessly reduce the number of questions you ask to the minimum needed for you to offer the functionality you're asking for.

- **Consider just asking for e-mail addresses.** Giving you an e-mail address causes your user less anxiety than anything else you might ask for, yet it gives you a way to reach them on an ongoing basis, which is about the most valuable thing you could get from the process. If you ask for more, you have to be offering a lot in return — and make it very clear why you're asking.

Part III: Creating Usable Web Pages

- ✓ **Get registrations from the real world.** If the value proposition — the tradeoff you're offering Web users — is really good, all your customers should want it, correct? If you're offering an e-mail newsletter, ask customers you encounter in the real world if they want to receive it, and to give you their e-mail address if they do.

- ✓ **Reduce clicks in registration.** When you've reduced your registration process to the fewest questions possible, reduce the effort required of the user to the fewest clicks possible. Either put the entire process on one Web page, or spread it across several pages that don't scroll and that the user can move back and forth in smoothly. Don't make the user scroll on each page and also enter data on several pages — they'll get lost.

- ✓ **Test your registration process thoroughly.** Users resent the effort required to enter data — and they feel a strong ownership of "their" data after they've entered it. Any bugs, surprises, or problems in the registration process cause them great frustration. Use standard quality assurance testing as well as user testing to identify and fix any problems in registration before you expose the process to real users.

Identity theft is a new kind of crime that your site could unwittingly contribute to. Identity theft is the process of getting enough information about a person to get credit or otherwise complete financial transaction in that person's name — then running up that person's credit card or other bill, leaving the victim holding the bag. If you gather name, address, and phone number information from users, let alone credit card numbers, you have data that's of great value to identity thieves — and you may be vulnerable to theft by hackers who steal the data from you online. Protect your users, your customers, and your organization by taking the utmost care with detailed personal information that you gather online. If you need to learn more, start at Verisign, one of the leading companies in this area. Their Web site is at www.verisign.com.

Shopping task pages

Online selling is a major opportunity for most organizations — yet it's also potentially hazardous to your financial health. It's expensive, time-consuming, difficult, and dangerous to sell online.

You can work through partners, such as Yahoo! and their online stores or eBay's online stores. Or you can build all the functionality for your site yourself. Or you can partner for some parts of the process, such as CyberCash for credit card processing, and handle other parts yourself. (Check out CyberCash at www.cybercash.com.)

Chapter 8: Designing Web Pages by Type 185

Recommended privacy policies

According to TRUSTe, the leading organization guaranteeing user privacy, your site's privacy statement should specify:

✔ Who you are — what organization is gathering the information.

✔ What information you're gathering.

✔ How you'll use the information.

✔ With whom you'll share the information.

✔ What options you'll give the user regarding use of the information.

✔ What kind of security procedures you have in place to protect user information.

✔ How users can correct the information they give you.

We recommend that your site specify all of the above, and anything else you think is relevant. We also have our own thoughts on what your policy should actually be:

✔ Gather as little information as possible. In particular, don't keep track of what specific individuals do on your site; the thought that you may be doing so makes people paranoid.

✔ Use the information you gather in a very limited way and only to carry out purposes desirable to the user. If you'll be doing something the user may consider intrusive — for example, having your sales department call them to follow up — make this very clear, limit the number of times and duration during which you may intrude, and make it easy for the user to opt out from being contacted.

✔ Commit not to share the information with any other company. Spam, junk mail, and junk phone calls are the #1 concern of users who give you contact information.

You should also consider getting a TRUSTe license for your site, though this is usually only done by larger companies. If you're interested in finding out more, go to www.truste.org (not .com; TRUSTe is a non-profit organization and therefore has a .org Web address).

The overall decision as to whether and how to best offer online selling is more than we can cover here, but usability concerns have a huge impact in maximizing your returns from online selling and reducing the dangers.

Start your quest for usable online selling by carefully reading the sections above about online search and online registration. Because your users are going to be searching for products, and because you're likely to be putting your users through a registration process before they can buy, everything we discuss earlier in this chapter should be of value to you.

Also consider every step of the sales process and just how much of the process you want or need to support online. For example, if you currently sell only through stores, you may want to offer most of an online shopping process on your site — but instead of completing the transaction online, offer a store finder to show the user where they can actually make the purchase. Your stores will appreciate it!

186 Part III: Creating Usable Web Pages

Make it clear to users what you're offering by calling the store finder "store finder" or some other recognizable name. You don't want users to think they can buy online when they can't. And be aware that users these days expect to be able to buy online — they may be irate if you don't offer this capability.

After you've researched what you want to offer in an online shopping experience and made the decision to go forward, follow these recommendations to get the most benefit out of your online selling experience:

- **Plan for full implementation.** Lay out all of your plans for a full implementation of online selling on your site. Do user testing on the core purchasing process and the steps leading up to it. Make sure all the information and functionality needed is present on your site before you actually offer anything for sale.

- **Start with a partial implementation.** The difficulty of recording and clearing transactions and fulfilling orders that you receive online, plus answering questions, handling returns, and other concerns have been a shock to more than one online seller. Figure out a way to limit the number of products you sell initially, the kinds of users you sell to, the geographic area in which you sell, and other factors to start with a small initial burden on your systems.

One important part of the online shopping process is clearing credit card transactions. You can actually accept credit card numbers online and then handle the clearing piece manually. It makes no difference to the user and lets you avoid some costs until you are ready to implement the full back-end process on your Web site.

- **Grow rapidly.** A partial online selling effort is clearly unsatisfactory, so scale from your initial, partial implementation to the full implementation you've planned for as rapidly as you can without problems. (But by starting smaller, you do give yourself the opportunity to go only as fast as you can do it right, and no faster.)

- **Protect privacy.** Carefully read the information above, in the section on registration task pages, about protecting user privacy. The information you gather during the online selling process is of great potential value to your users as well as to thieves, and you have the potential for serious responsibility if you abuse the user's trust in any way.

- **Keep the process simple.** Every step in the user's buying process is another opportunity for the user to make a mistake. The simpler you keep the process, the better you can test it, and the better the user can execute it.

Chapter 8: Designing Web Pages by Type

✔ **Track business as well as functional success.** The fact that you create an error-proof process is useless to your organization if the sales volumes you achieve fall short of expectations. Usability has a great deal of impact on the business success of the online shopping process; monitor both business impact as well as user impact of the online selling process. More marketing expenditures may be needed, for example, to bring in enough buyers — but your organization won't make that marketing commitment until the usability of the buying process is foolproof.

Figure 8-6 shows a page within the purchasing process at built-e (www.built-e.com), a site for the sale and purchase of environmentally friendly products. This page adheres to most of the principles describe in this book: simplified navigation for the shopping process; Web-specific content, at least for the key area above the fold; key information above the fold, where the user can make a quick decision without scrolling; key information also within the area that would appear on a printout of the page, as well as reproduced on a printer-friendly page just a link away.

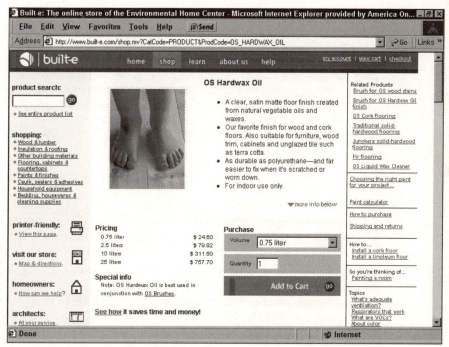

Figure 8-6: Built-e has built an easy shopping process.

Creating Usable Section & Home Pages

We have less to say about creating usable section front pages and overall site home pages than about task pages (described above) or content pages (covered in the next chapter). Why? Because section front and home pages must respect the rules you use for content and task pages — but less so. Because you may find yourself needing to accomplish so much on section and home pages, you may need to bend the rules you use elsewhere on your site.

You'll also find yourself designing section front pages and, especially, your home page, on a one-at-a-time basis rather than as templatized pages. Again, this is because these pages are so important within the site. You may even find yourself making commitments to advertisers, suppliers, or specific departments within your organization to put specific product mentions, photos, or other feature descriptions and navigation on a specific section page or home page, either above or below the fold. It's hard to set blanket usability rules for such valuable real estate.

You should still work, however, to create a template for section pages. Doing so will make it quick and easy to create a "good" section page, which you can go back and make into a "great" section page when you have time. For the home page, though, you have little choice; you need to create a "great" home page for your site's launch day. The home page is extremely visible, and as the old saying goes, you only get one chance to make a first impression. Creating a top-notch home page beginning on Day 1 will help you maintain the trust and support of all your stakeholders, from end users to senior management, though of course the home page can always be improved!

In creating a template that you'll use as a starting point for section pages and, to a lesser extent, the home page, start by answering these questions:

- **Where's the navigation?** Section pages are all about navigation. Simply by specifying all the site navigation and section-specific navigation that must go in each and every section page, you'll have done much of the job of designing your section page template.

- **Borrowed content or Web-specific content?** Never use borrowed language on section front pages and the home page, they're too important. Write new, brief content and carefully edit images to fit within what you're trying to do on the page.

- **Long or short pages?** Section front pages and the home page will almost always be long, because there's so much you're trying to accomplish within them. Make sure that navigation and popular information and tasks are briefly described and linked to in the area above the fold. This gets new users up to speed faster and helps experienced users quickly head deeper into your site. Put less valuable content lower on the page.

Chapter 8: Designing Web Pages by Type *189*

Sectionizing your site

Section pages are organizational "front pages" for the sections of your site, and they help to orient and guide the reader. They aren't destinations, like content pages, and they don't help you get anything done, like task pages. They're organizational, like home pages (explained in the next section), but more focused because they only apply to one part of the site.

Like content pages, a section page can draw on familiar models from the print world, but like a task page, a section page is also new to the reader's experience. The familiarity has to do with the role of the page: Organizing information and guiding the reader to it is the role of several elements from the print world such as the front page of a newspaper, the Table of Contents of a magazine, or the index of a book. What's new is the Web's ability to link directly to desired content.

Section pages may be the most interesting Web pages to design, as well as the most difficult. Why so interesting, yet difficult? A few reasons:

- ✔ **Section pages are familiar, yet different.** It's useful, in designing section pages, to draw on existing models such as the front page of a newspaper, but you're also subverting the existing model by taking advantage of Web functionality like hyperlinks, which overturn the sequential-page model of print. If you make the right choices, your section pages will combine the familiarity of existing models with the power of Web-only capabilities (but it's easier to fall short of this goal than to meet it).

- ✔ **Section pages enforce, and subvert, navigation.** Section pages are nothing so much as expanded navigational sections with pictures. As such, they reinforce the navigational structure of your site, and serve as a guide to it. But they also "hot-wire" the navigational structure by bringing special attention to parts of the site that you want to make it easy for users to find, usually because they meet your goals for the site (such as user registrations) or for your business (such as product sales). Every time users click a link in your section page that's not part of the site's regular navigation, you've just taught them again how to not use the regular navigation to get things done.

- ✔ **Section pages are complex.** Section pages may be the most complex on your site. Their job is to entice the user further into the site, either through regular navigation or through links to intriguing content or important tasks. So unlike content and task pages, which are ends in themselves, section pages must be attractively designed, interesting to look at, highly graphical, yet fast loading and easy to use.

190   Part III: Creating Usable Web Pages

With all these concerns interacting at once, it's no wonder section pages are hard to design well and receive so much attention during the design process. Follow these recommendations to create great section pages:

- **Create section pages throughout your site.** Users expect each major section of your site to have a section front page — they're used to this from newspapers and from other Web sites, among other examples. So meet expectations. Create a section page in the front of each major section of your site.

- **Use the section page to highlight the key assets of the current section.** We'll allow you one "What's Hot" or similar area to lead users from the front of a section to other places of interest in your site. Besides that, focus the content of the section page on what's of interest in the current section. If there isn't much in the section, consider posting a brief article or story relating to the section's topic — after you've pointed out the section's highlights first.

- **Keep section pages small.** Section pages get a lot of attention, so it's tempting to make them crowded — and therefore slow to download. But users are visiting your section page on the way somewhere else, so they want it to pop up quickly. Keep your section pages small so they download quickly.

Create an overall template for your section pages and an example for one particular section. Get feedback from the design team and users on both. Use what you learn to modify the template, and then use it to create section pages for all the sections of your site.

Figure 8-7 demonstrates the principles that apply to section pages as realized on the front page for the Find Recipes section of the Web site of Godiva Chocolatier, seen earlier in this chapter. The core, central part of this section page features content found only in this section and nowhere else on the site. The top and bottom of the page are navigation and links to the rest of the site. The user's eye naturally falls first on inviting words like *brownies*, *cheesecakes*, *tarts*, and *truffles*, as well as a picture of a brownie sundae. You may not be able to achieve quite the same level of emotional impact within your own site — especially if your focus is something less appetizing like, well, almost anything — but it's worth trying to come close.

Making your home page not homely

The *home page* of your site — the first page users see when they type in the Web address that you publicize for your site — is simply a special case of a section page, yet it's worth extra attention and work. It's different from a *splash page,* which is a page that appears when you visit a site, shows a graphic or plays a multimedia clip, and then goes away. These pages are more for emotional impact than for functional use, so we don't go into detail about them here.

Chapter 8: Designing Web Pages by Type   191

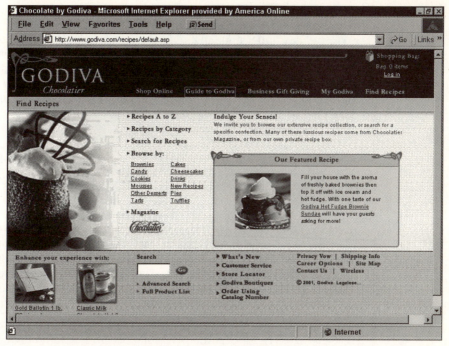

Figure 8-7: Godiva has the right idea on section pages.

There are two sets of reasons for giving the home page extra attention: outward-focused, or user-oriented, reasons, and inward-focused, or organizationally oriented, reasons. Let's take a quick look at the highlights of both sets of needs, and why you need to take both into account in designing your home page.

Here are the main reasons why your home page is so important to the user:

✔ **Your home page lets people know if they are in the right place.** Pity the poor user — millions of sites to go to, with a typical Web search turning up scores or hundreds of hits and little idea which site really has what they want or need. Your home page had better tell users exactly what they can get from your site, or they're likely to leave.

✔ **Your home page teaches users how to use your site.** A properly designed home page includes all the major navigational elements of your site. Users size it up to figure out how to get around your site. If your navigational scheme has problems, many users will be left puzzled — and are likely to go to another site as a result.

Part III: Creating Usable Web Pages

✔ **Your home page sets usability expectations.** The home page of your site sends many messages to the user. If it loads quickly, is attractively laid out, and has understandable overall navigation and specific links to topics and tasks of interest, the user will be optimistic about finding these attributes to hold throughout your site. If it's poorly laid out or begins their experience with a long wait for downloading or difficult-to-understand link text, users will develop low expectations of your site — and are likely to leave as soon as they get done on your site whatever they absolutely have to do.

Less obvious, but equally important, is the reason that your home page is so important to your organization: It's the best place on your site for you to get users to do things that are important to your organization —things that may be different than what they originally wanted to do when they came to your site. Let's take a look at some of the things you can use your home page for:

✔ **Getting users informed.** There may be important news that you want people to be aware of; for example, a positive review of a product or your organization's response to a story in the press. The home page is where you can highlight such news and draw people in to read it.

✔ **Getting users involved.** You may want users of your site to take some action to get more involved with the site or your company: registering for a newsletter, for example, or taking part in a promotion or survey. The home page is the best place to prominently display an invitation.

✔ **Getting users to be customers.** The home page of your site is where you can start the process of getting users to buy from you. Your site may offer a complete solution — online promotion, product descriptions, and purchasing. Or your site may only put up a special offer and instructions on how to find a store where the user can complete the purchase. No matter how the buying process is carried out, your home page is where you can get users started on it.

Recommendations are less pertinent to your home page than to other parts of your site; you're going to be giving this page more individual design attention than any other, so you are likely to consider all the good as well as not-so-good ideas that might apply to it before you're done. Here, however, are a few things you might want to keep in mind as you design the home page:

✔ **Don't oversimplify.** We prefer home pages with content as well as navigational links. Make sure your home page is worth the time it takes to visit it.

✔ **Include current news.** People just think your organization is out of it if something important is happening and it's not reflected on the home page of your site. Include a place for current news in the design of your home page — and consider doing something radical, like splashing a clickable banner across the top of the page, when something big happens that you want to bring attention to or respond to.

Chapter 8: Designing Web Pages by Type

- **Pack it all in.** Users want to get from your home page to the information or functionality they want in as few clicks as possible. Don't be afraid to have a busy home page or to offer pathways to the same area of your site in both the regular navigation and in a highlighted link of some sort. As you learn what users really do with your site, simplify the home page to emphasize the key elements of the site — but don't make it too hard for users to figure out whether the content or functionality they want is somewhere on the site.

Your home page is a good place to experiment. For example, the Sun home page, shown in Figure 8-8, offers many different navigational approaches to the site: a site map, resources by type of user, major site sections accompanied by graphics, and a pull-down menu of popular topics you can jump to. From the Sun home page, you don't see the details of how the site is organized — and you don't really care. You just know that you have a pretty good chance of being able to quickly get to what you want.

If you look at other home pages, you can find your own examples of the above purposes getting accomplished, well in some cases and poorly in others. Use existing home pages as models and examples — of what not to do as well as of what to do — before you create your own site's home page.

Figure 8-8: Sun shines several lights on site content.

Reprinted by permission of Sun Microsystems, Inc. Copyright (c) 2001 Sun Microsystems, Inc. All rights reserved.

194 Part III: Creating Usable Web Pages

Chapter 9

Designing Great Content Pages

* *

In This Chapter

▶ Creating great content

▶ Developing usable content pages

▶ Putting images in content

▶ Making printable pages

▶ Sending pages by e-mail

* *

Great content is a critical part of what brings users back to your Web site again and again. While navigation is critical to making your Web site usable, great content is the main reason anyone would want to even try to use your site in the first place.

Getting content pages right seems simple, but it can quickly become very complicated. There is a whole raft of features, such as the ability to e-mail, print, or order a related product, that users want — and are increasingly even coming to expect — on content pages. Add to that the demand by users for constant updating and how easy it is for you to make mistakes on your site in a "live" publishing environment, and you have an environment in which it's hard to do everything right.

Many of the issues we've talked about so far, such as knowing your users and their goals, are important in getting your site right from the "top down." Designing your content pages carefully, thoughtfully, and repeatedly — that is, going back to your content page template over and over again to fix problems and add features — is the key to making your site great from the bottom up.

This chapter describes the key issues in creating first-class content pages. If you work hard on these issues, your site will be very desirable to users, as well as very usable.

What Is Great Content?

Great content on a Web site comes from a combination of preparation and inspiration. *Preparation* means knowing your users and what your site can plausibly provide that will make them very interested in coming back again and again. That's the users and goals information covered in Chapters 2 and 3 of this book.

Preparation also means creating one or a few templates for content pages that support all the features needed to give users the feeling they can do what they need to with your site's content. That's the topic of this chapter.

Inspiration is when one or more people in your organization repeatedly and consistently make the right call about what to put on your site that will interest, enlighten, intrigue, fascinate, or otherwise serve the needs and interests of your site's users. Designing your site well, from setting appropriate goals and getting the navigation right to creating highly useful and usable content page templates, lays the groundwork for great content to be plugged into your site easily and, therefore, more frequently.

Who needs great content?

If you have a news, hobbyist's, or other kind of site that demands frequent attention, then putting up great content will seem like a natural interest for you. But you may be responsible for a simple company site, for example, that may seem like it doesn't need great content. Think again. Remember that executives, employees, and business partners — as well as customers, investors, analysts, and the press — will be checking your site for the latest on company products, services, financial results, and more. Great content is just as important for a "boring" company site as for a computer gameplayer's online hangout.

Content can be tied to commerce in interesting and valuable ways. For example, product information can serve both as content and as part of the task of shopping and buying online. You can also create content that supports the buying process in other ways. Figure 9-1 shows the "Elements of Gift Giving" page at Zumiez.com (`www.zumiez.com`), a teen shopping site that cleverly ties the ancient four elements — air, earth, fire and water — to gift-giving ideas.

It's true, however, that most content on a company or organizational site doesn't directly affect revenues or expenses. So the content part of your site is more a marketing, public relations, and — if you have investors — investor relations expense than a direct source of revenue or cost savings for your organization. So keeping expenses down is important. Standardization is the enemy of expenditure, so taking the time to design the content area and templates of your site well will save money as you operate your site.

Chapter 9: Designing Great Content Pages

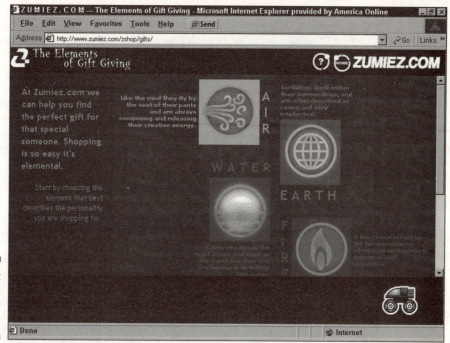

Figure 9-1: Zumiez ties content to commerce.

Writing for the Web

You can get whole books on writing for the Web. (We have one on our bookshelves called *writing for your website* — no upper-case letters for these Web purists, who have an ingrained cultural dislike of capital letters from the days when the Web only ran on Unix systems, which ignore capital letters — so we assure you we're not kidding.) But creating content for the Web really comes down to just a few questions:

- **Imported documents or Web-only documents?** If you want to present an existing document on the Web, you're going to lose the document's formatting, and the text will doubtless be too wordy for easy reading online. Consider providing a brief version on line and using an Adobe PDF file, which preserves the original document's formatting, for the full document. For more information about this format, visit Adobe at `www.adobe.com/epaper`.

- **Do you have time to write for the Web?** If you have time to rewrite existing documents for the Web or create new Web-only documents, just follow the rules below. Otherwise, use existing documents as is or (preferably) in PDF format.

Part III: Creating Usable Web Pages

- ✔ **Do you have talent to write for the Web?** You, or a designated person on your team, needs to be good at writing short, punchy text with lots of headings and bulleted lists that accurately summarizes the important points of much larger documents (not too different from the writing in this book, but shorter).

- ✔ **Are you going to use long or short pages?** A desirable way to present Web articles is to not force the user to scroll down to read; they are broken up into short text pages and provide a way for the user to easily page back and forth within the article. (We discuss making your Web pages printable in the section "Making printable pages" later in this chapter.)

- ✔ **Are you going to build a widget?** If you invest in creating a *paging widget* — text-based icons and code that track the page number that the user is on within an article — you can make it easier for the user to move through an article. You need a designer to make your paging widget look good and a software engineer to make it work right, but after you have it, you can reuse it over and over in your site. Figure 9-2 shows a paging widget example from a catalog for philanthropy in Washington State's Whatcom County.

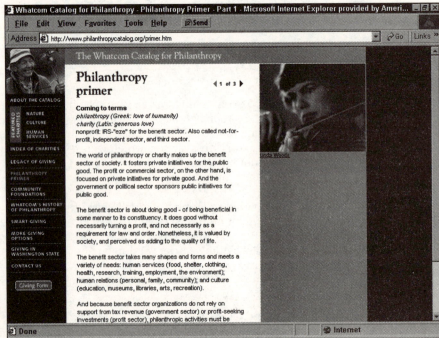

Figure 9-2: A philanthropy site does the paging widget right.

Chapter 9: Designing Great Content Pages

If you do have time and the ability to create Web-specific content, follow these rules:

- **Keep it short and simple.** Reading on the computer screen is much harder than reading from a book or magazine. So keep text short and simple. A newspaper level of complexity is about right. If you can't simplify to that extent, consider using a formatted PDF document for better readability.

- **Use many headers and lists.** Headers and lists break up text and make it easy to scan. Because it's hard to read from a screen, users are unlikely to read all your precious words — they'll scan them for high points. Make the high points obvious by using headers and lists that make them obvious.

- **Don't link out much.** Consider linking out to specific pages within your site that describe products and services you mention and to specific other companies and organizations when you mention them, which will usually be rarely. But don't link out to that interesting article on how skateboards are conquering the urban jungle from within your text. Instead, create an "Of interest" section at the end of your article and put such links there.

- **Don't create "webs" of information.** Some commentators recommend that you rewrite major pieces of text as interlinked "webs" that reference one another and even off-site resources in a heavily intertwined way. This is valuable, for the right kinds of information, but really hard to do well. Unless you're an expert writer, stick to traditional, recognizable formats such as articles, stories, and brochures — but shorten the content drastically.

If you need to provide longer text documents, provide a short summary on your site, then link to the fuller version. For example, "Foo.com respects your privacy. For more information review our privacy policy." The longer document can be in Web or PDF format.

- **Carefully proofread your work.** Because publishing on the Web can be instantaneous, there's nothing easier than committing typos, grammatical errors, and factual errors in content on your Web site. Set up a proofreading system to prevent these errors. Keep adjusting the system until you see no errors, or at least very, very few, actually reaching your live Web site.

Typos on your Web site indicate a lack of concern for, and interest in, your users that's very off-putting. Sacrifice a small amount of the immediacy you may otherwise be able to achieve for the accuracy that will allow your site to be taken seriously.

Why Web design advice is so confusing

Much of the Web design advice you'll see is contradictory and confusing because the people giving advice are talking about different kinds of Web pages — and different kinds of Web sites. But whereas both writers and readers realize that different sites have different needs, the split of Web sites into different kinds of Web pages is not widely understood, and neither are the different design and usability requirements of the different kinds of Web pages.

For example, you may have seen advice from various sources, including this book, to use a page size limit such as 25 Kb per page, in order to allow your pages to load quickly. But unlike other books, this one spells out for you that you can break the limit when the page in question is a content page, and the content is a high-resolution picture of something the user needs to see in detail.

For such a page, a long download time is acceptable if you've let the user know what's coming and the user has chosen to wait for it. On the other hand, designing complex, ever-changing navigation that's required on every page and that takes up more than 20 Kb all by itself is unacceptable, because it will make all of your Web pages — no matter how trivial and unimportant, or strictly functional, a given page may be — slow-loading.

As you run into different sources of design and usability advice, figure out whether it applies to content pages, task pages, section pages, or all of the above. Decide where the rules apply — and where you can break them anyway. Just thinking through the varying needs of these different kinds of Web pages as an exercise will help you do a better job of designing your own Web pages and making them highly usable.

Programming your content

As you design the content area of your site, you should also give some thought to "programming." This doesn't mean computer programming, it means programming in the television sense: filling designated areas of your site with up-to-date with fresh content, either as needed, on a regularly scheduled basis, or a combination thereof. For example, a company can make sure to issue at least one press release a month even if nothing that would normally be press-worthy is happening. The company then has to make sure to do something worth writing about at least once a month, which is a whole other issue.

In designing the content area of your site, think of what happens as new is created and old content is retired. How will new content be highlighted on your home page and elsewhere on your site? Will there be an archive for certain kinds of old content, such as old press releases or articles? Will new content be included in the index of your site's search capability as soon as it's added to your site? Asking these and similar questions can solve potentially nasty problems before they arise, improving the usability of your site for the people keeping it updated as well as for the people using it.

Even if you intend to leave your site relatively static, you very much need to have a plan for quickly adding breaking news that affects your company to your Web site. When your company has a new product, a new strategic partnership, a positive (or negative) press story, or other news that affects you, people will go to your Web site within minutes to see what you have to say about it. "Nothing" is not an acceptable answer these days. Have a spot on your home page and an internal location designated for breaking news and quickly address anything major that happens regarding your company.

Creating Usable Content Pages

You should have one or a few templates for content pages in your site. A *content page* is a destination page that a user may visit to see or learn something. The content page doesn't "sell" anything, and any actions taken as a result of viewing a content page are taken offline.

However, to be specific, a content page typically doesn't contain a *call to action* — a request for the user to do something. If you find yourself putting a call to action in a Web page, it's probably not a content page; it's a task page, where the task is completed offline. Task pages are described in the Chapter 8.

Content pages have many types, depending on whether they contain all text, mixed text and images, mainly images, or (shudder) multimedia. (We shudder because of the raft of usability and design issues that multimedia content brings up, not because it's a bad thing overall.) We discuss multimedia in more detail in Chapter 10.

The purpose of content pages

Content pages are generally provided to meet users' needs. Users come to your site seeking certain kinds of information; content pages provide the information to them. Therefore, thoughtfully designed and carefully user-tested content pages play a crucial role in the user's satisfaction with your site.

However, content pages don't generally play a strong role in producing revenue for your company or organization. Therefore, it doesn't make sense to spend a tremendous amount of money on them. You should come up with a simple, usable content page design — or a few related designs for different types of content — and create each individual content page from your template, with little or no new design work needed for that specific page.

Questions for content

In designing a content page template, ask yourself the following questions:

- **Where's the navigation?** The design of content pages is greatly affected by where the navigation is. If you have navigation at the top and bottom of the page, you have the entire width of the page to use for content. But if you have left-hand navigation, your options are seriously restricted. If your site is heavy in content, especially text content, try to avoid left-hand navigation. If you have to use left-hand navigation, you'll have to make careful use of the width of the page.

- **Wide or narrow pages?** Content pages should be narrow, so as to be easily printable. You can get around this by providing a wide page for general use and a special, easily printable version, if you're willing to do the extra work. Chapter 7 discusses these issues in detail.

- **Borrowed content or Web-specific content?** If the content you're providing users is mostly borrowed from non-Web sources, it's probably "written long," using a lot of words where a few may do and using unbroken blocks of text rather than shorter text blocks with lots of bulleted lists, headers, and hyperlinks.

- **Long or short pages?** This is a tricky question for content pages. If you can write Web-specific content, use short, non-scrolling pages and chop longer content into separate pages. If the content you're providing is copied in from other sources — not written specifically for the Web — you probably need to use long pages. Adopt an overall page-length limit, such as four times the length of a short page, and take the user to additional pages after that limit. See Chapter 7 for information about acceptable page lengths.

Figure 9-3 shows a content page from the For Dummies site, using content from the book *Web Design For Dummies,* published by Hungry Minds, Inc. (which we recommend as a companion volume to this book). Notice how few words appear in a single pageview — about 250. A magazine page that we checked, by contrast, holds about 1,500 words — and you can read them all without scrolling. Clearly, if you put text-heavy content from print sources online, the user is going to have to scroll or page through a lot of screenfuls of text to read all of it.

Chapter 9: Designing Great Content Pages 203

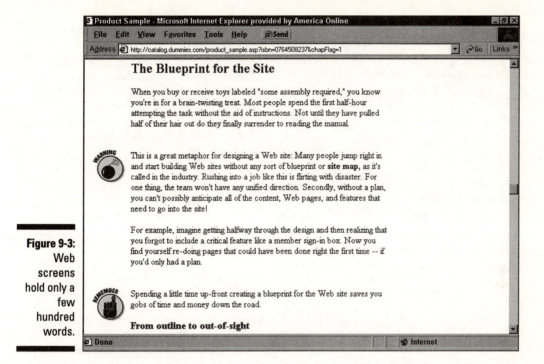

Figure 9-3: Web screens hold only a few hundred words.

Types of Content Pages

A key concern in designing content page templates is the mix of text and images on a given content page. You need separate templates for content pages depending on whether they're image-free, use a small image to create interest, or provide a large "payoff" image that's a destination in and of itself.

Images in content

As we describe in Chapter 7, images on the Web don't work that well — they're ugly because they're compressed and made small for fast transmission, and clumsy because no matter how small they are, a user is still going to have to wait extra time for them. Still, a carefully selected, cropped, and compressed image can often liven up content without imposing an unacceptably heavy burden on the user.

Generating pageviews

Many Webmasters and people in related jobs proudly point to the pageviews generated by their Web site as a measure of the site's success — and their own importance.

As business and other organizations get more sophisticated about the Web, however, generating pageviews is becoming less accepted as a goal in and of itself. Pageviews that provide interesting information have some value, but only a little. Pageviews that reduce the need for users to call or write your company have more value because calls and correspondence generate costs. Pageviews that are part of a shopping or buying process that generates revenue have correspondingly greater value.

Keep track of overall pageviews for your site, but only as one measure of success. Track pageviews per section and tie them into concrete business goals like costs avoided and, most importantly, new revenues earned.

Follow these rules for creating templates for images that liven up a story or marketing piece:

- **Predefine a place for a small image.** Set up a standard template for a small image embedded above the fold in a story, article, or other document. Specify a specific image size or a set of sizes that can be accommodated in any one template.

- **Keep the image small.** A typical news story on a Web site typically includes an image perhaps 50 x 70 pixels in image size — a bit larger than a postage stamp — severely compressed to perhaps 5 to 7K in file size. Along with the content's text, page navigation, and an ad, this keeps the total Web page size manageable.

- **Link to larger images.** If the image that you want to display is large, put a thumbnail (small, preview) version of it in the standard template for a small image, then link off to a larger version. (See the next section for details.)

The easy way to create a thumbnail is to simply reduce the whole image. But better than that is to crop a smaller representative piece of the large image and then reduce *that* as the thumbnail. The result is a more "readable" image and a more interesting larger image (more interesting because it shows more information, not just more resolution).

If you appreciate high-quality images, these rules may seem harsh — but remember, when you're putting an image into text content, the image is a preview or highlight, not a full representation. And remember that, no matter how large you make the image, it's going to be a backlit, low-resolution thing anyway — for a truly good image you need either print or reality.

Images as content

When you want to display a larger image, treat it respectfully. Give it the whole display space. Add some text beneath it as explanation, if needed, but put the image front and center.

What about download time? When the image is the main point of the page you're displaying, don't worry about it much. Use a larger, higher-resolution, less-compressed image to really show the object or person in question to best advantage.

This is a Web image, of course, so don't go overboard. It's stupid to show an image that's too large to see without scrolling —seeing only part of the image at once is irritating, and the result is absolutely unprintable. (And what your users say after waiting to see an image that they can't view in its entirety or print in one piece is likely to be unprintable, too.)

Figure 9-4 shows a medium-sized, relatively high-resolution image shown as content from the Whatcom philanthropy site. Cleverly, the site developer — we admit, it was one of the authors (Mander) — used a high-resolution black and white image, giving a high-quality result from an image with a small file size — just under 10K.

For products, you should use even larger images — color images, in most cases. Reduce the file size as much as you can, but it's still acceptable to use an image 30K or 40K in size. But, you say, won't a home user connected by modem get upset while waiting 15 or 20 seconds for an image of that size to download? Not if you warn them first.

Database-driven content

Advanced Web sites today — and even some fairly simple ones — drive their Web sites with content databases that provide information on request and format it "on the fly" for display on the Web. These systems are confusing — ever wonder why the address of an article can be `www.budznews.com/article/YYY333?=2wwehike` instead of something sensible? Because the article is being searched for by a database system that uses a query, rather than a hierarchical structure, to retrieve the article. It is possible to provide comprehensible URLs within such a system, but it's a lot of extra work.

Sophisticated database-driven systems can handle formatting issues such as those described here and seamlessly add features such as e-mail capability and easy printability. If you have such a system, use it. If you don't, consider upgrading to one — but in the meantime, be glad you have comprehensible URLs for your articles.

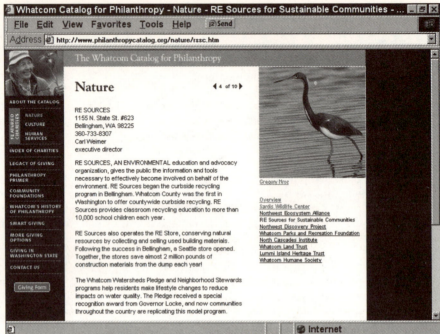

Figure 9-4: Even small pictures can be worth a thousand words.

On a typical, text-focused content page, put a thumbnail of the image, then the words "click for larger image." Users will understand that you used a small image the first time to save them a long wait — and that they should expect the larger image to take some time to load.

Adding elements to content pages

You can "complexify" your content pages in some interesting and, possibly, valuable ways. Despite what some people think, though, this is not a necessary thing to do in the first version of your new Web site. Content pages are relatively low-value; spend time making sure the navigational scheme works well and your task pages are fully optimized before spending time upgrading your content pages.

The starting point to extending your content pages is to know what they're doing for you. For each of the possible additions you can make to a content page, we've added a description of what kind of Web site the new element fits in:

- **Related links box.** You can embed this box in the article — further reducing the number of words from the article that display in a given screenful of content — or in the right-hand rail. Related links can include

Chapter 9: Designing Great Content Pages **207**

other articles on the same topic, message boards, or even off-site links. Use a related links box if your goal in the content area is to generate lots of pageviews or to educate the user. (Don't link off-site very often if your goal is to generate pageviews.)

✔ **Products box.** Like a related links box, you can embed a products box in your article or put it in the right-hand rail. Don't try to make the products specifically relate to the article — it becomes obvious you're stretching, especially when a story is important or tragic, which makes attempts at "contextual commerce" seem cruel. Use a products box if the main purpose of your Web site is to sell products.

✔ **Site highlights box.** When users reach a content page, they've completed a task, even if the task was just to find out more about that interesting link on the home page. A site highlights box gives users an alternative to going back to the home page to look again for something interesting or useful on the site. You can mix links that fit your goals for the site with links that users commonly find of greatest interest.

Special Features for Content Pages

There are certain special features that are becoming standard for content pages, at least on large, content-heavy Web sites. You should consider adding these special features to the templates for content pages on your Web site as well.

Making printable pages

In Chapter 8 we describe how to make every Web page on your site printable. However, you may have made design choices, such as using a wide template, that make printability of all pages impossible. Never fear, you have an alternative: Separate, printable versions of your Web content pages.

Even if you've kept your pages narrow, you may well want to provide separate printable versions, for some or all of the following reasons:

✔ **The content is too long.** Often a relatively short story, article, or other piece of content takes up a lot of vertical screen space when it's "poured" onto a page with left navigation and perhaps even right-column ads or related links. A printable page will put the key content on a much smaller number of printed pages.

✔ **The content is split.** You may well split long articles — or even relatively short ones — over several pages. This makes printing an article very difficult and frustrating. A printable article solves the problem.

208 **Part III: Creating Usable Web Pages**

✔ **Readers want an alternative.** Your users will sometimes go to your printable page as an alternative version to the one that they read online! It gives them a break from the busy formatting and frequent scrolling or clicking links needed on your regular site pages.

You can support printable pages with a *print widget*. This is simply an icon that leads to a printable version of the page. The printable version should have your company logo and enough headings and descriptive information that someone finding the printout a year from now will know what the article's about and where it's from.

Put the print widget icon in a consistent place on each printable page and spawn a new window with the printable version of the information. See Figure 9-5 for an example. (You can make your print widget more complicated if you have a database; if so, find out what it takes to pull up a simpler version of the article from your article database.)

Making e-mailable pages

It's really hard for users to e-mail content from your Web site to each other. They have to perform a difficult cut and paste operation, then worry about page breaks and other formatting issues that bother the recipient.

You can solve this problem with an e-mail widget, but be forewarned: An e-mail widget is actually a smallish task like those described in Chapter 8. It takes planning, work, and testing to make this work well.

Consider doing this if you have information on your site that people will want to share — or that you will want them to share. For example, you may want to drive referral sales on your site by making it easy for users to send your brochures to themselves or each other.

The e-mail widget is basically a Web form that supports several features:

✔ **The icon:** Each e-mailable page has an icon and a text message such as "e-mail me" in a similar location on the page.

✔ **Form element 1:** User's e-mail address. The sender has to be asked for his or her e-mail address. Also use this as the reply-to address for the e-mail message you send.

✔ **Form element 2:** Recipient's e-mail address. Where the message goes. If at all possible, support multiple recipients, with the e-mail addresses separated by commas — this is what the large sites do, and users are accustomed to it.

✔ **Form element 3:** *Prepended* message (a message that precedes the article). Give the user a chance to write a brief introductory message that you'll put in the e-mail message before the actual article.

Chapter 9: Designing Great Content Pages

- **Extra features:** You can give users a checkbox to copy the e-mail message to themselves. You can allow the user to sign up for additional things such as a newsletter. You can offer to let the user send just a link to the article instead of the full article. (Most people would rather have the article.)
- **Privacy policy:** Briefly state your privacy policy for this activity; the user-friendliest one is that you promise not to use the e-mail addresses that the user enters for any purpose except sending the e-mail message.
- **Nirvana version:** The best implementation we can think of would show the user the fully addressed and assembled e-mail message in the form in which it will be sent to the recipient, along with the option of copying the message to user.

Sun Microsystems uses a very simple e-mail page on its site. Each product description includes a link to a datasheet in PDF format, a link to a printer-friendly page, and an e-mail icon labeled "E-mail this Page." Figure 9-6 shows the form Sun uses to let users specify where to send the e-mail. You can launch with a simple e-mail feature like this one, and then add features as users or internal needs require them.

Figure 9-5: Built-e offers printable versions of most pages.

Part III: Creating Usable Web Pages

After you've gathered the information from the user, you'll need to create a computer program that gathers the data and sends out the requested e-mail. Test this relentlessly, but don't be scared off from offering the feature: this is a very valuable capability that makes the information on your site more flexible and more usable.

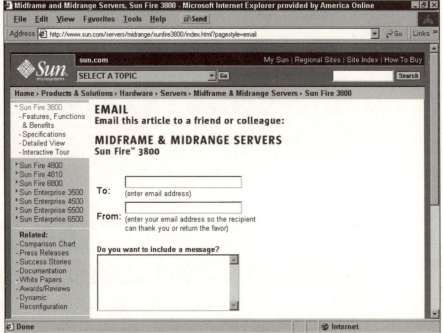

Figure 9-6: Sun uses a simple e-mail form.

Reprinted by permission of Sun Microsystems, Inc. Copyright © 2001 Sun Microsystems, Inc. All rights reserved.

Part IV
Reaching a Broad Audience

In this part . . .

This part shows you how your site can meet the needs of a wide variety of users, including people running various kinds of computers and people from countries around the world. After you address all of those needs, it's time to test. This part also tells you how to test usability in many different ways, from using site logs to see which tasks get completed to sitting users down in front of a computer and watching them try to get things done on your site.

Chapter 10

Broadening Your Site's Appeal

In This Chapter

▶ Dealing with different hardware and software
▶ Making multimedia usable
▶ Going global
▶ Empowering disabled users
▶ Supporting power users

*W*eb site design has been the topic of many spirited ongoing discussions, including one that affects all Web designers and users: taking advantage of new technology versus reaching the widest possible number of users. Most software developers have been in the new technology camp, wanting to create and use Web sites that take advantage of fast connections and the most advanced features found only in new versions of Web browsers. This approach often leaves many users, who lack fast connections and the newest versions of Web browser software, behind.

Usability advocates, not unreasonably, want to go the other way and make sure that Web sites work for all users, including those with slow connections and older browser versions. Some usability advocates, though, go to extremes, and will "dumb down" a Web site so that it's uninteresting and unattractive to most users, just to make sure that absolutely no one is ever excluded from using it. Such an extreme viewpoint neglects the fact that an attractive layout is positive for usability as well as for aesthetic value, even if that attractiveness comes at some cost in performance.

For the most part, we side with the usability advocates — and so will you after the first few times you have to deal with angry or, worse, heartbroken users who can't access your Web site using an old computer, a WebTV unit, the latest version of Linux, or some other non-mainstream system. But we also acknowledge that business and practical considerations, not ideology, need to drive your decisions. In this chapter we take a look at all the different audiences you may need to reach and tell you how to do what needs to be done — within reason — to reach them.

Dealing with Different Systems

Nowadays, a mainstream computer is a PC with a fast Pentium processor — over 500 MHz — with 32 MB of RAM and several gigabytes of hard disk space, a monitor with 1024 x 768 or better resolution displaying thousands of colors, running Windows 95 or better, and with Internet Explorer 3.0 or a more recent version of Internet Explorer as the browser. Life for usability experts would be much easier, though perhaps less interesting, if all users had a system with at least these characteristics.

The truth is, though, that the site(s) you work on are going to have to deal with a complicated world. There are almost as many different computer hardware and software setups as there are users. And those users will blame you, not their computer setups, if your site runs poorly on their system. (After all, Yahoo! runs fine on their computer; why shouldn't your site?) Let's take a look at the different kinds of hardware and software elements you may have to deal with and how they affect usability.

Dealing with different hardware

The main reason that the Web became so popular is that it runs on all different kinds of computer hardware. Early Internet and Web users were willing to install software and even, in some cases, to run different operating systems in order to get online, but few of them were willing to change their hardware. So the ability of people to use the Web on different kinds of computer hardware has been critical to its success.

Let's take a look at the different kinds of hardware that you may run into — except for monitors and display subsystems, which we describe separately in the section "Dealing with different monitors" — and how far you should go to address hardware-related usability issues:

- **Computer workstations.** Computer workstations are powerful computers that typically run the Unix operating system. Fewer than 1 percent of all computers in use are workstations running Unix and, more important, workstation users often see it as their problem if they can't access your site, not yours. Unless your site has a very tech-savvy audience, you don't need to test on, or worry much about, Unix workstation support.

- **The Macintosh.** The Macintosh once made up more than 10 percent of computer sales, though that number is now down to 3 to 4 percent. But you can't ignore the Mac: its users are somewhat numerous, extremely vocal, and well-represented among journalists and industry analysts who may criticize you publicly if they can't run your site well. Yet some

Chapter 10: Broadening Your Site's Appeal

pages look really odd on certain browser versions running on the Mac, and some software (especially from Microsoft) that does cool stuff on a PC doesn't work as well or at all on a Mac. Despite the inconvenience, you need to test your site on a Mac and be responsive to concerns raised by Mac users.

- **Slow connections.** The toughest usability issue for Web site designers is pleasing users with slow as well as fast connections. And little wonder — connection speed varies by more than ten times among users and dramatically affects users' Web-surfing experience. Even users with fast connections sometimes experience Internet or local network slow-downs that reduce their connection speeds to a crawl. As mentioned throughout this book, you need to keep your Web pages small in total file size — 25K is a good maximum for most pages — in order for them to work well for users with different kinds of connections.

- **Slower PCs.** Computer processor speed affects overall page-loading speed, especially if a page has lots of images — JPEGs in particular require some processing power to decipher. But many users have no idea how fast their computer systems are and think that your site is buggy if it loads slowly on their slow PC. You should test on a low-powered — say, 100 MHz — Pentium to see if there are any undue delays, and be ready for some complaints about page response time if you make your pages extra-complicated.

Users will not change their computer hardware or networking connection just to run your site better, so your site has to have high usability on almost all the systems out there, and acceptable usability — perhaps lacking some advanced features or experiencing some ugliness but no actual usability breakdowns — on the rest.

For example, if your audience is primarily business users with fast connections, you can put large, high-resolution images on your site — but be sure you warn people before they click on a link to such an image so that home users on slower connections can "think different" and perhaps avoid waiting for an image that takes too long to appear.

The corporate user and the home user are often the same person — the "home user" can be a businessperson doing work at home or in a hotel room. Unlike consumers, these users can't just go to a different site if they can't get at something — they need to use the same sites from home or the road that they use at work, even if the site is so slow as to be nearly unusable. Make sure your site works well for "home" use even if your primary audience is corporate.

Dealing with different monitors

Users running different kinds of monitors — not monitors alone but different display subsystems, which combine the monitor and the graphics hardware supporting it — have very different Web experiences. Surfing the Web on a big, high-resolution monitor with a fast display subsystem that supports thousands of colors is much different than logging on via a slow portable with an 800 x 600 resolution screen. Yet Web pages need to work well for both kinds of users.

Making things worse is the tendency of people with Web-related jobs to have large, high-resolution monitors (as well as fast connections). The people creating Web sites therefore have much different online experiences than many of the people in their target audience. They naturally tend to create sites that look good and work well on the systems they and their colleagues use.

True story: One of the authors (Mander) took a group of site designers to someone's home to show them how slowly the site loaded and responded over a typical home 56K modem. The designers, never having tried this, were predictably horrified by the results and immediately began simplifying their designs. Try to make sure that you and others on the site development team regularly try accessing your site via a typical modem.

To create Web sites that are usable for the broad range of users, you need to look carefully at each aspect of display systems that you're likely to run into:

✔ **Low-resolution display systems.** You need to make sure your Web site works very well for people running at 800 x 600 resolution. You also need to make sure that navigation and core content of your Web page are usable at 640 x 480 resolution, though it's acceptable to have non-essential content in a right-hand column that isn't entirely visible without the user scrolling horizontally to see it. Table 10-1 shows the total number of pixels available at various screen resolutions. This is a pretty good indicator of the difference in how much information users are seeing at any one time. Figure 10-1 shows the relative size of various resolutions graphically.

Table 10-1	Pixels Available at Typical Monitor Resolutions	
Resolution	*Total pixels*	*Comparison to 1024 x 768*
1024 x 768	786,432	100 percent
800 x 600	480,000	61 percent
640 x 480	307,200	39 percent

Chapter 10: Broadening Your Site's Appeal

As someone working in usability, you should do much of your own Websurfing, and most of any designing or testing that you're involved in, with your monitor set to 800 x 600 resolution. This gives you a view of the Web most like that of most Web users.

- **Low-color-depth display systems.** Many users surf the Web using systems that only display 256 colors. Many computers, especially older portables, are incapable of more; in other cases, users have set their screens to 256 colors to speed up screen updating, or have used a game program set the color depth to 256 colors and don't know that they need to change it back. With only 256 colors, colors used in graphics can be displayed in very odd-looking patterns. Web graphics pros restrict themselves to the 216 "Web-safe" colors that work correctly on both Macintosh and PC 256-color graphics systems. See *Web Design For Dummies* (published by Hungry Minds, Inc.) for details.

- **Small monitors.** Small screens, such as those on many portables, create their own problems. Many users run small screens at high resolutions, making the type on many Web pages tiny. Others have small screens that only run at 640 x 480 or even, in the case of WebTV systems, 544 x 376. These users will see very little of what you'd consider a full Web page.

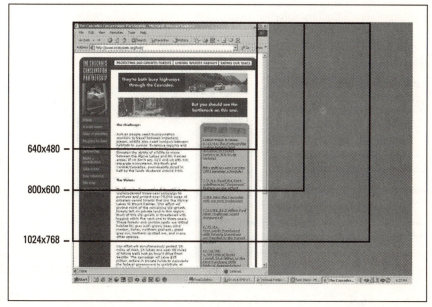

Figure 10-1: Relative screen size at 1024 x 768, 800 x 600, and 640 x 480 resolution.

Part IV: Reaching a Broad Audience

Versionitis reductus

Versionitis — the necessity of dealing with endless new versions of software, in our case browser software — is getting to be a less serious disease. Many corporate IT departments have standardized on Version 4.0 of the popular browsers. Many users have Version 5.x of Internet Explorer because it came with their computers, but from a Web designer's point of view, it's not that different from Version 4. Netscape skipped Version 5 of Navigator in an attempt to move the version number ahead of Internet Explorer's, and Version 6 was buggy and little-adopted. So you can keep your main development focus on Version 3 and Version 4 of the popular browsers, on both Macs and PCs, with extra testing at the end of all the versions from 2.0 up so you can learn about and fix any specific problems.

The wide variation found in display systems creates a very difficult situation for Web designers and usability pros, who would like to create attractively laid-out pages for most users only to find that the resulting pages are inaccessible to some. Do some research into your user base to find out if they are more prone than others to have small or low-resolution screens and then pick a design point — usually 800 x 600, with graceful degradation at 640 x 480 — and stick to it.

Don't forget to test at the low end of your design target. Many companies that have a lot of money invested in Web site development simply have no way to test what a site will look like from a typical home setup; access from outside the company is blocked during development, and for some sites it's never allowed except through special, secure connections. This means it's very hard for developers to even get a look at their site on a slow, small-screen — that is, normal — computer system.

Work hard to set up a PC with a modem that you can use to access your site while it's under development. Set the screen at 800 x 600 resolution and 8-bit (256 color) color depth. Work through your site while it's in progress and review the design. Make sure that important controls are visible, check on the speed of the site, and work hard to get appearance as well as performance to an acceptable level on this system.

Dealing with different software

There are some software differences that are also hardware differences, so we've dealt with the differences between Unix-based workstations, the Macintosh, and PCs in the hardware section above. But what about software differences on specific platforms?

The main variations you have to work with for usability purposes are 1) different versions of Microsoft Windows, and 2) different browser versions. Almost all Web users on PCs run Windows 95 or greater because it's been out almost (but not quite) as long as the Web has been popular; later versions of Windows are very similar to Windows 95, so you don't need to worry much about that. The main differences you have to worry about are among browser versions and the various levels of support they have for HTML, for JavaScript, and for multimedia.

✔ **Netscape Navigator (the original).** NCSA Mosaic was the first widely used browser, but it was quickly swamped by the first version of Netscape Navigator, a fantastic piece of software for its time that made using the Web easy and fun. Navigator is a lot like Internet Explorer, the current leader, but it has some differences — especially on the Macintosh, where it held its lead longer. Make sure that your Web pages are usable on Navigator 3.0 or higher (and not just on Internet Explorer) on both the Macintosh and PC.

✔ **Internet Explorer (the new champion).** Microsoft's Internet Explorer (also known as *IE*) took market leadership from Navigator a few years ago and never looked back. IE is great for Web developers because it's so popular and because it supports ActiveX controls, described below. While you need to check usability on all versions of IE from 3.0 upward, remember to test on Navigator (above) as well.

✔ **Javascript extends the browser.** Javascript is a programming language used to provide common Web page functionality such as second-level navigation that pops out when you roll over it. However, the IE and Navigator versions of Javascript differ from each other, as do versions for different releases of the same browser. Javascript bugs are very ugly — they cause anything from odd error messages to random system crashes — and a major cause of complete usability breakdowns. To ensure usability, you should keep reliance on Javascript to a minimum, test on a wide range of software platforms, and make sure to alert users as to what computer systems and browser versions you've tested on.

✔ **ActiveX controls extend Windows browsers.** ActiveX is a Microsoft-controlled software standard for extending browsers, but it runs best on IE on PCs — it's not fully supported on the Macintosh, and not at all on Netscape Navigator on Macs or PCs (let alone Unix). ActiveX controls, as ActiveX programs are called, download and install themselves smoothly and are more predictable in behavior than Javascript programs. But if your team wants to use ActiveX, you will have to just say no — telling all Navigator users and most Mac users that they can't use the full functionality of your Web site is too big an accessibility hindrance.

Part IV: Reaching a Broad Audience

Scratch 'n sniff the browser?

Many sites use *browser sniffers* — software routines that check what browser is being used to access the site — to determine which of several different versions of a site to show the user.

In our experience, this is more trouble than it's worth. This may seem strange for us to say — we are, after all, consultants who usually like (and benefit from) complexity — but even for us, it just ends up being an awful lot of trouble to maintain multiple versions of a Web page over months and years. It's hard enough to make everything work right on a Web site with just one version; mixing and matching various versions of pages in real-time is just asking for additional trouble.

Though it's tempting to do whatever it takes to serve up the best-looking possible page to users, try to avoid the need for browser sniffers in your site. You'll save yourself a lot of work and possibly a lot of mistakes as well.

One case in which a browser sniffer may be worthwhile is to create a separate version of your site for use on WebTV. Consider this if your site has a large number of WebTV users. (You'll likely find this out by hearing from them via e-mail.) WebTV is so different that it's very hard to create a site that looks good on both WebTV and personal computers. With a browser sniffer you can provide an excellent personal computer version of your site and a reasonably good WebTV version.

✔ **RealPlayer, Windows Media Player, QuickTime and Flash multimedia support.** Multimedia, as exciting and lively as it is, creates many potential problems for the usability of a site. One big problem is whether the user has the correct player application for the multimedia content you put on your site. Various versions of IE and Navigator have included various versions of these media players, and millions of users have downloaded some version or another of one or more of them — a very confusing situation, to say the least. One reason to avoid or sharply limit use of multimedia in your site is that, if you include it, you'll have to support your users in downloading and installing the appropriate, up-to-date player — a big burden for a site to bear. (You can simply refer your users to the site of the maker of the player software, but this leaves many users dissatisfied — with your site, not the player maker's site.)

Usability Notes for Multimedia

Usability for Web multimedia is a potentially huge topic; after all, a personal computer can potentially embody the capabilities of a radio, CD player, television, even a movie studio, all in a single box. Trying to take advantage of all this functionality causes users huge problems. At least one company (the one named after a fruit) made TV commercials making fun of how hard multimedia was to use on other computers.

Chapter 10: Broadening Your Site's Appeal 221

Our #1 rule for multimedia usability is to avoid using multimedia, if at all possible, until the basic purpose of a Web site is well-understood, its goals are agreed on, and the site is up and meeting at least some of its goals. That's because the potential for spending huge amounts of money only to inflict massive usability problems on your users is so high when dealing with multimedia. We both worked together on Apple's Quicktime team, so we're well aware of the potential power of multimedia, but we think it will be some time before it's truly easy to deploy and use on a Web site.

When you do deploy multimedia, use it initially as icing on the cake — not to deliver core content, but as a fun and interesting way to see and hear optional information or entertainment. This approach prevents many of the problems that come from multimedia; if users can take or leave a given piece of multimedia content, it doesn't cause them nearly as big a problem if that content doesn't always work as advertised.

We do have a few observations about the usability of specific types of multimedia that may help you decide when to jump in — and to have greater odds of success when you do:

- **Audio clips.** Sound quality of Web audio varies from awful to not bad. Brief audio clips can liven up a Web site. Just be aware that many users can't or won't play them — they either lack the equipment to do it, they have the equipment but don't know how to turn it on, or they work in a crowded environment and are unwilling to inflict the sound on others. So use audio clips to liven up your site, but if the information is vital to users or customers, always offer the same information in text format.

- **Video clips.** Web video clips make regular TV look great by comparison. Many users can't play them back or, for the reasons stated above, can't hear the audio that goes with the video. Small, jerky, and slow to download as they are, video clips should be used only for optional information, with the same information provided by text. But even with all these problems, video clips can be a lot of fun for the people who can play them back. They can also provide a preview that can inspire users to buy a VHS videotape or a DVD movie, or even get them to go to a new movie in a theater.

- **3D and other multimedia.** There are some 3D formats, such as QuickTime VR, that are supported by existing multimedia playback software; other formats require a special player. Some sites have used 3D to good advantage for showing off products or providing an immersive experience, but these are still few and far between. Consider 3D only if it adds in a major way to meeting your site goals, and make sure the same information is available in other formats — static JPEG images, for example — for users who don't want to try using 3D. Figure 10-2 shows a how the Monterey Bay Aquarium provides a still picture of world famous kelp tank along with a thumbnail on the right provides access to a panoramic QuickTime VR image taken within the tank. Users can click on the thumbnail to access the panorama.

222 Part IV: Reaching a Broad Audience

Figure 10-2: QuickTime VR is a powerful 3D format.

✔ **Flash animation.** Macromedia Flash is an intriguing animation technology that livens up a Web site while keeping download times within reason. However, many users lack the playback software, and the benefit of downloading the Flash software is usually not worth the somewhat mild level of pizzazz that it adds to any one site. Many Webmasters use Flash to create fancy introductory sequences to their site that only interfere with users being able to get to the information or services they came to the site for. In most cases, Flash doesn't add enough to a site to be worth the usability problems that it causes.

Much of the above doesn't fully apply if you've made the decision to create a multimedia section of a site, or a full multimedia site, to meet business, organizational, or creative needs that can't be met any other way. If this is your situation, carefully identify your target market and let your users know what you need them to have in order to fully use and enjoy your site. This kind of advance notice will do a great deal to keep users happy. If you're providing enough value, some of your users may even be willing to upgrade to the specifications you spell out, as long as users know what they are.

Chapter 10: Broadening Your Site's Appeal   223

Intranet and extranet usability

An *intranet*, just to be specific, is a Web site intended for use only within a company or other organization; an *extranet* is a Web site intended to be accessed by users at partner companies, for example to conduct business-to-business purchasing or to check order status. A *public-facing* Web site is a typical World Wide Web-style Web site that anyone can access.

Usability considerations for intranets are just as demanding as for public-facing sites, though intranets often get far less attention. For most companies, no audience is more important than employees, and serving them well with an intranet can save all concerned tremendous amounts of time and trouble. Partners, executives, and other "insider" users of these sites are important, too.

It's fun to do usability work for an intranet because most users have fast connections and most have relatively standard hardware setups. So you can push the envelope a bit in terms of page design, functionality, even multimedia. You can even use an intranet site as a testbed for possible advanced features for a public-facing Web site.

Usability considerations for extranets, on the other hand, sometimes focus around eliminating Web usability as a concern. That may sound funny in a Web usability book, but here's why: Many tasks performed by people using an extranet can be made into automatic tasks handled with little human intervention between machines. Taking the user out of the equation completely is the ultimate usability coup. Another use for an extranet is publishing information that people at partner companies need. However, this function can sometimes be accomplished just as well by using automatically generated e-mail updates, again reducing the amount of effort humans have to expend to get needed information.

Going Global

Both the authors of this book have significant overseas experience — one (Mander) is a native of New Zealand, the other (Smith) grew up partly in Australia. And each of us has been involved in international business, both in the "real world" and on the Web. So we're well aware of the need of businesses to operate in a global environment and to adapt to specific countries in which they do business. However, we're also aware that half-hearted — or worse, underfunded — efforts to serve the needs of a global audience can be worse than no such efforts at all.

Every Web site is automatically a global site — it is the "World Wide" Web, after all. For better or worse, there's nothing you can do to prevent your site from being visited by anyone in the world with Internet access. This is not always positive — companies that have different prices for their products in different regions, for example, have a very difficult time selling on the Web because it's nearly impossible to enforce geographic restrictions on pricing online.

Most U.S.-based companies can go a long time — even, in some cases, forever — with an English-only, U.S.-centric Web site. This applies even to companies that do a fair amount of business overseas. English is still the language of the Web, and a surprising number of non-native speakers either know English fairly well from school and work or have learned enough written English to be able to puzzle their way through an English-language Web site. There are even free Web services like the Babelfish service on AltaVista that will provide a rough translation of Web content into a wide range of languages, further helping non-English-speaking users get by.

If you want to try Babelfish, go to `babelfish.altavista.com`.

Sun is one of many American companies that makes many of its Web sites and specific Web content available in many different languages and even in country-specific versions. Figure 10-3 shows the French-language version of the Sun Switzerland site; there are versions for Switzerland's other languages as well.

English is also the first or second language of most journalists, analysts, government officials, and other decision-makers who use the Web to understand what's going on in the world. Whenever a company or other organization makes news — willingly or unwillingly — the world press needs to be able to access an English-language Web site for background and, hopefully, ongoing updates on whatever's happening. So while it may be of secondary importance for an English-language site to be translated into other languages, it's very important for sites in other languages to have a Web site in English.

However, many organizations have a strong need to reach non-English-speaking users and will have to implement one or more non-English-language versions. Carefully consider the details below before planning how to create a highly usable Web presence in another language.

Doing a "quick and dirty" translation of your Web site into another language and putting the result on the Web is almost certainly worse than not doing internationalization at all. Don't let your organization join the many that have embarrassed themselves and alienated, rather than impressed, non-English-speaking users by doing a poor job of preparing a translated site. Do a careful job of translation, but also of true internationalization — taking into account the culture and preferences of the country or countries in which your translated version will be used. If you lack the requisite expertise in your company, hire a consulting firm to do the job — and another consulting firm, or a savvy local or two, to check their work before you go live.

Chapter 10: Broadening Your Site's Appeal 225

Figure 10-3: The Sun never sets in Switzerland.

Reprinted by permission of Sun Microsystems, Inc. Copyright ©2001 Sun Microsystems, Inc. All rights reserved.

About international users

The United States is the only large country in the world wherein more than half of all households are online, and thereby the only one in which the Internet is truly a mass medium. In other countries, to varying degrees, the Internet is still used more by the young, male, and well off than by the population at large. (The same was true in the U.S. until recently.) This has a few important implications when considering internationalization efforts:

- **International Web users are really sharp.** Web users in other countries are often among the best-educated and brightest people in their countries, and they've often gone to a lot of effort and expense to be online. Don't waste their time with a bad site. Better that you make your English-language site highly usable — many international users will be able to struggle through it — than that you do a poor translation of an old version of your site so you can call your Web effort international.

- **International Web users are accustomed to English.** Throughout the PC revolution, international users have had to deal with computer software and manuals that are mostly or entirely in English, as well as English-language Web sites. One of the authors (Smith) still remembers an early-90s visit to a Japanese software store in which software was available in every conceivable mix of straight English, straight Japanese, English software with Japanese manuals, mixed English and Japanese screen instructions and manuals, and every other variation. Many PC users are accustomed to working their way through or around a certain amount of English.

✔ **International Web users are hard to pin down.** International Web users are a mobile and sophisticated group. Residents of other countries travel much more than Americans, and young, well-off Web users travel more than their peers. Even current Web conventions like representing a German-language site with a German flag are simplistic; German-speaking Web users may be Austrian or Swiss in nationality and may at any given time be living in or visiting almost any country on Earth. The older, more stable burgermeister who has rarely left Germany is not yet on the Web, even if his American counterpart is.

✔ **International Web users expect the best.** When looking at content in their own language, international Web users have an odd view of the Web. They either visit carefully translated versions of truly excellent sites, like Yahoo! and Amazon.com, or truly home-grown sites conceived as well as written within the context of their own language and culture. So an outdated, badly translated version of part of your site is not going to impress most international users, no matter how much of a struggle it was for you to create it and put it up.

The upshot of all this is, again, that the typical American strategy of giving non-English-speakers some translated content and nothing else doesn't work well on the Web, if indeed it works well anywhere. Before going international, you need to carefully strategize your overall approach as well as what you'll do within each country or language group, even if the audiences you're trying to reach are quite small compared to your English-language audience.

Have your full international strategy worked out before you create your first non-English-language Web site because things get complicated fast. For example, your French customers will probably not appreciate it if you do a Spanish-language Web site and not a French one, even if you do have twice as many Spanish-speaking users. Be ready to reveal just when you expect to have that French-language site up and ready — or at least have a carefully crafted explanation on your site as to why you did the Spanish-language site and not a French one.

Usability and internationalization

Now that we've told you all the potential problems, there definitely is a case to be made, from a usability point of view, for translated and localized sites. Users whose English skills are less than the best are certainly going to feel more comfortable working in their own language. They're likely to make fewer mistakes, be better able to recover from the mistakes they do make, and feel more satisfied with the site overall if it's in their own language.

Chapter 10: Broadening Your Site's Appeal *227*

Testing international sites

Part of the reason for thinking carefully before you create translated versions of your site that are localized to certain markets and/or countries is the tremendous amount of work involved in getting it right. Even though the site may be reaching a much smaller market than your main site, it still has to be just as up-to-date and accurate as your main site or you risk doing more harm than good by having the site at all.

The testing process is where you may catch a number of problems that otherwise would have reduced the value of your site in reaching international users. Use the testing process to look at your site very broadly — look at things like whether you have the URL, layout, and features that a user in your target language and/or country would expect, not just whether the links work. Spell-checking and grammar-checking take on extra importance here.

Have someone familiar with the specific dialects of a language used in your target area check the site; broadly used languages like Spanish vary even more from country to country than does English between, say, England and America. Chinese has multiple dialects, and if you choose to use only one, you may irritate the hundreds of millions of Chinese who speak the others. These are the kinds of issues you should consider in testing, if not before. See Chapter 2 for a list of the number of users online for each major language group (but be aware that such lists don't address differences in dialects).

However, international users are on the alert for differences between the site they're using and the English-language version of a site. And all the usability advantages we just described erode quickly if a site is incomplete, out of date, or poorly translated. Little things, such as misspellings or seemingly minor mistranslations, count for a lot — and it's just those little things that are so hard to get right and to keep right as the translated version of a site is updated and improved over time.

So, for each translated version of your site, you need to be ready to make a usability effort that's sufficient to catch and address any problems, preferably before the site is launched. (As with the English-language version, the "buzz" about your site will form very quickly after you launch and be quite hard to change afterward. So get it right before you launch it.)

Internationalization is an issue for your main site as well. If you're using an English-language site to support significant international business, you can take steps to support international users without launching entire new sites. Add translated documents in the languages that are important to your customers to your site. Link to them from the front page of your site — even if you can just give up a few dozen square pixels for one or more of those little flag icons — so users don't have to use English-language navigation to get to content in their own language.

If you take care to avoid offending people in your main target market, it's unlikely you'll give great offense to people in other areas. But if you push the limits of good taste, as you understand them, in your home market, you risk deeply offending people in other areas who may have stricter or just very different cultural or religious standards than you do.

Empowering Disabled Users

Much of what you do in making your Web site usable for all your site visitors makes the site more accessible to disabled users as well. Investing a moderate amount of additional effort in considering the needs of disabled users may open your site up to many people who would otherwise encounter great difficulty in using it.

The lowered curbs found at street corners throughout the U.S. are a good "real world" example of this. This lowered curbing, placed to make it easier to navigate the streets in a wheelchair, also makes life easier for skateboarders, bicyclists, and anyone whose knees or back are less flexible than they used to be. Most of the changes that make a Web site more usable for the disabled make it more usable for the population at large, and vice versa.

The term *disabled* is a bit too narrow here for our purposes. Many users who don't consider themselves disabled still have physical challenges that make it difficult for them to use some Web site features. Some of the tiny text that you find on the Web, for example, is a challenge to any but the sharpest eyes. And the amount of coordination needed to use some kinds of rollover navigation may be considered enough to make for a pretty challenging video game. Paying attention to usability for your broad audience gets you a good part of the way to making it usable for people who fit into traditional disabled categories as well.

The U.S. Government has recently created a set of guidelines for Web site use by disabled people. You can find the guidelines at `www.section508.gov/final_text.html`. Many of them are simply repetitions or extensions of good usability principles. These guidelines are increasingly being used as rules when creating government Web sites and may eventually be required of sites used by government workers as part of contracts with the government — for example, the online FAQ documents used to support software purchased by the government.

People who are disabled use special programs called *assistive software* to help them access computer software as well as Web sites. The best-known type of assistive software is a screen reader program that tells a blind person what's on the screen. Many of the government guidelines are intended to make sure that assistive programs have enough text provided, through ALT tags and other means, to help them interpret complex and highly graphical pages for the visually impaired.

An *ALT tag* is a hidden field within a Web page that specifies what text should be shown when a user has graphics turned off. Modern browsers display the ALT tag content for an image when the user rolls his or her mouse over the image.

Site-level changes

The following government guidelines for access by the disabled apply to Web pages and to Web sites overall (additional rules specific to graphics are described below):

- **Readable without a style sheet.** Web pages need to be readable without the need for their associated style sheet. This means that, while a style sheet can improve the look of a Web page, the page still needs to make sense without it. Check your Web pages for this.

- **Usable without color.** If information is conveyed by color, the same information needs to be conveyed without it. This helps both color-blind people and people with other visual problems, because assistive software has trouble describing color or ascribing meaning to it.

- **Mark tables carefully.** Identify row and column headers for tables, and make sure that it's clear, for tables with multiple sub-levels, which headers go with which data. (Avoiding multiple sub-levels in data tables may make more sense for usability for all your users anyway.)

- **Title frames.** Put titles on frames to make identifying and navigating them easier. For maximum usability, it's probably best to avoid frames in most cases anyway. Chapter 5 describes some appropriate uses of frames.

- **Provide text equivalents to scripting.** Like ALT tags for graphics, provide text in your Web pages that explains what scripts (such as Javascript programs) are doing and offer other ways to get the same information or effect.

- **Provide text equivalents to difficult pages.** Provide an equivalent text-only page when needed, and keep it up to date — but do this only if the main site pages can't be adapted. Disabled people would much rather access the "real" pages of your Web site, even if a text-only equivalent would be easier to access. Such substitutes are almost always a subset of the actual Web site and are likely to become outdated as well.

Graphics and multimedia

Not surprisingly, an additional group of government requirements apply to graphics and multimedia, which are much harder for assistive software to translate than text:

- **ALT tags.** Use ALT tags or other content to fully describe graphics and other non-text elements.

- **Multimedia text.** If you provide text or other alternatives to a multimedia presentation, do so in a way that's synchronized with the presentation.

- **Use client-side image maps.** Use a client-side image map wherever possible; only irregular-shaped areas require a server-side image map. If you must use a server-side image map, provide a text description of each active region.

- **Don't make the screen flicker wildly.** Keep screen flicker between 2 Hz and 55 Hz; higher or lower frequencies of flickering may induce discomfort or even a seizure in sensitive individuals.

- **Keep plug-ins compliant.** If your Web page requires a plug-in or other helper application, that helper application needs to comply with these guidelines as well.

- **Support form completion.** For online forms, make sure all directions and cues are in text and can be read by assistive technology. If a timed response is required, in a form or elsewhere, give the user a way to ask for more time.

- **Skip repetitive navigation links.** Because dealing with navigational levels can be a challenge for the disabled, allow a way to quickly get to highly desired content and tasks.

Supporting Power Users

In the computing world, a power user is someone who is really good at using a computer. A power user of a Web site is a little different. A power user is someone who frequently uses *your* Web site. And often, the power user actually has some power over what happens at your company or organization or with the site itself.

The first thing power users will consider when visiting your site is the basic competence of your organization. If your Web site is bad they'll think poorly of you — period. So if your pages load slowly or navigation is hard to decipher or they can't find a needed fact or even if you haven't posted the latest news within a few hours of when it happens, they'll think your entire organization is run by incompetents.

Chapter 10: Broadening Your Site's Appeal

Power users also like the little things that make a site more useful. Having a form page treat the Enter key as a command to submit the current content and move on is one example. Others are trimming fields and screens that make a process longer without adding much to it and putting shortcuts to your most popular content right on the home page of your site.

Most of the advice we've given you so far in this book is extremely helpful when dealing with power users. A fast-loading, well-organized site that's easy to navigate and that helps people get things done will be well-received. However, some power users like multimedia and "glitz." Often these requests are appropriate in that they make your site more interesting and exciting. Responding positively to these requests in a way that doesn't interfere with the overall organization and usability of your site may be the best thing to do.

Reporters and other press people

Reporters depend on the Web a great deal. They'll come to your site whenever they're writing about your organization — or the industry or area of endeavor it's part of. Reporters are very facts-oriented and very "now"-oriented. They often are working over slow connections in a hotel room or home office and don't appreciate slow-loading pages. They do like pertinent photos and multimedia clips that let them see or hear from someone they're writing about.

Provide images on your site for press people to use. Provide a set of thumbnail images that give an idea of the content, and then provide high-quality full-sized images linked to the thumbnails. Also provide contact information for reporters to use to quickly get a hardcopy photo as well. And ask them to contact you to let you know when a story about you is coming up!

Making your site usable for the press is extremely important. The easiest angle for a reporter to take on a story is a negative one, and there's no sense in having your Web site make you look incompetent. Luckily, following the recommendations in this book will ensure that your site meets the "are they aware?" test that reporters use in sizing up an organization. Your usability-tested site will help reporters start off with a positive bent toward you.

The most important thing about your site, to a press person, is that it be up-to-date. Press people are very involved with what's happening *now*, and it's incomprehensible to them that others may not be. So making sure all the information and data on your site are up to date is crucial. One outdated product description ensures that a reporter will look askance at anything and everything else your organization has to say.

232 Part IV: Reaching a Broad Audience

Besides expecting your site to be thoroughly up-to-date, press people want to find actual news on your site. This includes:

- ✔ **PR and other contact information.** If your organization is of medium size or larger, you should have a PR contact available during business hours (an hour or two extra on either side doesn't hurt) and have PR contact information easily available on your Web site. If you put up a phone number and an e-mail address and make (and keep) a promise to respond within, say, two business hours to all legitimate press inquiries, press people on deadline will love you forever.

- ✔ **Press releases.** If your organization puts out press releases, you must provide the press releases, or at least links to them, in an organized, accessible list on your Web site. If your organization doesn't put out press releases, it should start — they're a great thing to put on your site. Press people will scan your site's home page and the titles of your press releases and very quickly form an overall opinion about your company. (Scary, but true.) Never put out a press release without linking to it from your Web site. Consider having an area on your site's home page where you can prominently post a link to the latest press release for a week or so after it comes out.

- ✔ **Articles about your company.** Reporters like to know what other reporters think. If your Web site is good, they'll assume that other reporters like your organization, and they will, too. If you have links to positive articles about your organization on your site, reporters will really be inclined to like you — you've just proven that you care what the press thinks, while showing that other people who've researched your organization like it too.

- ✔ **Responses to news stories, rumors, and scuttlebutt.** Organizations often find themselves caught up in a swirl of rumors, online comments, and negative stories — sometimes for good reason, oftentimes not. Reporters will find out about rumors, whether online or directly, and come to your Web site looking for a response. If this kind of "swirl" happens to you, consider putting out a brief press release — usually from the CEO or, if it's a financial matter, the CFO — addressing the rumor in a straightforward way. ("XYZ Corp. denies reports that its VP of Operations is a space alien.") Put the press release on your site. If the swirl is getting more than a little attention, link to the press release from your front page.

- ✔ **Financial results — and summaries of what they mean.** Like analysts and investors, reporters know that financial results are important; but unlike analysts and investors, reporters have little idea what all those numbers mean. Along with any financial information, provide context — let people know whether the investment you just got was a record amount, or typical; tell the reader whether your profits were above, below, or about even with expectations. And don't be overly negative, but do be honest; press people will actually treat your organization better if you set the context for them than if they have to dig up bad news about you themselves.

Ich bin ein Reporter

The late president John F. Kennedy once declared his solidarity with the then-beleaguered city of Berlin by declaring, "Ich bin ein Berliner." In a similar sense, we are all, in a way, reporters. Many people who are not actually reporters will look at news and press releases when they come to your Web site to try to figure out what's going on with your company. People who will look at press info include current and potential partners, investors, employees, and other people who have a strong influence on your company. Serving reporters well means you make your site more usable by all these other "infonauts" who are surfing the Web looking for the latest happenings.

The press loves the press; a reporter's favorite thing to find on a Web site is links to articles others have written about you, along with a link to someone at your organization who wants to hear about the story he or she is writing and who can add it to the list once published.

Industry analysts and investors

Analysts and investors are much like press people. *Industry analysts* are an eclectic group including financial analysts who work for large investment firms, think-tank and analyst company employees, competitive analysts, and a smattering of other folks. Investors range from the person down the block who is thinking of buying a few shares to people who can swing your stock price several points with a single buy or sell order.

Analysts and investors, like reporters, are very much interested in what's happening now. But analysts and investors are almost exclusively interested in financial impacts rather than in product, service, or customer satisfaction realities. They do want to see that kind of news, but they'll almost always be reading between the lines looking for what something means to the near-term financial future of a company. A quarter is a really, really long time to these people.

Figure 10-4 shows investor information as shown in the Investors area of the Web site of SonoSite, a medical equipment company. Note that other important audiences, such as the media and distribution partners, also have their own buttons in the navigation

234 Part IV: Reaching a Broad Audience

Figure 10-4: SonoSite has details for money types.

In addition to the things that press people look for — press releases and new information, constantly updated — analysts and investors have their own expectations:

- **Front-page links to information.** Investors and analysts are, if possible, even less patient than reporters. They expect front-page links to information. This should include, at least, an "Investors" or "Financial information" link in your navigation, backed up by actual relevant facts, and prominent front-page links to any updated information on your site that has a financial impact.

- **Context, context, context.** Industry analysts see the world by industry or major area of endeavor. Individual investors are often frustrated because they know this but don't have enough pieces of the puzzle to understand how one company's progress compares to others with which it can legitimately be compared. If you link to analyst reports or news stories that place your company in context within its industry, you'll be helping set expectations appropriately and making investors less likely to be disappointed by what they should see as positive results.

- **No hype.** Whereas reporters are put off by hype, investors who feel that overly positive statements on your Web site have misled them will call a lawyer. Be sure to avoid overly positive statements and firm predictions on your site. Also look out for words like "dominate" that have antitrust implications.

✓ **Competitive comparisons.** While you don't want to overemphasize competitors, you should make it possible for people visiting your site to find out what the other prominent companies and product offerings in your industry are. Not only investors, but also customers will be more receptive to what you're offering if they feel that they've been able to check out the competition.

Even if your organization is not a public company — or is not a company at all — there are still people interested in its financial health and well-being. Take a look at your site through the eyes of an investor to see whether you've provided the kind of information that will make current and potential partners, investors, employees and others feel good about getting involved with you.

Executives and employees

Executives and other employees of your company or organization are probably the hardest people to gracefully accept feedback from. They have a wide range of opinions, too often based on a poor understanding of your customers and goals, let alone usability imperatives. And, frankly, it's hard to hear criticism of your work from colleagues, let alone upper management. "Your" Web site is the most easily accessible and detailed public face of your company, and it's bound to attract criticism — hopefully, but not always, in a constructive vein — from people you work with.

Luckily, most of the things we suggest in this book will make executives and fellow employees happy, just as they will mainstream users of your site. Maybe even more so — it's a real relief for a member of an organization to find that their Web site avoids the major usability problems common on so many sites. Relentlessly improving your site so it works best for all users will have a positive effect on the opinions of coworkers as well.

Focusing on users also gives you a positive way to deal with the innumerable suggestions you're bound to get from executives and fellow employees as well. First of all, be sure to take down these suggestions and put them in your database of problems. Employee and executive feedback is important in and of itself, and often insiders can give you clear, well-stated, detailed descriptions of problems that you may have needed a lot of time and effort to discover any other way.

But you can also use the process to protect the process. Make clear to anyone making suggestions that you take in a lot of input before changing the site and that you have a well-defined process for identifying, ranking, and implementing the most important suggestions each time you revise your site. Let them know that your respect for them is genuine, but doesn't extend to any special boost for their ideas when you're considering changes. They'll go in the same hopper with other feedback that you get.

You may have to go a little farther to work constructively with executives. Many times executives have ideas that they have trouble stating clearly, especially not until they see a mock-up or even a live Web page that they can react to (meaning "that they can criticize"). Be ready to go through a cycle or two of build, get reaction, and respond before successfully implementing an executive's idea on your Web site.

Then the executive's idea gets put through the same sieve as everyone else's: Does it help you reach the site and business goals that you've set? By focusing on your goals, as we suggest in Chapter 3, you give yourself an objective metric for measuring the success or failure of all the ideas you implement. Keep track of how well new content and services on your Web site "perform" so you know what's worth additional effort as you move your Web site forward.

Don't ignore executive feedback. It's tempting to just smile and nod when you get executive feedback and then ignore it. Don't do that. Executives are busy, and the thing that drives them most crazy is to feel like their input wasn't heard. Good executives would much rather hear "We decided not to do that" than "Whoops — we forgot." Treat executive feedback as important — track it and let the executive know whether or not you decided to include his or her suggestion, and why. This will build trust that will help you get the support you need for the next round — and prevent embarrassing "stop the presses" hassles when you're about to launch a site and your favorite executive notices that her suggestion was "forgotten."

Chapter 11

Testing, Testing, Testing

In This Chapter

▶ Performing the user test

▶ Testing Web sites, both unpublished and "live"

▶ Crafting a prototype

▶ Testing competing sites

Testing is the *sine qua non* of usability — the core part of the usability process, and the part without which none of the rest really works. Testing tells you how well your Web site is working for real users and gives you guidance on how to improve it. *Usability testing* is the whole range of ways that you can test your site, and we discuss it in depth in this chapter and the next.

Out of the many ways in which you can test your site, the main method we recommend is simply called a *user test*. In the usability business, a user test means bringing in several people who are representative of your intended customers and having them try to use your product. Each user says what he or she is thinking while trying to accomplish tasks on your site.

It's simply amazing to see the kinds of problems people have with all kinds of products. Things that seem obvious to the people who create products are very often downright mystifying to users.

A user test is the most powerful method of usability testing. Why? Because it comes closest to allowing you to capture the actual experience real users will have in using your Web site. And by asking people to talk through what they're thinking as they use the site, you're able to understand what is really going on in people's minds — and how you may improve the site to make it more usable.

In this chapter we describe the basics of a user test and the most important variations of the process so you can implement user tests all through development — even in early stages when you don't yet have even a working prototype of your site. User testing allows you to get close to the "right" design faster and more effectively than anything else you can do during the site development process.

Part IV: Reaching a Broad Audience

Usability testing saves time and money

The most common reasons given for not doing usability testing are "we don't have enough time" and "we don't have enough money." In most cases, usability testing actually saves time and money. We've heard companies and other organizations that use usability testing results in their project planning rave, time and time again, about how much easier and faster it is to get project work done after usability testing has helped get the ball rolling.

Not all of a project's time is spent, as you may have assumed, in having skilled professionals — your organization's employees and consultants — doing things they're skilled at. Instead, a great deal of time is spent in having these same professionals try to figure out what they should be doing — something they're not very skilled at. Besides the time spent making decisions, or waiting for decisions to be made, additional time goes into rework as new people weigh in with alternatives. What one person considers completed work, others consider an experiment to be reconsidered and redone as more people see it and are exposed to it.

Senior managers are often the worst at this. They tend to be visually oriented people and are almost always pressed for time. As a result, they tend to have a hard time giving their ideas, input,

and constructive criticism during a project's planning stages, which is when it's most needed. Instead they don't react until the product is, in the opinion of the people creating it, nearly done. When they can actually use the product — the Web site, in this case — they tend to a) not like it and b) want it redone, to a greater or lesser extent, immediately. This process drives everyone nuts, from the senior managers themselves on down.

Usability testing does two things. It tends to make the Web site actually work better, so negative feedback at each stage is likely to be less. And it shows what the problems with the Web site really are from the user's perspective and not from the perspective of insiders. This means that you're likely to get less criticism from insiders — because the site will actually work better — and that the criticism and suggestions you do get can be weighed against what actual users said was needed. Usually the user opinion wins.

How does this save time and money? Simple — projects become much simpler when the people doing the work have a reliable, external source of input as to what they should be doing. And projects tend to end neatly when everyone involved understands that the most important opinions — those of actual users — have been incorporated into the project from the start.

However, user tests aren't your only source of usability information about your site. They're a powerful tool to help you learn how to improve your site. But user tests, because they test only small groups of users and are only semi-structured, aren't statistically valid. You'd need to run a user test on hundreds of users — and use more structure and less interactive discussion with the users — to have a chance of attaining statistical validity.

Other testing methods, such as using site statistics to see what hundreds or thousands of users are actually doing on your live site, or surveying people on- or off-line, are good for other parts of the process and for achieving statistical validity in results. We describe these additional methods in the next chapter.

Doing Usability Testing

In our work with our clients' customers, we are constantly reminded of how badly designed many Web-based products are and how nonobvious many Web interfaces are. User problems with today's Web sites are more the norm than the exception.

Usability testing is, more than anything, a way of looking at things. If people involved in the project could forget what they already know, much of user testing would be unnecessary. You could simply tell yourself "think like a novice user," start using a working site or a prototype, and immediately run into most of the problems commonly encountered by novice users. Then you could remember all of your expertise again and start figuring out how to solve all the problems "newbie you" just encountered.

As you work in usability testing, some of this may actually happen to you. You are likely to develop two complementary abilities: an expert's ability to recognize common problem areas on a site and steer around problems, as well as — if you're lucky — the ability to achieve "beginner's mind," a state in which you forget some of what you know and see things again as a beginner would. As you develop these abilities, you'll be able to help a Web design effort avoid common problems and even some uncommon ones. Design work that you're part of will get toward its goals much more quickly.

However, the ultimate resource on what a product is like for a typical user is always the same: actual, typical users. No matter how much you learn — or how much you are, when needed, able to forget what you've learned — you'll always need to go back to real users and try out your Web efforts on them.

What a user test is

A user test is a specific type of usability test. It's a structured session in which individual users are given the opportunity to try to accomplish tasks with a product — for our purposes in this book, a Web site. The purpose of the user test is to identify problems in the user's ability to complete the assigned tasks.

The term "user test" is a bit controversial; some people prefer "usability test" because it doesn't imply that the user is what's being tested. Trouble is, the term "user test" is very, well, useful — people know just what you mean when you say it. So we'll keep saying "usability test" in this book to mean any kind of usability check, and "user test" to mean a structured session with real users.

There are all sorts of things a user test *isn't:*

- **A test of the user.** A user test is a test *with* users, not a test *of* users. The purpose is not to find out how good users are; it's to find out how good the Web site is.

- **A goal-setting exercise.** A user test doesn't tell you what your goals for the site should be — that happens before you design the site, in meetings within your organization.

- **A focus group.** A user test doesn't tell you what users would like to be able to do at your site — that's the purpose of a brainstorming session with users called a focus group, which is often confused with a user test (see the sidebar, "User tests versus marketing focus groups").

- **A traffic-building exercise.** A user test doesn't tell you how to get people to your site — that's marketing's job. (But usability work does help marketing's efforts by making it more likely that people who visit will come back to the site again.)

The user test simply tells you the following: If a user comes to my site with a given task in mind, what problems is he or she likely to encounter in trying to complete it? Identifying problems like these, and fixing them, is the core of the value that usability as a discipline brings to a Web project. So getting approval for and setting up user tests — and analyzing, interpreting, and disseminating the results — is the most important thing that a usability person does.

Figuring out what tasks to test

One of the points in the user test process where the expertise of a usability person really matters is in figuring out what tasks to test. (Try saying that three times fast!) If you are testing an already-working Web site, there are two major areas to consider when looking for things to test:

- **Broken stuff.** A rich source of testable tasks is areas in your site that are known to be difficult for users. Check in with any user support people you have for your site to find out their "hit list" of major problems relating to your site. (Support people often have a cheat sheet for use on the phone or a set of pre-written e-mails that address common problems. These are invaluable resources in identifying problem areas.) Ask people who use your site about their problems. Think through your site yourself and identify the three worst things about it. Using this and any other research you can think of, list the major problem areas.

Chapter 11: Testing, Testing, Testing **241**

User tests versus marketing focus groups

Executives have gotten in the habit of asking for focus group research before committing to a development effort. People doing the actual work, though, often are more interested in doing a usability test. So the most common question that potential customers ask a usability company is this: Should we do a user test or a focus group? It's easy to confuse the two — but also easy to understand the differences.

A focus group — also known as a marketing focus group — is a brainstorming session in which users are gathered together in a room to discuss, *as a group*, various questions that relate to their likes and dislikes. People in them often think focus groups are fun.

Users in a marketing focus group are usually shown or told about a product and asked what they think about it. The purpose is to find out whether users want the product "as is," and whether they'd want it more with certain changes. Marketing focus groups are about measuring, and increasing, *desire*.

Like a marketing focus group, a user test also involves users, but it's a testing session in which users are asked, *one at a time*, to complete specific tasks. People in a user test rarely think it's "fun," but often do enjoy it, because they've been asked for their feedback. (Most of Zanzara's user testing participants volunteer to come back and do another test sometime!)

In a user test, each user is given a product — or a mockup or prototype — and asked to complete various tasks with it. Sometimes users are asked marketing-type questions at the beginning and end, but the purpose isn't really to find out what users want; it's to find out what users are able to do with the product. User tests are about measuring, and eliminating, *frustration*.

User tests and marketing focus groups are similar enough that it's easy to understand why they get confused. Both involve calling up and recruiting current or potential users of a product. In both cases, users are paid — usually $100 or so. Both exercises often involve getting users into a room and having observers sit behind a one-way mirror and watching. But the differences are clear as well.

Focus groups are marketing-focused groups that find out what has to be changed in a product to make people want to buy it. User tests are individual exercises that find out how a product has to be changed to enable people to use it. Web sites generally need user tests more than they need focus groups — but there's nothing wrong with doing both.

✔ **Important stuff.** Refer back to your goals for the site. (You did write those down, as we mention in Chapter 3, didn't you?) Consider your business's goals. Look on your site for areas that involve helping people buy or that involve getting information that supports the buying process. Find areas on your site that help users solve problems with your product or services. Think through the site yourself and identify the three most important things in it. Draw on all these resources to list the most important capabilities.

242 **Part IV: Reaching a Broad Audience**

After you use these two sources to create your overall list of tasks that you may want to test, plot the tasks on a chart as shown in Figure 11-1. The chart has two different descriptions of tasks: Important stuff versus unimportant stuff, and stuff that works versus stuff that doesn't. (At this stage, use your own understanding of your site to identify what works well and what doesn't.) After dividing things up into important or not, and works well or not, you'll have four areas on your chart, each of which requires different action:

- **Important stuff that works.** People tend to test only what's broken, but you should also test the most important of the tasks that you believe work well. You'll often find that they don't work as well as you think they do. And even minor improvements in important tasks yield big results.

- **Important stuff that doesn't work.** This is where a lot of testing gets done, with good reason. Test as many of these tasks as possible. Finding out what it will take to move tasks from the "Important stuff that doesn't work" area of the graph to the "Important stuff that works" area is the most important result you can accomplish in a user test.

- **Unimportant stuff that works.** Leave these tasks alone. If a task is unimportant you can apply the old maxim — if it ain't broke, don't fix it.

- **Unimportant stuff that doesn't work.** It's surprisingly common that certain content or functionality is allowed onto a site with little review because it's considered unimportant — then, when it doesn't work, is simply left there, again because it's considered unimportant. Don't test this stuff, but do consider removing it from the site.

When you've considered the importance of each task and how well you think it works, make a list of the tasks you plan to test. Circulate it among people involved in or responsible for your Web site to get their feedback.

You may also want to generate scenarios for your tasks. For each task, cook up three to four situations in which you could imagine some specific user undertaking the task in their own way. For example, you may imagine a 25-year-old man who just bought your company's high-tech corkscrew but can't get it to work. He needs to get the bottle of wine open before his dinner date comes over. He comes to your site looking for a customer service number and hours because it's after business hours. Will he find the number quickly? Better, can you provide a link to the answer online so he doesn't need to call you?

Scenarios such as this allow you to make tasks much more real and to better identify the key tasks you most need to test. You can also use the scenarios in actual user testing. For example, you can tell a user, "Imagine you just bought our company's corkscrew and can't make it work. You come to our Web site . . . ." Such storytelling gets the user past his or her anxiety about being in a test environment and into helping you with your job of identifying problems on the Web site.

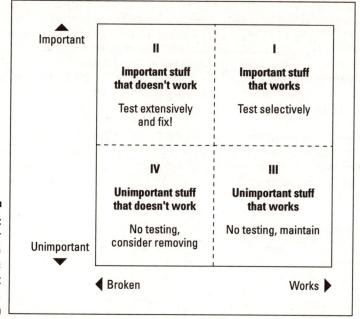

Figure 11-1: Plotting your testable items helps you set priorities.

Anticipating likely results

Part of the art of user testing is setting up a test in the most helpful way possible. Like a scientist, you're basically creating various hypotheses and then testing them. The most interesting hypotheses for user testing are the extreme cases: tasks that users complete easily, and tasks that users have a lot of problems with.

For each task you're testing, imagine what the best and worst imaginable results would be. For example, for a registration process, the best result would be that you get the information you need from the user with a minimal amount of work and hassle on your part or the user's: Users fly through the screen(s) entering their information, proudly hit the Submit or similar button at the end, and then tell you how easy it all was.

For registration, the worst result would be that users have a great deal of trouble filling in the information and that many users fail to successfully complete the registration process. (There isn't much that's more agonizing than watching a user flail about, paging and scrolling frantically around a process that you helped create, looking for missing information or trying to make an error message go away.) But in a way, these are the best results of all — because you've identified a problem area that would have been frustrating to your users for a long time to come if you hadn't identified it.

Part IV: Reaching a Broad Audience

Set up your tests so that the opportunity is there for either the best results or the worst results. For registration, this would mean putting the user in front of the first screen in the process and asking him or her to fill it out. In order to let results happen, good or bad, you'd have to be quiet and not help users while they proceeded, except when asked. (And make a note when they ask — these are areas where the process has problems.) Then see how various users do. You'll quickly know whether you have a good, bad, or mediocre registration process.

One way of subjectively scoring usability tests is to create a best and worst scenario for each test. Then draw a line with "worst" and the appropriate description at one end, and "best" at the other. Assign each user's try at the test a value somewhere between best and worst. (You may also ask users to do the same thing for themselves.) You'll be able to quickly identify the broken, so-so, and highly usable tasks among the items you're testing (see Figure 11-2).

Figure 11-2: Plot your users' experiences.

```
         1   2  3         4    5
Worst ◄----------------------------► Best

Worst: User enters wrong information      Best: User quickly and easily completes
or sees error messages they can't clear.  registration with the right information.
```

User 1: User couldn't figure out how to work the "Mr./Mrs./Ms./Miss" pulldown, got frustrated, entered other wrong information.

User 2: User quickly went through the process but put the city in the wrong box, entered a phone number that our system won't recognize – but got no error messages.

User 3: User successfully completed registration after four retries to fix error messages. Complained that she didn't get to check her entries before committing them to the database.

User 4: User slowly and cautiously worked registration, completed it with no problems. Said there was too much scrolling and paging.

User 5: User quickly worked through registration and completed it with no problems. No negative comments, but no positive ones either.

Statistical significance

Statistical significance is a poorly understood term. It's an important issue in usability testing, however, so it's worth taking a minute to understand it.

If you want to know what users think is the best method of doing something, you would ideally like to ask all your potential users. Then you could say, with authority, "66 percent of our potential users think buying on our site is very easy."

However, you can save a lot of time and money by asking only a small group of your users. The trouble is, does the group you select represent your user base with statistical validity? It depends. You have to trade off among the number of users you ask (more is better), the number of options you offer for each question (fewer is better), and the difference in opinion that you get from users among the options (a greater difference is better). In general, you can get a statistically significant result for a yes/no question from a sample of several hundred users. But you need to get a statistician to tell you for sure what it would take to get statistically significant results for the questions you're asking.

User tests — getting one or more users to try using your Web site — don't yield statistically significant results because they involve too few users. They're anecdotal evidence. What you're trying to find in these tests are specific trouble spots that you may expect many of your users to have trouble with. But you can't credibly use percentages or other numbers that imply any degree of statistical validity to the very small numbers of people involved in most usability tests. Use common sense: If a user test turns up a problem, and you can see how other users may run into the same problem, fix it. But in some cases one or two testers will have trouble with something on your site that most people won't run into a problem with. Prioritize your site fixes accordingly.

Most other usability testing does not yield statistically significant results either. If you put up a survey on your site, the users who take it are people who decide to take the time. These users may tend to be different from your typical user — for example, you may get a large number of students, who have more time on their hands than working people. This can render the results of the survey statistically dubious. You can still use the results; just realize that they may not be capturing the point of view of all of your users.

Site logs, which capture the activity of all users in a given time period, do yield statistically significant results. (If your user base changes quickly in a short time period, you can't project what users did in one time period onto what your fast-changing user base is likely to do in a different time period.) We describe how to use site logs to identify areas for usability improvements in the next chapter.

Testing Web Sites

It's a lot of fun to do a usability test for a real, working Web site. (Whether the site is actually in use by real users doesn't matter much, as long as it works well enough to do a test.) Everyone has his or her own theories about what makes a Web site usable or not. This is your chance to find out whether your predictions about what will and won't work on a given site hold up with real users.

The actual process used in bringing in users and running them through a test is described concisely in Chapter 14. The process in Chapter 14 applies to any kind of Web site usability testing. However, there are differences in the process depending on whether you have an actual, working site to test or a prototype.

Testing alpha and beta sites

An *alpha* version of a site is one that is not yet all that close to being ready to release. It's unlikely to have its final look and feel and may have one or two areas of functionality that don't yet work.

Performing a user test on an alpha version of your site can be very valuable because you get input while you still have time to make changes and fix problems. However, the results of a test on an alpha version of a site need a fair amount of interpretation. Users who run into alpha-type problem areas are likely to get flustered and be less effective in completing any of their tasks. And if the site doesn't have its complete look and feel yet, they're less likely to have a positive opinion of the site as a whole or of any particular area.

Working with site developers on getting a site ready for an alpha test is a real challenge. There is a universal tendency among developers to tell you that a site is more ready than it really is. You only have to go through one user test on a site that keeps crashing to understand how big a waste of time this can cause. Protect yourself and your test subjects by double-checking that the site will be ready enough to test in time. Insist that you get a testable version of the site locked down a couple of days before the actual test. If it's not, in your opinion, "ready for prime time" by the promise date, postpone the test.

Also, make sure the developers leave the site alone during the user test. Developers should resist the urge to fix usability issues they observe. The test is more useful if the site is kept the same for all users.

A *beta* version of a site is "feature complete" — either because all the work got done or because you decided to move some features to the next release. It has its near-final or final look and feel, and has no important areas of functionality that don't work.

Performing a user test on a beta version of a site is easier for the user and more challenging for you. It's easier for the user because the site is nearly "real"; it has fewer rough edges and works better. It's more challenging for you because no one, yourself included, wants to hear bad news about a site just as it's nearing completion. You have to make an extra effort to ensure that you hear everything that users are telling you — and to make the appropriate tradeoffs between pushing for fixes immediately versus supporting the planned launch date of the site, or something close to it.

Working on beta software is also a real challenge. Anyone who gets early access to a site — technical writers, paid testers, even adventurous marketing people — is familiar with the sinking feeling that comes when you find that your long-awaited "beta" is really still in an alpha stage and that no one involved is going to admit it. As with alpha software, insist that the beta version you'll use for the test be locked down a couple of days before the test date. At that point, evaluate it yourself, and postpone or modify your test if needed.

User testing on pre-release sites, whether alpha or beta, is easier on everyone concerned if you have a well-managed site development process. Such a process makes it easier to ensure that the crucial problems discovered in user testing get fixed before the current release goes live — and that the slightly less crucial problems only get put off one release into the future, not forgotten about forever. Contribute to the process by keeping your own careful notes of usability testing results and the work that needs to be done to address problems.

Testing live sites

As we mentioned previously, testing a live site is a lot of fun. Your usability testing work on a live site often helps determine the size, scope, and timing of the effort going into the next release of the site. And you have site statistics and user feedback, described in the next chapter, as additional usability input to help you test the right tasks and put the results you get into context.

Getting developers involved

In testing alpha and beta sites, you will benefit greatly from having one or more of the site's developers watching. They'll notice things that are not working right and may be able to tell you how to get around areas of the site that are not working.

It's often quite difficult for a developer to watch a user test. Developers are problem-solvers, so they want to either explain to the user how to do something or fix the problems in the site right away. They're also personally embarrassed by problems, whether they're "bugs" or usability problems. This makes the test hard for them to watch — but also ensures that they'll keep usability concerns in mind forever after.

We've had the experience of going to lunch after a hard morning of user testing and finding that, while we were gone, a developer has changed the site to fix problems!

You need to educate developers that no one user's feedback is crucial and not to jump to conclusions about what needs to be fixed.

248 **Part IV: Reaching a Broad Audience** _____

When testing a live site, go all-out. Get a wide range of people involved in your learning process about the site's history and goals and in the job of deciding what is and isn't going to get tested. Allocate a lot of time to make sure your results get disseminated to everyone who needs to know about them. Follow up to make sure that as many of the problems you identify as possible are indeed fixed in the next release.

Site developers are especially valuable people to involve in testing a live site. Like other creative people, site developers are usually not the easiest to work with just before a deadline — in their case, in the alpha and beta stage. Between release crunches, site developers can be more open to what users are saying, and contribute valuable ideas on how to solve problems. Things that site developers see during a usability test of a live site will stay with them for months and inspire them to do excellent work in the following release (see the sidebar, "Getting developers involved," for more).

Rapid Prototyping

Rapid prototyping is a fast, repetitive process of creating a mockup of a Web site or other product, getting user and stakeholder feedback on the mockup, and then using the feedback to create a better mockup for more feedback. By the time actual development begins, everyone involved has a very good idea of what the final product needs to be like.

Unfortunately, rapid prototyping is often just used to mean somehow completing the same old clunky development process faster. In this case, the "prototype" is real software, just incomplete. When users suggest changes, the changes either get made slowly because changing real software is difficult — the "rapid" part goes away — or they don't get made because changing real software is so hard — the "prototype" idea disappears.

People who do real prototyping treat it as a completely separate task. For example, car prototypes are made of clay, wood, or as rough computer models. Car manufacturers realize that if they're using their everyday assembly processes to create something, it's a "concept car" — a real car, no longer a true prototype.

How do you know if you're really doing rapid prototyping and not actual Web site development? Real prototypes have the following characteristics:

 ✔ **Looks and feels different.** Like those car prototypes made with clay, a prototype has to look and feel different than a real Web site. A prototype is for inspiring the imagination; if it looks "real," it won't get the right kind of response.

Chapter 11: Testing, Testing, Testing

- **Made with different tools.** A real prototype is made using different tools from the final product. You may not be able to avoid some HTML in a Web site prototype, but if you're writing Javascript, you're probably developing a site, not creating a prototype. If you build your prototype with real tools, you may be unable to avoid the temptation to try to use the prototype as an alpha version.

- **Not made for reuse.** Developing for reuse is a basic element of training for today's Web and software developers. However, a true prototype is thrown away at the end of the prototyping process. The graphics in a real prototype are too ugly, and the HTML too clumsy, to consider reusing them in the real site.

Real prototypes are "noble hacks" that are created in a "quick and dirty" fashion. After you communicate clearly to your developers what you need and why, they'll enjoy the process of creating and modifying prototypes.

Fat-marker prototypes

For Web site development, useful prototypes can be very, very rough. A good usability person can get useful feedback by showing a user a kind of prototype called a *fat-marker prototype* — a prototype created by drawing with a marker on blank sheets of paper. (We show an example of this back in Chapter 2; see Figure 2-3.)

If you can use your marker to write small text, it's not fat enough for a fat-marker prototype.

How many fields should be in a registration process? Should you put all the fields on one scrolling page or spread them out on several non-scrolling pages? You can get useful feedback on these kinds of questions with fat marker prototypes.

Clickable prototypes

A *clickable prototype* is a roughly laid out Web page, or series of Web pages, that model or provide a mockup of a process. You can start a clickable prototype with a fat marker prototype; just scan in the sheets of paper, use HTML to make large areas of the image clickable to different destinations, and let users work through them. The cartoonish look of this kind of interactive mockup sets the right tone in terms of getting users to look at the big picture rather than the details.

Part IV: Reaching a Broad Audience

> ## Working with a testing consultant
>
> As more companies come to see the importance of usability testing, there's increasing use of consulting companies to do usability work. Companies that do have in-house usability staff sometimes turn to consultants for overflow work or for a different perspective.
>
> Using a consultant helps in-house staff stay focused on the big picture: Project management for the site development effort, setting and refining site goals, and making the tough calls about what to keep, change, or drop will keep internal staff very busy just before a site is due to go up. There's a lot of drudgery in making user tests happen, and in-house staff is sometimes better off focusing on the other aspects of site-building. A really good consultant also brings a fresh perspective due to the fact that he or she isn't tied to past practices or existing designs. The consultant also has experience in making top-level recommendations, not just suggestions for detail-level changes, but about how to improve your Web site.

You can also create a clickable prototype in Microsoft Word or, better, Microsoft PowerPoint. These tools produce a somewhat more slick result, but their output still looks much different than a real Web page. If you're comfortable with either of these tools, consider using it to create clickable prototypes. Just going through the process of creating the prototype will make you take a fresh look at what you're trying to do.

Fully interactive prototypes

To create a prototype that's just as functional as a real Web site — maybe even more so — without resorting to your actual Web development tools, consider Macromedia Director. This is an interactive multimedia tool that allows you to do astounding things — including some you wouldn't try using Web development tools because they would be too hard to implement for a mere prototype. Yet the result still looks and feels different enough from a Web page that you can keep thinking about how the process should work rather than details of the site's look and feel.

Competitive Site Testing

After you've earned your spurs by leading or supervising usability tests, you may want to try something different. Competitive site testing gives you a fresh perspective on the usability of your own site and new ideas to use in simplifying — sometimes radically simplifying — how tasks are done on your own site.

Start a competitive site testing exercise by identifying four to six sites that are in a similar state of development to yours and that belong to organizations competitive with, or highly comparable to, your own. Make a matrix of all the elements in your site and theirs — a made-up example is shown as Table 11-1 — and think about the comparison. Are all the elements in your current site and near-term plans really needed? If so, how are some of your competitors getting by without them? Similarly, identify elements in competitors' sites that you lack, and ask yourself if you should have them as well.

Table 11-1	Competitive Comparison: Wristphone Company Sites		
Site	**Dick Tracy Wristphones**	**Wearable Walkie-Talkies**	**Watchphonia**
Home page: What does the organization do?	√√√ "They manufacture and sell wristphones"	√√√ "They make wristphones"	√ "Wristphones? I can see the company makes wristwatches"
Home page: Describe major site elements	√√√ "Products," "Technology," "Company," "Jobs," "PR"	√√ "Users," "Stuff" (products?), " About Us," "Success Stories"	√ "Cool Flash animation, not sure yet what's on the site"
Find company phone number	√√√ "Right there on the home page"	√√√ "Clicked on About Us and there it was"	√ "I can't believe it! No phone number on the site"
Find description of top-selling product	√√√ "I guess they just sell this one thing linked from the home page"	√√ "It was the first thing I saw after clicked on Stuff"	√√√ "Every page shows the product — and a chance to win one!"
Find the dealer nearest me for top product	√√√ "Cool — I just entered my zip code and there it was"	√√ "Easy to find list of dealers by state, hard to find my city"	N/A "No dealers — I guess they just sell online"
Buy top product online	N/A "I would have liked to buy one online — no dealer nearby"	√√ "Cool — buy from a dealer or online. But online buying was hard."	√√√ "Very easy to buy online; wish there were other ways, though"

Part IV: Reaching a Broad Audience

Users versus customers

Traditionally, usability professionals refer to people who use a product or service as "users." However, in many cases it's better to refer to them as "customers." In this book, we're advising people who are creating many kinds of Web sites, such as a university's site, as well as businesses. So we use the more general term "users." However, if you're working on a company site that's primarily about marketing and selling products or services, it's accurate to use the term "customers." Do so when it makes sense — "customers" is a powerful term that quickly gets management's attention, and it reminds everyone involved why it's so important to make the site more usable.

Then the fun begins. For each major element, which of the sites — your own versus the competition — is most usable? Do user testing across sites on elements like finding company information, finding a specific product description, or completing a purchase. Pick two to three examples for each type of element — don't try to test every site on everything.

Competitive site testing is bound to have a marketing aspect to it, so get marketing involved. (If you leave them out, they may resent your whole effort.) Have a marketing person sit in on user tests and participate in analyzing the results. Find out if there's anything they can make happen in the short term to improve on areas of weakness until you can make more far-reaching changes in the site.

The reporting part of a competitive site-testing project is also fun. Middle and senior managers who normally couldn't care less about usability get very involved when there's a competitive angle involved. Expect cheers for the areas where your site is best, and groans when a competitor comes out ahead.

Use the comparison to identify two to three key needs on your site, and put them in the hopper for the next Web site revision — along with needs identified through scanning for trouble spots and identifying areas of crucial importance to your organization. Make sure to compliment the people responsible for the areas of your Web site that hold up best against the competition.

Chapter 12

More Usability Testing

In This Chapter

▶ Testing insiders

▶ Testing by using site data

▶ Looking at a first site

▶ Using surveys and polls

▶ Working with other disciplines

*F*ormal user tests with individual, outside subjects, as described in Chapter 11, are the most important form of user testing for Web site development, but luckily there are a lot of other ways to test as well. Many measuring tools originally devised for marketing or engineering purposes can also be adapted for usability. Even the time you spend using your own site can become a kind of usability test.

In some ways, usability testing is a state of mind as much as a specific set of techniques. If you take on as your main job the task of making your site easier to use for all the people who visit it, you'll find more ways than you can count to improve it.

Unfortunately, you'll also find more ways to improve the site than you can get on the engineering schedule. Working with engineering — which means everyone who is hands-on in creating parts of the site, not just software engineers — is part of the overall art of usability work. So is working with marketing. Getting your stuff put on the schedule — and making sure everyone else's stuff is done right before it goes out —greatly increases your impact on the usability of your site.

Testing Insiders

The formal user testing process described in Chapter 11 is very useful and very powerful, but if it's the only usability testing you ever do, your site will improve very slowly. To improve the usability of your site more rapidly,

254 Part IV: Reaching a Broad Audience

members of the site development team should be thinking about and working on usability all the time. Part of that effort includes small, easy, inexpensive usability tests.

What makes these informal tests easy and inexpensive is that the test subjects are yourself and people around you. The things you learn from informal testing make your site better and your formal user tests more productive.

You can do informal tests opportunistically whenever you have a chance to talk to someone and have access to your Web site. (But you may want to leave certain occasions, like important business meetings and family vacations, test-free.) The people you can ask to help with these tests include:

- **You and only you.** You can actually conduct a fairly useful user test on yourself. The main trick is to not rush ahead when you hesitate or get stuck, but to carefully note areas where you weren't sure what to do — and where someone less familiar with the site than you may do the wrong thing.

- **Testing colleagues and customers.** Coworkers and customers are a lot like you — they understand the overall context your organization is working in and what your site is trying to accomplish. So they'll make fewer mistakes than typical users — any mistakes they do make when you watch them work on your site should go high on the "fix-it" list.

- **Testing friends and family.** Friends and family are great test subjects because they often know absolutely nothing about your site and what it's trying to accomplish. Therefore, they can be counted on to make mistakes of omission, commission, and incorrect submission. It's very painful to watch people you care for stumble aimlessly around your carefully crafted Web site. Take careful notes and try not to cry.

The informal testing process isn't nearly as structured as a formal user test, but some structure is helpful to get the most out of it. In order to make tests on "insiders" useful, follow a few simple rules:

- **I've got a little list . . .** Have a short list of a few areas of your site that you're concerned about. An example of such a list may be: Overall navigation; finding company phone numbers; completing a purchase. If you have a list, you can keep coming back to the same few items, building up enough focused information to be useful.

- **. . . and they'll none of them be missed.** Make sure you test all the items on your list several times. It's easy to focus on brief tasks and on the buying process, but also be sure to look at other areas; overall navigation is one crucial element. A good test for navigation is to ask users to complete a task; then, when they're done, ask them to return to a screen they saw early in the task.

Chapter 12: More Usability Testing — 255

- ✔ **Listen to the user.** Really open your mind to what the user is saying. User complaints usually get one of the following responses: "All you have to do is..."; "We had to do it that way because..."; "That's already on the list to be fixed." Practice seeing these problems as opportunities to learn. Ask the users to tell you more; don't try to quiet them down by solving their problems or by telling them it's already being solved. Even if you're hearing something for the tenth time, keep listening; you're likely to hear a detail or twist you haven't heard before.

- ✔ **Take notes.** Ideally, have a video camera going or a second person out of the user's line of sight taking notes. But in informal testing it's usually just you. Take notes just after the person finishes; if you find yourself missing too much this way, take notes while they're talking. (But beware that people will tend to keep talking about only the things that make you write a note.)

- ✔ **Communicate results.** Let others on the site development team know what you find out as you test users. Just send a brief e-mail note letting them know what happened after each informal test that yields interesting results. This will inspire your team members to focus on the problems you find and perhaps to do some informal testing on their own.

After a certain number of informal tests — say, three tests on some aspect of the site — write a mini-report. This will give you a record to use in improving the site and in doing formal usability testing. Follow up with a meeting to discuss possible solutions; often, there are serious business or engineering issues behind what seem to be simple usability problems, and the group discussion is needed to get action.

When doing informal usability testing or formal user tests, a good technique for testing navigation is to ask a user to return to a screen that came up earlier in the test. But try to avoid asking users to go "back" to something; they'll start clicking on the Back button in the browser window. In testing, you generally want the user to use your site's navigation instead, so ask them to "return to" the page you want them to find.

Testing by Reading Site Data

You can learn a lot about your site — and prove the importance of usability concerns to people who may otherwise be skeptical — by analyzing the *clickthrough* patterns of your site's users. A clickthrough is simply any click that a user makes on one page of your site that leads them to another page.

Web site producers who update content on popular news and entertainment sites fight to get users to click through to their particular pages. Headline text, picture choices, even font and color options are manipulated in order to attract users. Getting people's attention is crucial online, and producers at some sites are getting really good at it.

256 Part IV: Reaching a Broad Audience

For usability, you need to use the same kind of thinking for your whole site — or large areas of it, if it's a big site — that news and entertainment producers do for their specific sections. What pages on the site do you most want users to visit? How can you get them there? (Without trickery or flashing graphics, of course — this is usability, not advertising.) And conversely, when users want to get somewhere and can't, how can you reduce barriers?

Reading site data is a great answer. To get actual, specific clickthrough data for your site takes some tough engineering work, the details of which wouldn't fit here. Briefly, you assign a code to each and every link in your site; then you run a software program that analyzes your Web server's transaction logs and compiles a report of the number of times each link code appears.

If you don't have clickthrough data, you can get a very good idea of how users flow through your site simply by using pageview counts. The Webmaster for your site should be able to easily give you pageview counts for any period you ask for — a week is a good period of time for an initial analysis because it incorporates day, evening, weekday, and weekend use.

A *pageview* is the display of one page of your site on the user's screen. Pageviews may get counted slightly differently by different reporting software because an incomplete pageview — when the HTML file that sets up the overall page gets partly or completely downloaded, for example, but some of the graphics or other files in the page don't — may or may not be included in the pageview totals.

Pageviews and types of Web pages

Now let's look at an example of pageview counts for the home page and the front pages of major sections. Here are a few guidelines for pageview counts on these kinds of pages:

- **Home page.** The home page typically gets about 20 percent of all the pageviews in a typical small site. This percentage can be about the same even if it's occurring for one of two very different kinds of reasons. In a well-designed, interesting, engaging site, the home page gets a lot of pageviews because users return to it as a navigational resource several times during their long visit. In a poorly designed, less interesting site, users come to the home page, click a link or two to see if there's anything interesting, and then go away. In either case, about a fifth of the pageviews go to the home page.

- **Section pages.** A section page is the page the user sees after clicking on a major link in the navigation. Within a section, the section page acts somewhat like the home page does for the whole site — users going through a section of the site may return to the section page to check navigational options within the section. The section page should highlight the most important elements in the section — the ones users are most likely to want and the ones to which you most want to bring users.

✔ **Destination pages.** Destination pages have information or functionality that users want to access. For example, a page with your company's address and phone number is a destination page because users commonly look for this on your Web site. Content pages, described in Chapter 9, are destination pages as well. A page that begins a buying process is also a destination page — not that it's an endpoint, but it represents the user making the decision to at least start the process of buying something.

✔ **Task pages.** Task pages are single pages, or groups of related pages, that allow the user to accomplish some task that requires making choices or entering data. Usually, the goal for task pages is to get as many users as possible who arrive at the first page in a task to finish it.

Example: Zanzara's first site

Let's use pageview counts to analyze a simple site.

We'll use the first version of the Zanzara Design and Research site for our analysis. The current Zanzara site is much different, but you can access the initial version at `www.zanzara.com/old`, where we've posted it as an example.

The front page is shown in Figure 12-1. As you can see, there's a left navigation bar with buttons for five major sections. So users can get to the front page of any section of the site from any other section. This is convenient for users, but makes it a bit harder to track what path users followed to get somewhere. However, when you analyze pageview counts, you can assume that most users go from the home page, into a section, click around within that section, and then go back to the home page again.

The initial Zanzara site was a simple *brochureware* marketing site. The idea of such a site is that potential customers who have heard of a company or organization by word of mouth, by receiving direct mail, or by seeing an advertisement will naturally go to the company's Web site for more information. A brochureware site provides that information, thereby supporting the customer's buying process.

Let's look at the sections of the site:

✔ **Home page:** Brief description of Zanzara. Navigation is left navigation bar and same elements repeated as a bottom-of-the-page text navigation strip. Sections are Company, Services, Designers, Process, Portfolio.

- **Company:** Contact information. The page's text has links to the Portfolio, Process, and Designers sections.
- **Services:** Descriptions of six services. Internal links within the page take the user to a brief description of each service.
- **Designers:** Biographies of Zanzara's two principals.
- **Process:** Six-stage description of Zanzara's process. (An early version of the Usability Design Cycle.)
- **Portfolio:** Projects sub-page comes up first. (These days, we'd do an overall Portfolio page and keep the Projects page as a separate sub-page.) Additional Clients sub-page lists all clients and quotes from several; Papers sub-page lists papers, articles, and pending patents.

This is a fairly robust version of a "brochureware" site — not nearly as robust as the current site, but not bad in terms of meeting user needs. However, it doesn't do much more than provide support for the company's marketing and sales efforts. (To see the current version of the site, go to www.zanzara.com.)

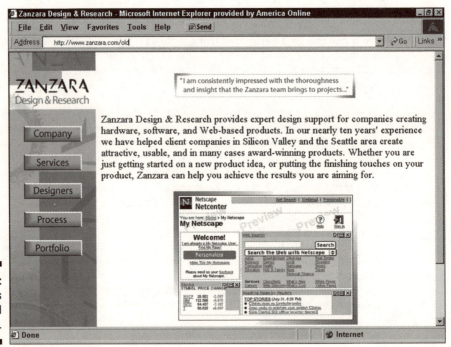

Figure 12-1: Zanzara's site started simply.

Traffic flow on Zanzara's first site

Now let's look at a week's traffic flow for a typical brochure-type site, using the Zanzara site as an example. Figure 12-2 shows a map of all the links within the Zanzara site and a typical week's traffic for each page. Major navigational links are shown as dark arrows; the three links within the site, from the Company page to the Designers and Process sections and to the Clients page within Portfolio, are shown as lighter arrows.

Now let's take a look at what's popular within the site. We know that only the front page of the site was publicized, and there were no major external links to any page in the site, so most users will come first to the home page and then click around from there. As expected, the home page gets the most traffic, but the Company page gets almost as much. We assume that most people visiting the site are coming to the home page first and then going straight to the Company page for the company description and/or contact info.

The Services page is also getting a lot of traffic. This is good because Zanzara wants people to know about its services as part of educating themselves before buying. The Designers and Portfolio page gets less traffic, and the Process page gets far less. Within the Portfolio page, the Projects page gets the most traffic, but this is to be expected because it appears whenever someone clicks Projects. The Papers page gets the least traffic on the site.

In reviewing the site's pageviews, we get a few ideas about ways we may want to improve it to better meet Zanzara's goals:

- **Highlight contact information.** From the pageview totals we guess that people are coming to the site and then going to the Company page to look for contact information. In a revision, we'll highlight contact information for the company's two offices straight from the home page.

- **Highlight clients.** Zanzara's list is very impressive — IBM, Microsoft, and a host of others. But the Clients page is one of the least-visited pages on the site. In a revision, we'll highlight client news on the home page and add a client news area. We'll also rename this section Clients, move Projects and Papers to lower levels, and add the client news area as a subsection parallel to them.

- **Improve the Services area.** We want people to see Zanzara's services, and the area is getting good traffic. In a revision, we'll give each service its own page so we can provide more detailed descriptions.

- **Get more business.** All of the changes so far are designed to highlight "money pages" — pages on the site that are most likely to improve the bottom line. Because Zanzara doesn't sell or do customer support online, the money pages are those that help people understand what's offered and get in touch with the company. In a revision, we'll put a contact e-mail link directly on the separate Services pages. We'll also create an Ask for a Quote section asking someone to enter a brief description of their needs and we'll contact them to get them a quote.

Don't "balance" pageviews. There's a natural tendency when analyzing site traffic to want to be Robin Hood — to want to take traffic from the "rich," or areas of the site that have a lot of traffic, and give to the "poor," the less-used areas of the site. Don't do this — it makes a site less usable. Instead, strive to make the imbalance worse — help users get to key pages in fewer clicks and get tasks done with as few pageviews as possible. That's real usability work.

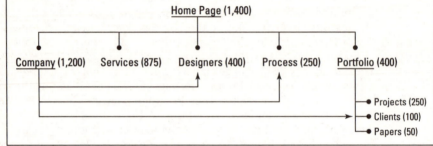

Figure 12-2: The Zanzara site gets solid traffic.

Getting more traffic to a page

After you get the pageview count for the pages in your site, you'll no doubt want to get more traffic to certain key pages — as in the Zanzara example above. Good usability practice sets certain boundaries on what you do to get more traffic to a page; you don't want to trick people (with a misleading link), annoy them (with blinking text or an extra-large clickable "ad"), or keep them from completing a task. What you can do is attract them to the desired area. There are several ways to do this:

- **Linking from the home page.** The most valuable space on almost any Web site is the area on the site's home page and "above the fold" — high up on the page in the area visible to users when they first bring the page up. Putting a direct link to a page in your site increases traffic to it. Make sure that the link text is brief, informative, and interesting without being annoying.

- **Linking from navigational pages.** You can link to a desired page from any navigational page — the section front page for the area the desired page is in, or another section front page, or pages such as the site map or search results pages. Users are presumably on these pages because they're looking for where to go, so for you to suggest a destination is not intrusive.

Chapter 12: More Usability Testing **261**

Hard sell or soft sell?

When you're trying to bring traffic to a specific area of your site, it's tempting to use a "hard sell" approach — maybe create a link that says "Click here for deals!" or some such. Strong sales-oriented language is usually not appropriate for the Web. The Web is a "cool" medium — very informative but not, for the most part, very emotional.

Most company and organizational Web sites are mixed in purpose — combining general marketing information, and possibly investor information, with product, service, and sales components. Again, such a site has to have a calm overall tone. Hype on the selling page doesn't mix well with legalese on the investor's page.

Some sites solve this problem by making nearly the entire site a selling site, using somewhat sales-oriented language throughout, and banishing "official" information to a small corner of the site or even a separate site. (It's often quite hard to find basic company information on such sites, because making it easy to find may interfere with selling.) Unless you create such a sales-oriented site, keep the language and graphical treatment on your site low-key and informative. Even in a selling site, don't go overboard.

✔ **Linking contextually.** If a user is reading a product description, it's not only contextually valid, but also actually helpful to provide a link to information about how to buy that product — whether it's an 800 number to call, a list of dealers to contact, or an online buying capability. Look for other such contextual links, but make sure the contextual fit is good so you keep the user's trust in what you're providing.

✔ **Creating a "Favorite pages" area.** One powerful technique for redirecting traffic within your site to key pages is to create a "Favorite pages" block that fits conveniently in any extra space, perhaps as a strip across the bottom of a page or as a block in the right rail. This makes it easy and fun for users to click around to interesting parts of your site without having to guess on their own what may be interesting, and without having to click every page on the site to see what's there.

✔ **Getting external links.** The overall issue of getting traffic to your site isn't a usability concern overall, so we haven't addressed it here in detail. However, there is one usability concern about the various techniques for getting traffic to your site: they usually point directly to the home page. You can increase the usability of such external links by having them point directly to the page that does what the incoming user wants. Or create a transitional page, in your site's look and feel, that links to areas that fit the interests of people coming to your site from different sources. These techniques help the user and increase traffic to the specific pages in your site that you want to target.

Don't try to run up pageviews for their own sake. Pageviews are not, in and of themselves, a good thing. First of all, they cost you money. Secondly, many pageviews in a typical Web site visit are "bad" pageviews, generated by a frustrated user who hasn't yet found what he or she is looking for. Make your site work better, meaning that each task the user completes takes fewer pageviews. Then try to make more tasks available to the user and work with Marketing to get more people to the site. Then you'll run up "good" pageviews that make users happy and help you meet your business goals.

Finding trouble spots in tasks

You can use pageview data to find trouble spots in tasks. Just make a map of the task, putting the task pages in a row, and see what the pageview numbers are for each page. Wherever there's a sharp drop in pageviews, your site may have a usability problem that's causing users to stop in frustration.

Before looking for the reason for a drop-off, remember that pageview counts measure pages *seen* by the user, not *completed* by the user. So the page that causes users a problem is probably the page *before* the one with lower numbers. The page with the problem gets viewed — but the next page in the task doesn't, because the problem with the prior page keeps users from ever getting to it!

Figure 12-3 shows an example of the kind of map you may make to identify this kind of problem. This map is schematic — you could accomplish the same thing on the wall of a meeting room by taping the actual pages up on the wall and putting the pageview count on each page. Note that it's the page before the drop-off that you have to examine for problems.

Many such problems will be more complicated than our example. For example, the process of buying something often takes multiple steps. You need to look at the total drop-off from the first page of the process to the last, as well as the drop-off at each step.

When you do find a problem, there are two ways to proceed. The first is by trial and error; the second is to conduct a usability study to help identify problems. Both are valid. Try the process yourself; then have several others on your Web site development team do the same. Then meet and discuss what problems you found. Consider putting up a new version of the troublesome page and see if it gets better results.

Also consider conducting a user test, as described in Chapter 11. In a user test you can look at the entire task, with special attention to the page that's causing the drop-off. (You may not want to let the user who's participating in the test know that there's a problem with a specific page, since he or she may then overemphasize minor issues in an attempt to be helpful.) This may give you not only the information you need to fix the problem but also data that helps you strengthen the process as a whole.

Chapter 12: More Usability Testing **263**

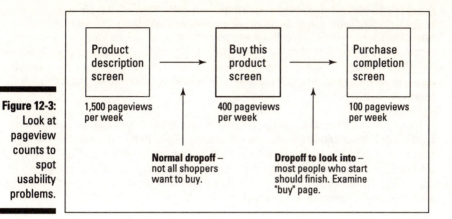

Figure 12-3: Look at pageview counts to spot usability problems.

In analyzing data and doing follow-up testing and repairs, realize that no task is going to get 100 percent completion. In entering a shopping process, for example, users may be looking for information — product information, information about the purchase process itself, or what the final price will be after sales tax, shipping, and other costs. Part of the reason that people like to shop on the Internet is that there's no one watching them if they want to change their mind at the last minute.

Tasks can also be interrupted when the users themselves are interrupted or distracted by outside events. A certain amount of drop-off within a task is unavoidable. What you're looking for when you first use pageview counts to analyze tasks are big problems — things that are preventing many of your users from completing tasks that they fully intended to finish.

After problems are solved, you can use usability data to work with marketing to make selling-related tasks enticing, not just usable. For example, you may find that removing some data entry fields from a task greatly increases the completion rate, and this is likely to be a worthwhile tradeoff. You can even go all the way over to the "dark side," as engineers sometimes call marketing, and employ your usability skills specifically to improve completion rates within tasks that have no obvious, major problems at all. At this point you aren't exactly doing usability anymore, but you're certainly making a difference in the bottom line.

Using Surveys and Polls

Surveys and polls are marketing techniques that can be adapted for usability work. Though the words mean almost the same thing, we'll use the word "survey" from here on out; see the sidebar, "Which is better: A survey or a poll?" for the reason why.

264 Part IV: Reaching a Broad Audience

A survey is a good way to find out people's opinions, but it has its limits as a tool for usability work. A problem has to be pretty firmly fixed in a person's mind for him to be able to give a useful response about it; yet people quickly forget most of the little annoyances and problems that usability people spend their time fixing. That's why you have to listen so closely when doing usability studies — you're trying to get people to tell you something before they forget it.

A survey also forces people to put responses in writing — albeit using electronic ink if the survey is online — and people are hesitant to write things that may make them or others look bad. So even if users know they have a problem with part of a site, they'll be hesitant to say so in a survey. Or, when users do finally say something, they tend to say it with a lot of pent-up anger and hostility, obscuring their point.

Surveys work best for finding out from people what they want. More exactly, surveys work well for finding out from people what they *think* they want — and from that list, the survey also tends to extract only what people are *willing to admit* they want. So you may find some users who are willing to admit in a survey that your registration process is hard to use, but you're less likely to get people asking you to please just scrap the whole thing, even if that's very much what they would prefer.

So use surveys as part of an effort to research what users want in a planning effort toward creating or improving a site. Such an effort is usually done in cooperation with marketing. (For more information on how to work with marketing people, see the section, "Working with other groups," below.)

As a usability person, you can help with both the phrasing of the questions — making sure they're exact enough to map to features that are practical to add to your Web site — and with the use of the answers. If users want to be able to buy on your site, for example, you can work with marketing to help determine what such a capability should look like on your site — then do usability tests starting early in the process to make sure that the solution you end up with really works.

Which is better: A survey or a poll?

The words *survey* and *poll* both mean a sampling of opinion, though each has several other different meanings. You can use the words interchangeably to a certain extent, but the word "survey" sounds a bit more serious. On the Web, a poll is often a partly humorous, fun distraction from news or other information. So call your opinion sampling a "survey" to convey that you mean to use it for a serious purpose. (However, you may also be called on to put on your usability hat and improve a poll — the lighthearted, fun kind — that's not working well!)

Usability and Other Disciplines

Usability is an emerging discipline within Web site development. That means it's fairly new as a separate effort and that most Web sites are still created and implemented without anyone who calls him or herself a usability pro being involved at all.

Usability pros have to establish their role in a site development methodology that has, up to this point, largely evolved without them. That methodology is, in important ways, broken, because so few Web sites meet the needs of their users effectively. But the current participants don't have much interest in saying that the process they've been a part of for so long doesn't work well. This makes establishing the importance of usability work in Web site development a bit tricky.

There are three sets of requirements that must be met in order for a site to work well:

- **User (also known as customer) needs.** The user is, in essence, the customer, and organizations of all kinds are finding anew that treating the customer as #1 works. The user needs that get met, though, are the ones that the specific business or organization is most interested in solving. If the site doesn't meet user needs, use of the site fails to grow or declines, and the site is unlikely to be expanded or even maintained well. If the site does meet user needs, use of the site expands, and the site is likely to be expanded as well.

- **Business needs.** The needs of the business or other organization that puts the site up and maintains it must be met for the site to continue to get funding. If the needs of the business don't get met, the site doesn't grow and eventually is cut back. If business needs are met, the site grows in size and capability. The requirement that business needs be met as a site is developed is often forgotten by usability folks, which is the reason that we've emphasized business-related goals so much in this book. Usability people need to remember to wear their "company hat" and advance company goals as they help the user.

- **Site capabilities.** Both user needs and business needs can only be met within the bounds of what a Web site is capable of doing. A Web site can't read a user's mind, respond to his or her expressions, or talk back and forth with the user (yet). A site can, however, provide easy access to important information and allow the user to do business online quickly and easily. A site that's well designed and maintained to meet both business and user needs is likely to be expanded accordingly.

Part IV: Reaching a Broad Audience

How disciplines work together

Up until recently, these three different sets of requirements — business needs, user needs, and site capabilities — have been addressed by two groups: marketing on the one hand, and design and engineering on the other. In fact, both marketing and design — which is by rights part of the engineering effort — claim sometimes to be the "voice of the user." But both have limits on how far they can go to really listen to the user because of their prior commitments to business concerns, for marketing, and technical concerns, for design.

An important reason for the increasing importance of usability as a separate discipline is to meet the need for someone to truly represent the user — to get user input, in a structured way, and to apply it intelligently to the needs of the business and to the capabilities of the site. Here's how the three groups can best work together:

- **Usability.** Usability takes over the *vox populi* — voice of the people — role, backed by formal user testing, informal usability tests, and accumulated experience. The benefits of usability's role are only gradually accepted as projects are completed faster and have better results with usability involvement.

- **Marketing.** As usability comes into the mix, marketing is pushed back a bit into being more purely the voice of the business. Most good marketing people with whom we've worked find this confusing at first, then liberating. They become much more focused on identifying and meeting the needs of the business, knowing the users' needs are in the hands of experts.

- **Site engineering (including design).** With usability clearly stating user needs, the design group becomes more technically focused, more driven by metrics like page weight, response time, and clickthrough percentages. They also can do a better job on appropriate aesthetics, the "look" of the site. The rest of the engineering group is likewise more focused on problem solving and less responsible for problem definition. Most topnotch designers and engineers find this a welcome change and can do their work faster and better when usability work is done well up front. Later in the process, design controversies that once took up much time and energy can quickly be resolved by getting user feedback.

Figure 12-4 shows the relationship among the three groups graphically. Usability is responsible for user needs and how those needs interact with business needs and site capabilities. Marketing defines and pursues business needs as they interact with user's desires and things the site can be made to do. The engineering group and design team concentrates on making the site do what's needed to meet the needs of the business and users.

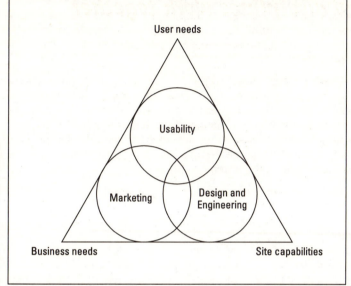

Figure 12-4: Usability, Marketing, and Engineering have to work together.

Hurdles for usability to overcome

Emerging disciplines always have some problems in working with established groups. There are several reasons why this is so. In the case of Web usability, areas of potential friction include:

- **Lack of perceived value.** For any new discipline, people are unlikely to recognize automatically just what value it adds. Usability is, by its nature, hard to define — in fact, the more usable something is, the harder it is to find much to say about it! (Think of hammers, pencils, even TV remote controls.) People think that things that are usable are that way through common sense — and that, because they themselves have common sense, anything they create will therefore be usable. In reality, most technological products that are highly usable have benefited from extensive usability research.

- **Concern about added time and cost.** Usability work takes time and costs money. We believe that the time that usability work takes is saved later in the project, as design and engineering work proceed faster and with less risk. And we also believe that the money that usability costs is more than made up by the site being more effective much sooner than if it had improved only through a trial and error process. But it takes a few positive experiences with usability before people in other disciplines come to believe this.

268 Part IV: Reaching a Broad Audience

- ✔ **"That's Marketing's job."** When it comes to users' desires, marketing views itself as the experts. Explaining to them that usability is more focused on helping users when they *can't achieve* their desires should help. Marketing people are usually the first to come around to the value of usability.

- ✔ **"That's Design's job."** Web site designers, as the ones who best know how to put up a Web site, often usurp not just usability work but also marketing, engineering, even the overall decision-making role that properly belongs to upper management. It sometimes doesn't help that usability people are former designers. It will take a series of usability "wins" to get designers to fully accept that there's a valid role for usability as a separate functions.

- ✔ **"That's Engineering's job."** Engineers should be experts in *how* to build things, but they often end up deciding *what* to build as well. This is actually marketing's job first, and usability's job second. Engineers are usually the slowest to accept a role for usability work — and the biggest supporters when they do accept it. Engineers are typically very much overworked, and anyone who can credibly help them refine the plan for what needs to be built, or brings in new information that helps them choose between two ideas on how to do things, will be viewed as an ally.

As you can see, there is a whole raft of potential problems in getting recognition and support for the importance of usability work in Web projects. We'll talk about how best to work with various groups below. But here are a few general rules for getting acceptance for the role of usability:

- ✔ **Don't be a jerk.** It's easy to get frustrated by the number and size of the usability problems in a typical Web site and to sound dismissive and arrogant when you talk about how bad the problems on a given site are. Don't do this! Instead, take it slowly, get lots of people involved, and stay positive. (For example, whatever you're testing is not a "bad design" — it's just a design that many users have a hard time understanding.) It's only after colleagues go through the full cycle of usability testing and resulting improvements that they'll begin to see the value of what you bring to the process.

- ✔ **Solve small problems first.** It's usually much better to try for a couple of base hits when you first come up to bat as a usability person — save the home runs for later. Identify small, relatively obvious problems that users are clearly having difficulty with. Figure out the smallest and easiest fix needed to solve the worst of the problem. Make sure to let people know how things improve after. A couple of wins like this will give you a good base for going after bigger fixes later.

- ✔ **Get credentialed.** There are various classes and programs you can participate in to get credits, a certificate, even a degree in various aspects of usability. (See Chapter 16 for details.) Any start you make on this process will help your own credibility and that of your discipline within your organization. Actually achieving a credential, certificate, or degree will make a world of difference.

✔ **Emphasize testing.** Formal usability tests are pretty impressive to all involved, and usability tests of all kinds are really the only place from which you derive solid information rather than just a well-informed opinion. Bring formal and informal usability tests to bear early and often, and always let people know whether your opinion on an issue is grounded in actual testing results, or is just your opinion — based on your overall experience but not on specific testing results.

Working with other groups

Working with other people is one of the challenges in any team effort, and Web site development is a team effort unlike just about any other. There are many different kinds of people, playing various professional roles, who have a voice in a Web site development project — and every single one of them will use the resulting Web site when you're finished! It's easy to overdo any kind of generalization about people, but we have found certain common threads in our shared decades of experience working with many very bright and highly motivated people in the high-tech hotbeds of Silicon Valley and, more recently, Seattle. Use the information in this section as a starting point to working constructively with some of the key people you depend on — and who depend on you.

Working with engineers

Each of the authors has been in professions — including high-tech marketing, usability, and project management — that are entirely dependent on engineering to get anything done. We could write a book on how to work with engineering - and a follow-on book about what happens when that isn't done well. But we won't write either of those books at the moment — we can, however, give you a few useful generalizations about engineers and how to work with them:

✔ **Engineers love data.** Engineers love "real" information. The results of your formal user tests and informal usability studies, properly presented, will be treated as solid data — though with some degree of uncertainty due to the small sample size. That's okay; the data you present will be much more than marketing ever gives them.

✔ **Engineers love "the truth."** Engineers love simple declarative statements that clearly state facts or inferences. "Three of the users who tried this process were unable to complete it." Don't give engineers statistics; they'll derive statistics themselves if needed. Just tell them what happened and they'll draw useful conclusions.

270 Part IV: Reaching a Broad Audience

✔ **Engineers hate — and love — being there.** Engineers love to watch user studies, but they are always "too busy" the first couple of times you ask them. This is because they don't feel they're really working if they aren't producing code, specifications, or designs, and engineers are conscientious about work. If you have trouble getting engineers to attend user studies, get their managers to order them to show up; it will be a relief to all concerned. Or tell them you need them at the first session so they can help you fine-tune the study. Whenever they attend, they'll use what they see in your current project and talk about what they saw for years to come.

✔ **Engineers like — and dislike — clear directions.** Engineers get very vague instructions from marketing, which frustrates them but also leaves them with a lot of freedom in how to do their jobs. They'll like the clearer instructions you give them but will find that your involvement limits them a bit at first. But after a project or two they'll find new areas where they can focus their creativity and find it hard to imagine not having you involved.

✔ **Engineers like people who can work with users.** Many engineers find it hard to talk to users at all, or when they do, they tend to turn the conversation in a technical direction. Yet they understand the value of user input. When engineers see your ability to keep users talking about their problems come into play, they'll appreciate your talent — and the information you derive.

✔ **Engineers will become your best friends.** The real story about working with engineering is that you are, as a usability person, stepping into the middle of a long, ongoing confrontation between engineering and marketing. Expect to end up with a few bruises of your own. Engineering will end up liking you better than they do marketing, though, because you have data, and because you make their job easier. Engineering will also try hard to take on the user's point of view and will eventually learn to address many usability concerns before you even ask them to.

Working with designers

What about designers? More and more, designers are part of the engineering group, just as they are on non-Internet software projects. Design is the group within engineering that you're likely to work with most directly, and the rules above apply to them as well as to others in engineering.

There's an additional concern about designers: They're the group most likely to have been trying to address usability concerns before an actual usability person stepped in to do it in a more focused way. The differences are that designers have too many other fish to fry to do the job fully, and that designers are unlikely to have actually done usability testing to get definitive input from users. You'll need to work carefully with those designers who've previously taken on some of the usability role; it will take them time to adjust to having you do the work instead.

Chapter 12: More Usability Testing 271

 Ask designers for help. Designers have many good ideas about usability — and about how to creatively solve usability problems that you identify. Just keep asking them for help and they'll adjust to not being the only ones concerned about the user. (Or they'll switch hats and become usability people along with you!)

Working with marketing

How about marketing? Marketing is the group engineering loves to hate — and can't live without. We can give you a few useful generalizations about working with marketing as well:

- **Marketers love people.** Some marketers are business analysts in disguise, but a typical marketer would describe him or herself as a "people person." Marketers will really like it that your usability work focuses on real, live users. They can often tell you the major usability problems of the site themselves and are upset that engineering never asked them what they were.

- **Marketers need conclusions.** Just as engineers love facts, marketers love conclusions. Business needs are stated as conclusions, so marketing needs additional conclusions — dates, percentages, bug counts — from engineering and usability so they can calculate how best to get the business needs met.

- **Marketers love — and hate — being there.** Marketing people will always tell you they'll be there to watch your user study, but will either come late and leave early, or beg off entirely. That's because marketing people like users but don't like user encounters that they're not in charge of. Also they're very busy and don't feel productive if they sit in one place too long. Keep inviting them, but also give them a good summary when you present your results.

- **Marketers like clear presentations.** Marketers are accustomed to speaking for the user and won't like it when you, to a certain extent, take over that role. But with marketing, the most important thing is that you present what you have to say clearly, both in a written report and, more importantly, in an in-person presentation. They'll take the ball and run with it from there.

- **Marketers will become your best friends.** Marketing will accept you in your role as a usability person fairly quickly. They will then like you more over time as you cut through the usual fog between engineering and marketing and actually help meet business needs by making things better for the user. Marketing, like engineering, will eventually be relieved that you've stepped in to fill some of the gap between them and serve as a true voice of the user.

Working with senior management

Senior management operates more like marketing than like any other group, but they have some of the skepticism of engineers. The things that will impress them most are for you to focus on business goals and for you to get the engineers and marketers to say good things about you. However, if you do really excellent work, greatly improving the usefulness and ability to meet business goals of your Web site, you'll get the ultimate executive compliment: a senior manager in your organization will take the credit him or herself, saying something like: "I sure whipped that Web site situation into shape."

One thing to add about senior management. Senior management are responsible for identifying goals and then making sure that systems are put in place to achieve them. In doing this, they are always interested in seeing and hearing about how well the goals are being met. As a usability person, you have a very interesting role in that you get to spend a lot of time with users — much of the time business goals have a direct relationship to meeting the needs of a business's customers. So, you'll easily be in a position to be noticed by senior management because you're familiar with the needs of the user.

One thing to watch though is to not be too much of a maverick about usability. This may sound strange coming from the authors of a book on usability. The point is that senior managers like to listen to people who are rational. When you're explaining what you see in usability tests, make sure your company hat is on and remember you're part of a larger team that includes marketing and engineering. Refer back to our discussion of goals and use this as a guide to how you structure the results of your usability tests.

Part V
The Part of Tens

In this part . . .

There are official International Standards Organization (ISO) standards for what makes up a usability test! Learn this and dozens of other (mostly) useful facts in our Part of Tens chapters — where you not only can find out how to become a usability expert, but have fun while doing so.

Chapter 13

Ten Do's and Don'ts

In This Chapter

▶ Do have goals for your Web site

▶ Do check back with the user

▶ Do manage your Web site like a real project

▶ Do "think different" when writing for the Web

▶ Do use PDF files to preserve formatting

▶ Don't ignore download speeds

▶ Don't try to do too much per revision

▶ Don't eschew large graphics and multimedia

▶ Don't listen to the HTML purists

▶ Don't skip actual user tests

In this chapter we identify ten do's and don'ts that represent many of the key things we have to say in this book and that are tied to most of the rest of the points we make. Use this list to impress on your colleagues the importance not only of our specific suggestions, but the whole idea that empowering the user comes first as you create and update your Web site.

Do Have Goals for Your Web Site

You need to have written-down, prioritized, agreed-upon goals for your Web site. Your Web site goals need to relate directly to your business or organizational goals. Put them on the wall of your office, and put up a copy on the meeting room wall when you have a site-related meeting. Whenever there's an issue, refer first to your list of goals.

This is hard to do, and few people do it. But without such goals, you'll never win an argument — because someone can always come up with a rationale by which it's a good idea to put updated pictures of the boss's vacation on the front page of your Web site every day.

Having your goals written down and prioritized is especially important. If your two major, equally important site goals are "increase sales" and "keep download speeds low," you'll never be able to decide whether to add a feature (such as a large graphic header for each page) that makes the site more attractive and presumably increases sales but also slows download speeds. Only if one goal is ranked above the other can you choose between them when there's a conflict. (Hint: In a business, "increase sales" almost always ranks first; but your sales are unlikely to increase if no one hangs around to view your slow-downloading pages.)

Getting everyone to agree on your goals is another matter. It takes a lot of time and energy to get everyone together in a room, from executive project sponsors to the people doing the work, and hammer out goals that fit the organization and the resources at hand. But investing the effort to do this is very much worthwhile. When everyone is heard and understands what the final goals are, work will go much more quickly and smoothly — and is less likely to suffer last-minute delays due to new players coming in and putting new things on the site's agenda.

Do Constantly Check Back with the User

The Usability Design Cycle starts with studying the user and ends with your site going live. After your site is up, it's time to start studying the user again. Except now you have many more interesting things to study!

After you get in the habit of treating your users as the ultimate authority about your Web site, it's important not to stop checking back with them. Keep checking. You can ask fellow employees, management, and people you know for feedback on your site. Get a look at all the user comments that come in through your Web site's e-mail feedback address. Develop a process for the customer support center to forward you a report of the customer calls relating to any issues on the Web site. It doesn't really take that long to scan through them all; you may also want to assign someone to organize them and keep score as to how often the same problems keep coming up.

It's also useful — if embarrassing for the person you ask — to get colleagues or friends to accomplish specific tasks on your Web site. Watch them try to find specific information. See where they hesitate, stop, or give up. Count the number of steps it takes. Time them. Use a benchmarking process to see if certain tasks get noticeably easier from one revision of the Web site to the next.

All this checking isn't to eliminate the need for formal user testing, which you should do at least once every time you revise your Web site. Informal testing helps you know what to focus on when it's time to do a formal user test.

Chapter 13: Ten Do's and Don'ts **277**

Do Manage Your Web Site Like a Real Project

As important as they are, Web sites tend to get treated as catchalls for many different people's ideas. Updates and changes happen in a haphazard fashion, with different people calling the shots at different times and for different parts of the site.

We think that this is exactly the wrong approach, that the ultimate toolkit for project management is perfectly appropriate for Web sites: the software development management approach. Although there are many ways to manage a software project, certain common elements such as agreed-upon, prioritized feature lists, regular project management meetings, and bug lists are found in all of them. Get people who are familiar with software development involved in setting up the process for managing your Web site.

Formal content management also becomes an issue after your site grows past a certain size and frequency of updating. (A site of more than a few dozen pages, updated more than once every month or so, is probably a good candidate for content management.) Use content management software already deployed elsewhere in your organization, or research what other people you know use. Work in editorial reviews and permission reviews and have a staging site where a nearly live version of even a minor change can get a last look before you push it live.

A Web site is like a play, performed every day on the biggest stage the world has ever scene (pun intended). Don't blow your lines.

Do "Think Different" When Writing for the Web

Writing is both an art and a craft, but on the Web, "craft" predominates, and "art" is out. You need to have at least one or two people on your site team who've mastered the art of writing for the Web. This means tossing out much existing material and writing very short text that's action-oriented and very much to the point. Put the key points first and the supporting evidence later. Use headings, bullets, numbered lists, highlighting, and links to make it easy for the user to quickly scan what you've written and get your point without having to work to find it. Consider breaking up your text into multiple pages that the user can easily page through — but never forget that the page the user is currently looking at may be the last chance you have to make your most important point before the user goes surfing somewhere else.

Do Use PDF Files to Preserve Formatting

The paperless office is a myth! People love highly formatted documents, especially if they have color illustrations and highlights — as long as there's a color printer nearby that they can print them out on.

Use your Web site as a means to help people find the documents that your organization already has. Take an inventory of all the documents you have that are suitable for public consumption and consider which should be accessible on your site. Create new formatted, printable documents where needed to fill information gaps. Be creative: Consider, for example, creating a printable version of the directions to your office, formatted as a PDF file and linked to the company information part of your Web site.

Don't Ignore Download Speeds

The easiest thing in the world — or at least, on the World Wide Web — to do when you're designing a Web page or Web site is to ignore download speeds. Initial design work takes place on your own hard disk, where download time is not an issue. Initial testing takes place over a local area network, where download time is still far faster than over a dial-up connection. Even remote testing, if and when you finally get around to it, is likely to feature highly motivated users (you or people who work for you), who quickly get key elements of your site cached on their hard disk, and who have nothing to do with their time but surf around on your site.

Try to keep in mind these key metrics:

- **3K/second:** The transmission speed that a user typically gets over a 56K modem.

- **10 seconds:** The longest a user is likely to wait for a page to download — *if* they know it's got something on it they really want to see.

- **30K:** The largest a page can be, in total, if it's going to reliably load in ten seconds over a 56K modem.

  A typical page on your site must be below 30K to be usable over a dial-up connection — and as more and more office workers use the Internet from a home office or a hotel room, even a corporate intranet will frequently get accessed over a dial-up connection.

Don't Eschew Large Graphics and Multimedia

"Danger, Will Robinson!" Robbie the Robot on *Lost in Space* sometimes said that when things got a little overwhelming. You may feel a bit like old Robbie on hearing us tell you to keep page sizes small, but not to avoid large graphics and multimedia.

We should probably say don't *completely* avoid large graphics and multimedia. For product shots, CEO speeches, and other high-impact deliverables on your Web site, there's nothing like a large, highly detailed photograph or a multimedia clip. Just make sure that you give users warning that they're about to download something that's going to take a little while to appear if they're on a slow connection. This way, users don't feel trapped, and they'll give you the benefit of any doubts they experience when that download time stretches on and on and on . . . .

It's also true that, in today's complicated world, it can be better to please a small group of people a lot than to please a large number of people a little bit. If you're willing to give up most of your target audience, you can consider creating an entire site just for people with high-bandwidth connections to access. Just let people know right up front on your home page — which downloads quickly, of course, even if your site's other pages don't — what to expect, and what kind of connection they need to have to be able to productively use or enjoy your site. Or offer low-bandwidth alternatives to the audio and video clips, high-resolution photos, and 3D experiences with which you plan to populate your site.

Don't Try to Do Too Much Per Revision

It's easy to overcommit when planning a new site or site revision. Even experienced pros who run, for example, well-known usability companies find themselves having to drastically scale back their original plans in order to get a site launched in a reasonable amount of time.

Try to keep your goals modest when creating a new Web site or revising an existing one. It's much better to do a few of the right things well than to try to do too much and to plan, design, and implement it poorly.

No matter how hard you try to keep your goals modest, you'll still find that sometimes you have less time and money than you feel you need. This is where your prioritized feature list is your friend. If you have in hand an agreed-on list of the must-have, want-to-have, and nice-to-have features on your site, you'll be ready for just about any eventuality.

To create this list, ask yourself "If I could only change one thing on this Web site, what would it be?" Ask yourself the same thing over and over. That's your initial list. Then drag everyone concerned into a room, have a massive and energetic discussion of what should be on the list, and in what order, and emerge with your final list. Get everyone a copy, then use the final list as your compass to guide you through the difficult waters of project management to your final — for this try — destination.

Don't Listen to the HTML Purists

Everyone has a pet peeve, and ours is the HTML purists who are heard so much in the Web design and usability fields. These people point out, rightly, that the Web was originally designed so that a Web page could be viewed on almost any machine, and so machines could process Web site content and make reasonably good guesses about where a given page should come up in, say, search engine results. If the Web was still only used for scientists to share badly formatted versions of the latest groundbreaking physics report, it would probably still work just like that.

Luckily, dozens of important innovations have occurred that have pretty much buried the original vision of the Web within a much richer and more interesting reality. META tags. JavaScript. Style sheets. Talented designers who torture HTML until it produces highly formatted, easily readable, interesting, and attractive pages that still work well on a wide range of machines — and that still get indexed appropriately by search engines.

Don't be afraid to use the tools at hand. Create Web pages that are highly usable — which includes being at least reasonably attractive — for your target audience. Don't let the HTML 1.0 specification be the starting and stopping point of your aspirations.

Don't Skip Actual User Tests

The basic source of authority for any usability expert is actual user tests of a given Web site. As you learn more about usability, including the many tips and tricks laid out in this book, you can certainly help any Web development effort that you're part of to avoid obvious mistakes. But in a sense, you, by yourself, don't know anything. Only watching real users struggle with a

Chapter 13: Ten Do's and Don'ts *281*

mockup or live prototype of your Web site will give you the ability to definitively choose between any two (or three) ways of doing something. Following up by watching the site data — and angry e-mail messages — generated by real users trying to get things done in real time will let you know if you chose correctly.

It's easy for usability experts to become pundits who can quickly give the "usability viewpoint" on just about anything. Avoid this temptation. Keep a certain amount of humility when confronted by the bright ideas of your colleagues and customers. Even impractical suggestions may represent a useful effort toward solving a problem you hadn't previously known your site had. A Web site can accomplish a great many things. Use actual hands-on user tests to help you choose the best way to accomplish each of them.

282 Part V: The Part of Tens

Chapter 14

Top Ten Steps to a Usability Study

In This Chapter

▶ Deciding what you're going to test

▶ Setting up your testing room

▶ Recruiting your testers

▶ Including other team members

▶ Getting off to a good start

▶ Taking the user through tasks

▶ Asking for final thoughts

▶ Getting ready for the next one

▶ Writing up the results

▶ Delivering the news

Conducting a user study is a fine art. After sitting through hundreds of studies with thousands of users, we feel qualified to sum up the high points for you. But don't forget to vary this routine for your particular needs. For example, we heard about a user test at a computer company where a user got a minor cut on her finger as she tried to open up a machine to add memory to it. She tried to complete the test while bleeding, crying, and apologizing for messing up the machine. That round of testing needed to be stopped immediately until the problem was fixed. But not every test needs a supply of bandages (and handkerchiefs) handy. Take our top ten steps to conducting a user study and add your own fine points.

Deciding What You're Going to Test

Decide on two or three areas of your site that you want to test. The tests take the form of tasks that you ask the user to complete. Create a dozen tasks for users to perform during the test. Put the ones that are most important to you first, and do all you reasonably can to make sure that all users complete a minimum number of these key tasks. (It can take some users, especially beginners or people who get nervous, an amazing amount of time to complete tasks you think are simple.)

Setting Up Your Testing Room

In high-end usability labs, there are cameras all over the place capturing the screen, the user, a view over the user's shoulder, and even one looking down from the ceiling. However, remember that your goal is *not* television production! The main reason to use a video camera to record testing is so that you can look back at the tape to get more details about something you missed in your notes.

Set up an area in which you'll conduct the user test. You should have a video camera focused on the screen so you can see what the user's doing. To reduce flicker in the videotape you create, make sure the camera is set at the same frame rate as the display. Or get a scan converter to intercept the video image on its way to the display and route it directly to a VCR for capture. (You'll still need to capture and synchronize audio.)

If you use an LCD screen attached to your PC, you can take a video image of the screen directly and not get any "flicker" on the video tape.

Optionally, you can use one additional camera focused on the users to catch their comments and facial expressions. However, it's rare these days to create a summary highlights videotape — even then, all you really need is a video record of what the users were saying and looking at.

Don't worry about glass walls to hide behind — they're nice, but not necessary. Conduct a couple of dry runs of the test to make sure the actual tasks are doable in a testing environment and that the taping equipment works.

Recruit Your Testers

Choosing subjects for usability tests is fairly easy. Identify people in the target group you wish to test and write a description of them — age range, amount of computer experience, products they own or have considered buying, and so on. Then start calling people in the area where you want to conduct the test and ask if they fit the criteria and if they'll participate. As you get some people signed up, vary the criteria for the additional people you accept so that the final group is fairly representative of typical users of your site. You can work through a local marketing company to get help with this.

Start off by saying that you're conducting a user test and offering $100 to qualified participants; this will keep most people on the phone long enough to query them fully. Do make sure to get a broad range of people, but don't worry about meeting specific statistical criteria for how the users differ; your

Chapter 14: Top Ten Steps to a Usability Study **285**

sample size isn't large enough to meet statistical tests of validity anyway. User tests are always anecdotal in nature — other kinds of surveys are needed to get statistically significant evidence.

Include Other Team Members in the Study

It's important that other members of the Web team buy into the user study and the usability design process. One important part of this is to make them a part of the usability study. If you can get them to watch even one user session, they will be much more likely to "buy off" on the results. However, you need to be careful how you manage your team mates during the usability study. Make sure they understand what you'll be doing in the study — give them a copy of the script. Remind them that the walls are not soundproof, so they should keep their voices down (laughter from behind the glass wall would be very disconcerting to the user). It can also be a really good thing to have one of the marketing or project managers introduce him or herself and individually thank users when they've completed the test and are leaving. At that point, other team members can also introduce themselves to the user.

Get Off to a Good Start

When users arrive for the test, make them comfortable. Offer them something to drink. Get their signed consent to conduct the test and appear on videotape. (Keep their last name out of your discussions and reports to protect their privacy.) Tell them what organization the study is being done for and give them an overview of what they'll be doing. Emphasize that it's the Web site that's being tested, *not* them. Any problems they have are indications of things that need fixing in the Web site and not the tester's fault. Ask the users to talk about what they're thinking as they work — tell them their candid observations as they go through the process are invaluable to you in making the site easier to use.

Start by asking users about their computer experience and other things they answered in "qualifying" for the test. This puts them at ease — clearly, they know the answers to these questions — and confirms for you where each user fits within the range of characteristics you're looking for. Then start describing the Web site and show them the home page; ask questions about what they know about it, what they think it's for, and how they may imagine using it. Even the answers to these basic questions may show that the organization whose site is being tested needs to do a lot of work on its overall image and on the home page of its Web site.

Take the User Through Tasks

Now it's time to take the users through actual tasks, one at a time. The main thing you need to do is be an active listener. Keep encouraging the users to talk about what they're thinking as they pursue each task. Note body language, facial expressions, and any non-verbal sounds the user makes — a live observer will pick these factors up better than someone who later watches the videotape. Don't talk; let the silence continue until the user speaks. (They will eventually speak, if only to break the silence.) After each task, ask the users what they thought; if the task was easy or hard, and are there any suggestions they can make about how to make this easier. (Don't be surprised to hear two common answers: "I'd rather do this by phone" and "This is easier on your competitor's Web site." Just grin and bear it.)

Ask for Final Thoughts

At the end of the task list, or when you run out of time, give the users their $100 and a copy of the consent form they signed. Then ask the user for any final thoughts. Are they satisfied with the Web site? What two or three things might they change about it? Are they satisfied with the study? This should be a short process, unless the users want to make a lot of comments. Thank them again and let them leave.

Get Ready for the Next One

There are a lot of mechanical things to do at the end of a test to prepare for the next one. First, add any observations or initial conclusions you have to your interview notes. Then, clean up. It's all too easy to let coffee cups and crumbs accumulate, but the resulting mess is very off-putting to later users. Label the videotape(s) you used, store them, and put in new ones. Clear the computer, clear the browser's cache and history files, and, if needed, clear any "cookie" files or other files that were written to by your Web site's software.

Restart the computer to reduce the odds it will crash during a later test.

Write Up the Results

When you've finished your testing, write up the results. The most important document here is the two-to-three page executive summary of your results. To write this, imagine yourself going through each stage of the test and think about what users typically said at each step. Then think about the main comment you would make about user's reactions at that step. State your main conclusions in the headers and one or two simple charts — many busy people will just scan the executive summary to get your results.

Make sure you capture screenshots of all the major screens your users landed on in the test, and include these screenshots in your report. This is very important because the site will change over time and no one involved will remember exactly how it used to look. Including screenshots in your report makes it much more useful as a reference in the future.

Don't use percentages in your report; say "two testers had problems with XYZ" or "seven testers completed the task quickly and with no problems." Percentages imply a degree of statistical validity that simply doesn't exist in this kind of testing. Behind the executive summary, do a full report with a brief description of each test, the results, and conclusions. Then create an appendix — not everyone needs to get this, just people who are likely to want to read it — with the blow-by-blow, user-by-user testing notes.

Deliver the News

The in-person delivery of your results is very important — many of the people who need to know your results will attend this presentation and leave with one or two key takeaways. Make sure you emphasize the most important points. Keep things positive; let people know that their interest in doing user testing puts them ahead of most Web site development teams. If you like, you can show *video clips* — short segments from all that video you recorded — to illustrate your main points. Then create a brief presentation or one-page summary that you go through as you speak. Allow plenty of time for questions and discussion throughout. Don't claim that your results are absolute, but do let people know that this kind of testing has proven its value over and over in finding usability problems. Finish on a positive note, and emphasize the benefits that will come from solving the key problems you identified in your presentation and written report.

288 Part V: The Part of Tens

Chapter 15

Ten Cool Tools for Usability

In This Chapter

▶ Your ears

▶ A laptop

▶ A room with an optional glass wall

▶ Solid writing skills

▶ A video camera

▶ A fat marker

▶ A graphics editing tool

▶ A prototyping tool

▶ A database program

▶ Walkie-talkies

It really doesn't take that much equipment to do usability work. Even the pros — see Chapter 16 for what it takes to become one — don't have a lot of gear. There are just a few things, most very affordable, that you need. Here are ten items that should go in every usability person's toolkit.

A Good Pair of Ears

The most important tool for usability work is a good pair of ears — and the ability to get people to talk to you so you can hear what they're saying. The thing that most impresses marketers, engineers, and others when they watch usability people at work is their ability to get users to talk, and talk, and talk about what they're experiencing. Most people feel some ownership of their products and get defensive when they're challenged, even by a bewildered user. The top usability people just keep using their ears — and keep their mouth mostly shut.

A Good Laptop

The most expensive piece of equipment for a usability person is a good laptop computer. Usability people spend a lot of time in rented rooms waiting for people to show up — plus additional time in airports and airplanes getting around — and a good laptop enables them to be productive during that time. It doesn't have to be a super-powerful machine — most usability work in the field involves taking notes or editing documents — but it should have both phone line and network connectors, for the times you're lucky enough to have some form of Internet access available, and long battery life in case there's no plug handy. You can also use your laptop for casual usability testing and as a backup machine for formal testing in a pinch. Oh, and by the way — unlike in design, a Mac isn't considered a requirement; a PC is fine.

A Room (Glass Wall Optional)

The mythology of user testing is that a glass-walled room is strictly necessary. But it really isn't; you can put the user, someone coaching her, and an observer/note taker in the same room with no big problems. The glass wall is more helpful if you want additional observers, such as marketing and engineering people, but you can also accommodate them simply by having a large enough room. The point is, don't let the lack of a glass-walled room stop you from doing your testing.

Solid Writing Skills

Usability work always starts with a plan and ends with a written report. You, or someone on the team who's closely involved in the work, need to have sufficient writing skills to communicate clearly and concisely what's happened and make a coherent case for your recommendations. We're not talking F. Scott Fitzgerald here — but we are talking about the ability to create error-free proposals and reports in business English and with a minimum of jargon. You also need Microsoft Word for opening other people's documents, as well as writing your own, and Flashit or a similar shareware tool for capturing and cropping screen shots. Go to CNET's Download.com site at `www.download.com` and search for "screen capture" to find Flashit or a similar shareware program that will work for you. (Some of us get by with using the PrtScrn key to capture the screen image to the Windows clipboard and then pasting the image into the free Paint program included in most versions of Windows.)

A Video Camera

You can create an instant usability lab just by setting up a video camera — okay, you'll need a tripod and an external microphone as well — and taping someone while she works. The main use of the videotape you record is for you; it turns out no one likes to watch hours and hours of users mousing around a Web site.

You probably want a two-tape VHS deck or PC-based equipment sufficient to create a brief highlights (and lowlights) tape, but you don't need expensive editing equipment. The video camera is all you need to get started. Eventually, consider adding a scan converter — a device that connects between the computer and the monitor and allows you to record the current state of the computer screen and the user's mousing around on videotape. This can be a useful record.

A Fat Marker

You need a fat marker — a marking pen with a tip too wide to draw thin lines or small text. Add plenty of blank paper and a clipboard for working on the scene and you're ready. Practice drawing quick, very rough prototype drawings to get feedback from users on how they'd like things laid out. The point isn't to draw something wonderful — it's to give the user something more to talk about.

A Graphics Editing Tool

You work with images quite a bit in usability, and you work with designers who do nothing but work with images. Adobe Photoshop is the industry standard for image editing. It can open many different kinds of image files that you may run into. Photoshop is also programmable, so you can create a simple script to, for example, convert a bunch of images to the same size and file format. There are cheaper tools, and you can try them if you have to or already know how to use one, but customers and colleagues will be mystified if you don't have Photoshop.

A Prototyping Tool

Somewhere along the way, between fat marker prototypes on paper and an actual working Web site, you'll probably need to make a working on-screen prototype. Macromedia Director is the professional's tool of choice. A time-based, programmable tool long favored by software development teams, Director and its add-ons will let you do almost anything. If Director is overkill for you, use Microsoft PowerPoint or even Word.

A Database Program

Usability people deal with a lot of disparate data. A database program — and the ability to set up simple databases — is vital to keeping it all organized. Filemaker and Microsoft Access are the two most popular tools, but you can get by with Microsoft Excel or even tables in Word.

Walkie-Talkies

We hesitate to mention these, because they aren't a requirement, but a two-person usability team can really get a lot of mileage out of a pair of walkie-talkies. The junior person, who's talking directly to the user, wears an earpiece and can get coaching from the senior person in real time. The senior person has to give brief, useful instructions such as "keep going" or "please move on." (Encouragement is good too; tell him "great listening" to encourage him to keep the user talking. This interaction takes a lot of skill, but it also makes the team very effective and allows the junior person to quickly gain expertise.

Watch out for observers, such as marketing people who've come in to watch the test, who grab the walkie-talkie from the senior person and start giving verbose instructions.

Chapter 16
Ten Resources for Usability Pros

In This Chapter
- Work experience
- *Usability Engineering*
- Education
- *Readings in Human-Computer Interaction*
- ACM *Interactions* magazine
- *Design Management Journal*
- ACM SIGCHI
- *The Design of Everyday Things*
- The Usability Professionals Association
- The Pencil

*W*eb usability is still an emerging field, so few people practicing it have a degree that says "usability studies," or something similar, on it. Many usability people are former teachers (such as Mander) or technical writers (such as Smith), two fields in which communication skills are vital. (Mander does have a doctoral degree in the field, though.) Others come from psychology, and a few are anthropologists. The rest come from almost any field under the sun — or the Apple, or the IBM, if you'll excuse the pun.

Buzzword alert: Usability draws on a number of predecessor and related fields with a wide variety of names. Among others, look for *time and motion studies, human factors engineering, computer-human interaction* (or *CHI*, sometimes pronounced to rhyme with "sky"), and *human-computer interaction* (same thing but putting humans first).

In this Part of Tens chapter, we describe some of the resources you can draw on if you want to move toward making usability your profession. But don't be discouraged if nothing we say describes you — the odd collection of skills and abilities that make someone good at usability work isn't limited to any specific education or professional background. Use these resources to make yourself more skilled, more credible, and more marketable.

The Right Work Experience

The three companies we joke about — Sun, Apple, and IBM — have had a huge influence on usability in the high-tech field. Microsoft has more recently poured huge resources into usability. A background in usability-related work at any of these companies carries great cachet in the rest of the high-tech world.

For example, the authors worked together at Apple and have each consulted for Microsoft. Mander has also consulted for Sun, and Smith for IBM. You don't have to have had a usability title at companies like these — they're so well recognized as actively involved in the field that any usability-related work experience earns you brownie points. But usability-related work at any company, in a field as new as this one, is also a plus.

Web development experience is also needed for establishing yourself as a Web usability pro. Web work is actually hard to break into at the moment because there are so many laid-off dot-commers out there competing for jobs. Build your own Web sites in off-hours and keep looking for ways to get Web development experience. Doing free projects for charitable organizations and other non-profits is a recognized way to build up your portfolio while also helping others.

Jakob Nielsen's Usability Engineering

Jakob Nielsen, who spent much of his career at Sun, is the best-known usability practitioner and creator of the useit.com Web site (`http://useit.com`), a well-known usability resource. His recent book, *Designing Web Usability* (New Riders Publishing), is an excellent resource, but it's his nearly ten-year-old *Usability Engineering* (Morgan Kaufmann Publishers) that the pros are proud to have on their shelves. Though focused on software design, most of it is applicable to today's Web sites, especially as they become more and more powerful (and less and less different from traditional software). This book is worth owning — and reading.

The Right Education

A bachelor's degree is nearly a requirement for professional employment these days; in Web usability work, it's not all that important which field your degree is in. Computer science, psychology, education, writing, communications, and anthropology are all well-represented among today's usability

Chapter 16: Ten Resources for Usability Pros **295**

professionals. A very few schools, such as Stanford University and the University of Toronto, now have human-computer interaction programs from which you can seek a degree. A much wider range of schools have extension or evening courses in computer science and Web design and development that have usability aspects. Any formal education you can get in the field — even a non-credit course or two — will help both your skills and your marketability.

Ronald Baecker's Readings in Human-Computer Interaction

Readings in Human-Computer Interaction: Toward the Year 2000 (Morgan Kaufmann Publishers), edited by Ronald M. Baecker of the University of Toronto, is another defining work in the field. If you haven't read this kind of professor-edited collection of papers before, be ready for some slow going, but getting through this one is a rite of passage for usability pros. The new edition is significantly updated; consider reading it even if you've gone through the first edition.

ACM Interactions magazine

The Association for Computing Machinery (ACM), a society for professionals and academics in computing, publishes *Interactions* magazine, subtitled "New visions of human-computer interaction." A bit dry and theoretical, *Interactions* is still a great resource for learning the current state of the art in usability. You can see much of the current content or order the magazine at their Web site at `www.acm.org/interactions`.

The Design Management Journal

The Design Management Institute Journal, to give its full name, takes on high-level design topics, many Web-related. The overlap with usability concerns is extensive. If you are coming to usability work from a design background, or if you work closely with designers, the *Design Management Journal* is nearly indispensable. Check out the latest issue at `www.designmgt.org/dmi/html/publications/journal/journal_d.jsp`.

ACM SIGCHI

ACM's SIGs, or Special Interest Groups, are famous within computing as homes for the highest level of thinking and sharing on advanced scientific and technical topics. SIGCHI, ACM's Special Interest Group for Computer-Human Interaction, is no exception. SIGCHI conferences are the resource for academically-oriented usability professionals and those in related fields to share the latest research and work. Learn more at `www.acm.org/sigchi`.

Donald Norman's The Design of Everyday Things

Initially published as *The Psychology of Everyday Things* (both published by Currency/Doubleday), Norman's book was a breakthrough in describing why so many items are unusable, from common doorknobs that turn the "wrong" way to computer programs. In doing so he laid out basic interaction principles that apply just as strongly on the Web as elsewhere. You'll see a copy of *POET*, as Norman referred to it, on the bookshelves of most usability pros. Get a copy of POET, if you can find it, or DOET, which is easily available, for yourself.

The Usability Professionals Association

The Usability Professionals Association (UPA) is the only professional group exclusively dedicated to usability. Top-level sponsors include Sun, IBM, and Microsoft. Their quarterly newsletter and annual conference are unique resources. Check out their offerings or join the group online at `www.upassoc.org`.

At the UPA Web site, you can get a copy of their poster, "Designing the User Experience," which is a one-sheet summary of the ways in which usability contributes to the development effort.

Henry Petroski's The Pencil

Anyone who thinks that common sense is enough when it comes to making highly usable products can learn a thing or two from Petroski's *The Pencil* (Knopf). This book shows the many, many steps that went into the creation of this most usable — yet still problematic, sometimes even dangerous — of everyday objects. And if you like *The Pencil*, you'll probably enjoy Petroski's *The Evolution of Useful Things* (Vintage Books) as well.

Glossary

56K modem. A modem is a device that allows a computer to send data over an ordinary "twisted pair copper" phone line. A 56K modem is the most up-to-date kind and sends data at just under 56 Kbps (about 56 thousand bits per second). In actual usage, most of these modems only achieve about 33K due to the quality of the phone line. See *broadband Internet access*.

216-color palette. The basic color palette on a Mac or PC is 8-bit, meaning each pixel or dot on the screen can be one of 256 colors. If you look at the Mac and PC 8-bit color palettes, there are actually only 216 colors that are exactly the same. So there are really only 216 colors you can assume are available on every Mac or PC. These colors are called the *216-color palette*.

Accessibility. Accessible Web sites are ones that can be used by people who have disabilities or other special needs.

Affordance. An aspect of a tool's shape or other design element that makes it easy to use for its intended purpose. A handsaw's grip "affords" grasping.

Alpha version. An early version of software or of a Web site. An alpha version of a Web site doesn't have its final look and feel nor all its functions in order.

Beta version. An early version of software or a Web site, but later than an *alpha version*. A beta version has its final look and feel, and all functions are intended to work, but the process of testing and fixing bugs is not yet complete.

Broadband Internet access. A fast, always-on connection to the Internet, not based on a regular phone line. See *56K modem*.

Browser. Software for accessing Web sites. The most popular types of browser software are *Internet Explorer* and *Netscape Navigator*.

Clickable image map. A graphical area that includes areas that are clickable. Clicking takes the user to a linked Web page or area within a Web page.

Clickable prototype. A roughly laid out Web page, or series of Web pages, that model or mock up a process.

Clickthrough. Any click on a link to another Web page.

298 Web Usability For Dummies

Contact information. Ways to reach a company, or individuals within a company. Can include, but is not limited to, phone number, fax number, address, and e-mail address.

Customer visit. A form of usability research in which members of the development team visit customers at their home or office and interview them in their normal environment. Used to understand what people need.

Downtime. A period during which your Web site is unavailable due to computer or network problems.

Extranet. A Web site developed by a company or organization for use by people at partner, supplier, or customer companies or organizations. Not intended for use by the public. See *intranet*.

Fat-marker prototype. A quick and easy-to-create Web site prototype created by drawing with a marker on one or more blank sheets of paper.

Focus group. A brainstorming session in which customers are gathered together in a room to discuss, as a group, various questions that relate to their likes and dislikes regarding a category of products or a specific product. Used to understand what people want.

Frames. Frames allow a Web page to be divided into separate areas that scroll and update independently. Often used to keep navigation fixed within the Web page while allowing other content to be scrolled.

Frequently Asked Questions (FAQ). A type of document commonly found on the Internet that lists common user or customer questions and their answers.

Global. A control that is accessible to users throughout your site. For instance, if a search capability is offered on your site, it should be made available as a global control.

Hits. A hit is the transfer of one file from a Web server to a user's machine. A typical Web page is made up of several files — at least one HTML file and a separate file for each graphic on the screen — so each page displayed causes several hits to be recorded. See *pageview*.

Home page. The first page that appears when the user links to the main URL of a Web site. The home page usually identifies the organization that created the site and offers navigation into other parts of the site.

HTML. HyperText Markup Language, the language used to format text files for display on the Web.

Hyperlink. Text or a graphic that connects to a location on the Web when the text or graphic is clicked; the new location appears in the user's browser.

Glossary *299*

Industry analyst. One of several different kinds of people who are responsible for understanding events and trends in an industry. Industry analysts include financial analysts, analysts for market research companies, think-tank analysts, competitive analysts, and some press people.

Information architect. An expert at the organization of information.

Information architecture. The process of organizing your site so the contents are easily accessible to users.

Internationalization. The process of converting a Web site to one or more other languages and making other changes appropriate to each country and culture that the site is intended to serve.

Internet. Short for internetwork, the Internet is the collection of all networks that are connected to, and share traffic with, each other.

Internet Explorer. The leading browser software, published by Microsoft. See *browser*.

Intranet. A Web site developed by a company or organization for use by people inside the organization. See *extranet*.

JavaScript (also spelled Javascript). A scripting language supported by recent versions of browser software that allows some graphics updating and data processing to take place on the user's computer. See *browser*.

Lead. Contact information for someone interested in a company's products or services.

Left navigation bar. A vertical strip of links to the major categories within a Web site, often implemented as a graphics file with a *clickable image map*.

Link colors. The colors used to highlight text that serves as a *hyperlink* to another Web destination. The default link colors are blue for links that have not been recently visited and purple for recently-visited ones.

Mockup. A representation of a Web page in a simpler form such as a different, less polished Web page or a hand-drawn image (see *fat-marker prototype*). A mockup is similar to a prototype, but the use of the term mockup suggests a cruder representation.

Navigation. The process of finding one's way around a Web site.

Netscape Navigator. The once-leading, now second-place browser software, published by the Netscape division of America Online. See *browser*.

300 Web Usability For Dummies _____

Newsletter subscribers. Not everyone who registers for your site will choose to receive your newsletter — if you're polite and give them a choice — or you may have more than one newsletter. So the number of newsletter subscribers may be different than the number of registered users.

Page load time. The amount of time it takes a page to download over the Web. The page load time for a user varies on the speed of their connection and the speed of the path, on the Internet, between the user and the Web server he or she is accessing. Page load time is typically, however, around 3K per second for a user connected via a 56K modem, the fastest modem available over a standard phone line. See *page weight*.

Page weight. The total size, in kilobytes (K), of all the files used to make up a Web page.

Pageview. The display of a complete Web page on a user's computer.

PDF. Portable Document Format, a standard for displaying formatted documents controlled by Adobe, a software company. PDF files can be read with Adobe's Acrobat Reader software (which can be downloaded at www.adobe.com).

Prototype. A representation of a Web page, usually as another working Web page that is less well-designed and/or less functional than the finished page will be. See *mockup*.

Rapid prototyping. The process of improving a design by quickly creating a mockup or prototype, getting user feedback on it, quickly creating an improved prototype, and so on.

Registration. The process of identifying yourself to a Web site in order to get some benefit, such as customization of the Web site, access to additional features, or a subscription to a newsletter.

Resolution. The number of pixels a graphics subsystem uses in displaying a Web page or other computer image. Resolutions commonly in use are 640 x 480, 800 x 600 (the most common), and 1024 x 768 (increasingly common). Also the relative number of pixels used in displaying a graphic; a more precise image is described as high-resolution, a less precise image is described as low-resolution.

Rollout. Making your site available to its intended audience.

Scan converter. A device which converts the monitor signal from your computer into a regular (S-video, or Composite) video signal you can record on a VCR.

Site map. A representation, usually in a single page, of the hierarchy of the sections and individual Web pages of your site, usually hyperlinked to the corresponding Web pages.

Stakeholder. Someone who is influenced by, or who influences, the success or lack of success of your organization. Stakeholders include customers, employees, investors, government regulators, and members of the press.

Step wizard. A combination of graphics and HTML functionality that A stepped process that 'walks' users through a process. A step wizard supports the use of 'Previous' and 'Next' buttons, or similar links, to move through the process in sequence.

Title. In *HTML*, a title is a feature of a Web page. The Web page's title does not appear within the body of the page, but shows up at the top of the browser window. People also call a large header at the top of a Web page the title of that page.

Under Construction. A notice placed on a Web page to indicate that the page, and possibly additional elements of the site, is still being worked on.

Unique users. The number of people who come to your site one or more times in a given time period.

Uptime. The time during which your site is available for use by its intended audience. See *downtime*.

URL. Universal Resource Locator, the name of a Web page or other named file on the Internet. Also referred to as the address of the file.

Usability engineer. An expert at working with users to test the usability of a site.

Usability testing. Broadly, the process of checking with users whether a Web page, a task on a Web site, or a site as a whole is easy to use.

User test. Bringing in a series of users who try to complete a series of tasks in a Web site to test its usability.

Visual Designer. A designer who is expert at visual design of information and who has detailed knowledge of color, fonts, and layout on the Web.

Walk-through. A way of systematically inspecting a site to get insights into how well it works.

Web site (also spelled Website or website). One or more Web pages that are logically related to each other and, usually, connected by an overall navigation scheme.

302 Web Usability For Dummies

Web usability. The art and science of making Web sites easier to use by a series of techniques that include obtaining feedback from actual or potential users.

WebTV. A device made by Microsoft for accessing the Web and e-mail using a TV set as a display.

Widget. A slider, button or other control on the screen.

Wireframe. A rough outline of a screen layout. Usually accompanied by with notes describing how the controls on the screen work.

Index

• A •

About.com, 144
Above the fold content, 159, 160
  on home page, 260
Accessibility criteria, 228–229
  definition, 297
ActiveX controls, 219
Adobe Photoshop graphics tool, 291
Advertising
  and home pages, 188
  by e-mail, 64
  highly trackable on the Web, 83
Alpha sites, 246
  definition, 297
working with developers on, 246
ALT tags, 229
Altavista.com, 180
  Babelfish on, 224
Amazon.com, 60
Analysts. *See* Industry analyst
Anecdotal evidence
  as user tests, 245
AOL Time Warner, 32
Apple Computer. 294
Art of Web design, 11
Asia as growing online market, 32–33
Assistive software, 228
  standards implementations, 229–230
Association for Computing
    Machinery, 295
Audience. *See* Users
Audio
  clips, 221
  quality, 157
Authors, 77
  contacting, 8

• B •

Babelfish, 224
Back button, 92, 161
  avoiding during usability testing, 255
Baecker, Ronald, 295
Banner ads, 165
Barnes & Noble Web site, 90, 145–146
Bellingham, WA Web site, 135–138, 142
Benchmarking user tests, 276
Beta testing, 246
  definition, 297
  locking site before user tests, 247
Books
  as information systems, 72–78
  conventions, 74
  establishing user expectations for Web
    sites, 75
  indexes, 73, 75
  making Web sites like, 76–78
  page numbering, 74, 75
  tables of contents, 73, 75
Borders.com, 90
Bots, 104
Bottom navigation links
  in multi-level site example, 139, 140
Breadcrumbs, 112
Broadband, 31
  definition, 297
Brochureware, 50
  example of, 258
Brainstorming site content, 97, 171
Browsers, 34–35, 220
  definition, 297
  sniffers, 220
Bug fixing
  in site development cycle, 174
  preventing during user test, 246

304 Web Usability For Dummies

Building Web pages, 13, 15
Built-e.com, 187, 209
Business goals, 4, 50–51, 54, 133
  agreed-on, 51
  example of meeting by improving site,
    259–260
  Extron example, 142
  meeting expections, 51, 53, 55–56
  reducing costs, 56–57
  relating to navigation, 136
  setting, 61
  stabilizing, 149
  tracking online sales as, 187
  translating into Web site metrics, 62
  Web sites being required to meet, 134
Business needs, 265
Business roles, 50, 232, 233–234
Business to business sales, 31
Buying. *See* Shopping

• C •

Caching, 123
Calls to action, 201
Catalog look and feel, 139–140. *See also*
  Products, Shopping
Categories, 21
  on left navigation single-level sites, 125
Chinese on the Web, 32, 33
Chunking, 143
Clickable image maps, 113–114
  definition, 297
Clickable prototypes, 249–250
Clicking, 87, 93
  for larger image, 206
  from home page, 193
Clickthroughs, 133
  as usability testing, 255
  calculating, 256
  definition, 297
Client-side information maps, 230

Clubs
  Web site metrics, 66–67
Color
  accessibility standards regarding, 229
  for link colors, 88
  palette, 151
  standard in links, 88, 89, 90
  support goals, 35
  usability and, 151–152
Communities
  building Web-based, 60
  competitor site evaluation, 38
Comparable Web sites
  as design source, 102
  identifying for competitive testing, 251
Competitive site testing, 250–252
  identifying key needs, 252
Competitive sites, 55–56, 57, 102
  functionality, 37–38
  identifying for competitive testing, 251
  reviewing during development, 47
  reviewing during walk-through, 18,
    24, 27
  setting user expectations, 37–39
Competitors
  information on, 235
Completion rates
  increasing, 263
Computer Professional for Social
  Responsibility Web site, 173
Computers
  configurations for Web use, 214–215
Connection speeds, 215. *See also* Load
  time
Contact information, 58, 60
Content
  above the fold, 159, 160
  calls to action and, 201
  creating Web-specific, 199
  database-driven, 205
  depends on user understanding, 196

great content defined, 196
identifying as part of walk-through, 21, 26
images as, 205
keep easily updatable, 80
links in, 161
of section pages, 188
of task pages, 179
offensive, 228
pre-check definition, 19, 23
purpose, 201
tieing to sales, 196
Content pages
consideration when writing, 197–199
content sources, 202
creating usable, 201–207
creation priority, 172, 206
critical to site success, 195
destination page type, 257
e-mailing from, 208–210
extension, 206
images on, 203
page length and, 169–170, 198
products box, 207
programming, 200–201
related links box, 206–207
site highlights box, 207
templates, 201, 202
types, 20
writing considerations, 199
Copyrights, 77
Costs
of usability, 267
per sale, 135
reducing by increasing reusability, 80
reducing with Web sites, 50, 56–58, 135
Web sites as a basic business expense, 55
Co-workers
suggestions, 235
using for internal testing, 253

Credit cards
external processing services, 184
Customer-centered design, 173
Customer satisfaction, 60–61
Customer visits, 40–46
debriefing staff after, 45–46
definition, 297
goals for, 42
interview techniques for, 44
using mockups, 42
Customers, 252
Customizability, 83
CyberCash
for credit card processing, 184

• D •

DaimlerChrysler.com, 38
Database-driven content, 205
Dead-end pages, 92
Delivering Web pages, 13, 15
Dell Computers, 59
Demographics
of users, 30–33
Design, 13–15, 61
best practices, 82–83
bottom up, 95–99
contradictory advice for, 200
external searches discouraged, 91, 182
for intranets, 223
for low-resolution monitors, 216–218
fundamental design rules, 172
helping users in, 159
professionalism in, 61
receiving most attention, 14
recommended order, 172
stakeholder input to, 96–98
usability and, 150–101, 266, 268
WebTV and, 170
Design Management Institute, 295

306 Web Usability For Dummies

Designers
  usability professionals working with, 270–271
  usually working with powerful systems, 215–218
  working with, 172–173
Destination pages
  pageviews of, 257
Development cycle
  bug fixing in, 174
Development teams
  and customer visit programs, 40
  for left navigation, single-level sites, 125
  for single-page sites, 104–105
  observing user tests, 247
  working on alpha sites, 246
  working on live site tests, 248
Development testing, 46–47
Dialects and internationalization issues, 227
Disabled users
  and accessibility standards, 228–229
Display system design, 215–218
Downloading
  images, 205
  inform users when large, 157, 279
  metrics, 278
  print pages, 207
Downloading software
  task pages, 178
Dummies.com usability walk-through example, 22–26

• E •

Easy-to-learn vs. easy-to-use, 16
eBay
  partner with online stores, 184
Ego graphics, 38

E-mailing
  advertising, 64
  from content pages, 208–210
  Sun Microsystems example, 209
Employees. *See* Co-workers
English
  on the Web, 32, 33, 224–226
Errors, 65
Europe as growing online market, 32–33
Executives
  input into corporate sites, 235–236
  saving time of by user testing, 238
  usability professionals working with, 272
Expectations
  meeting, 53, 93
  meeting customer online sale, 58
  meeting minimal, 36
  of load time, 162, 163–165
  set by experiencing other media, 75
  usability set by home page, 192
Exiting Web sites, 84, 162
Extensibility
  of content pages, 206–207
  of graphical nav bars, 114, 116
  of left single-level navigation sites, 121, 123, 125
  of text navigation links, 112
Extranets, 223
  definition, 298
Extron Electronics Web site, 140–142

• F •

Favorite pages block, 261
Feedback
  co-workers', 235
  executives', 236
Financial information, 231
  investors and analysts interested in, 233
  providing context, 234
  site example, 233

Index **307**

Flexibility, 84
Flicker
  accessibility standards for, 234
Focus groups, 39, 40
  definition, 298
  user tests and, 240, 241
Ford.com, 38
Forms, 208
Frames, 120, 126–127
  accessibility standards and, 229
  definition, 298
Frequently Asked Questions, 50
  definition, 298
Functionality, 265. *See also* Task pages
  community, 60
  global, 188
  important versus unimportant
    problems in, 242
  increasing completion rate, 263
  pre-check definition, 19, 24
  problems detected through user
    tests, 240
  search, 77
  translation, 224

• G •

Generating traffic, 65
Gibson, James, 16
Global, 137
  definition, 298
Global nature of Web. *See*
  Internationalization
Goals, 13, 14, 49, 51. *See also* Business
    goals, Site goals, User goals
  consulting during user tests, 241
  core, 51
  for customer visits, 42
  for non-business sites, 66–67
  for single-page sites, 104–105

identifying, 21, 25, 26, 27
pre-check definition, 18, 23
re-engineering, 21
usability, 64–65
Godiva Chocolatiers Web site, 121, 122,
    176, 177
  Find Recipes section, 190
Google.com, 165
Graphics. *See also* Images
  ALT descriptive tags for, 230
  appropriateness, 55
  turning off, 229
  use sparingly, 279
Groups
  Web site metrics, 66–67

• H •

Hardware. *See also* Computers, Monitors
  alternate configurations, 214–215
  configuration goals, 34–35
  optimal for Web use, 214
Headers in content, 199
Heidegger, Martin, 16
High-weight images, 153
Highlighting
  key assets, 190
  page content, 159, 160
  site features, 207
Hits
  as site metric, 62
Hobbies, 38, 196
  Web site metrics, 67
Home pages, 37
  20% rule on, 87
  advertising and, 188
  are busy, 193
  competitor site evaluation, 38
  create appearance last, 172
  definition, 298
  design requirements unique, 171

308   Web Usability For Dummies

Home pages (continued)
linking to, 86, 91
links for investors on, 234
most custom page, 192
orients users to site, 192
pageviews of, 256
search capability on, 180
set usability expectations, 192
Horizontal space, 122
HTML
changed very fast, 149
clickable image maps in, 113
coder on a small team, 104–105
coding, 15
definition, 298
different browser support for, 219, 280
in step wizards, 141
left bar harder to code in, 123
link formatting, 117
overriding user preferences with, 111
pageviews and, 256
strip link codes, 109
titles, 76
Human-computer interaction, 293,
294, 295
Hype, 234
Hyperlinking, 83. See also Links
definition, 298

• I •

IBM, 59, 294
Icons
internationalization, 227
used in book, 7–8
Identity theft, 184
Images. See also Graphics
and usability, 151–154
as navigation links, 91

as content, 205
disadvantages as navigational links, 152
download time, 205
keeping small, 204
links to larger, 204
on content pages, 203
on navigation bars, 113–118
printability, 205
Incoming links, 261
Increasing revenue by on-site sales, 57
Indexes, 73
Site Search on Web sites, 77
Industry analyst
definitions, 299
needs, 53, 233–234
Information architecture, 93–95, 150
definitions, 299
Information assets, 81
competitor site evaluation, 38
highlighting, 190
in newspapers, 81
making easily available, 92
pre-check definition, 19, 23
walk-through identification, 21, 25
Information professionals. See also Press
needs, Reporters
as stakeholders, 52
site needs, 231–232
Information systems
books as, 72–78
newspapers as, 78–81
Web sites as, 83, 84
Installing software
task page, 178
Internationalization, 224–226
icons for, 227
testing, 227
usability and, 226–228
Interview techniques
for customer visits, 44

Index *309*

Intranets, 223
definitions, 299
Investors, 233. See *also* Industry analysts

• *J* •

Japanese on the Web, 32, 33
Javascript, 35, 115–116, 164, 280
accessibility problems and, 229
definitions, 299
major cause of usability problems, 219

• *L* •

Language groups, 32
Language support, 223–224, 32–33
Leads generated
as site metric, 63
steps required for, 64
Leaving site , 84, 162
Left navigation
definitions, 299
multi-level example, 139, 141
using frames with, 126
Left single-level navigation , 120–127
advantages, 121
extensibility, 121, 123, 125
minuses, 122–124
when to use, 125
Libraries and Web sites, 80
Links
adding to section front pages, 260
colors, 87, 88, 90, 299
contextually, 261
defective, 92
in content, 161
incoming, 261
internal, 106–107
left navigation supports, 121
offsite, 92, 199

to larger images, 204
to long documents, 199
to printable versions, 143
top navigation graphical, 113–118
top navigation text, 108–112
strips, 108, 109
using standard, 88
within-page, 92
weak, 122
Live sites, 247–248
Load time, 54, 65
definition, 300
expectations of, 162, 163–165
minimized by using single-level
navigation, 119
of left single-level pages, 123
of text navigation links, 108
of graphical navigation bars, 114
metrics, 278
never ignore, 278
optimizing by combining links and
bars, 117
page download, 35
testing, 165
Low-resolution systems, 215–218

• *M* •

Macintosh computers
Web access and, 214–215
Macromedia Director prototyping
tool, 292
Macromedia Flash, 220, 222
Mailing costs, 57
Management. *See* Executives
Market research, 39
Marketing, 41
challenges, 71
involving in competitive site
testing, 252

310 Web Usability For Dummies

Marketing *(continued)*
  site engineering, usability and, 266
  to support online sales, 187
  usability and, 268
  usability professionals working with, 269–271
  working with to set site goals, 64
Media Player, 220
Metrics, 62–64
  and goals, 132
  meaning, 134
  reporting, 64
  types, 62–63
Microsoft, 32, 294
Microsoft PowerPoint
  using to create clickable prototype, 250
Microsoft Internet Explorer, 34, 219
  definitions, 299
  incompatibility with Macintoshes, 215
  optimal version for Web use, 214
Monetizing site traffic, 62
Monterey Bay Aquarium site, 113
Mockups, 29, 40, 42. *See also* Prototypes
  as user tests, 241
  definition, 299
Monitors
  resolution, 35, 216
  low-resolution, 215–218
  readability, 155, 166
  resolution, 155
  small, 217–218
Multi-language support, 224
Multi-level sites
  navigation example, 137–139
Multimedia, 221–222
  accessibility challenges, 230
  implementation when necessary, 222
  offering optionally, 157
  on Web sites, 155–157
  tools and usability, 220
  use sparingly, 279

• N •

Narrowband, 35
Nav bars. *See* Top navigation bars
Navigation, 54, 101–127. *See also* Left navigation, Top navigation bars, Top navigation links
  accessibility standards and, 230
  advantages of common schemes, 120
  areas on pages, 87
  Bellingham example, 136–137
  by Back button, 92, 161
  by clicking, 87, 93
  challenges of, 84
  definitions, 299
  determining site requirements, 102
  for content pages, 202
  for task pages, 179
  home pages and, 191
  intersecting levels of, 85
  Job One on the Web, 84
  levels, 102
  of single-page sites, 106–107
  optimizing by combining links and bars, 117
  pageviews tracked to determine, 63
  section pages and, 188, 189–190
  within-level, 102
Navigation Do scorecard, 89, 90
Netscape Navigator, 71, 219
  definitions, 299
News, 88, 192
  Web site attention crucial, 255
Newsletters
  registration as task page, 178, 182
  subscribers, 107, 133, 184, 300
Newspapers
  sections in, 79–80
  similar to Web sites, 78–81
Nielsen, Jakob, 294
Non-business sites, 66–67

Index **311**

Non-English Web sites, 32–33
  multi-language content on, 224
Non-profits
  Web site metrics, 66
Norman, Donald, 296

• O •

Online population characteristics, 30
Online sales, 31, 57–58, 60, 179, 184–185
  competitor site evaluation, 38
  increasing by site reading and redesign,
    259–260
  making enticing, 263
  product boxes and, 207
  separating sales information and, 261
  task pages, 178, 184–188
  tracking business goals on, 187
  usability concerns and, 185
  Web as cool medium, 261

• P •

Page download. *See* Load time
Page length, 112, 164, 168–170
  and top navigation bars, 116
  in multi-level example, 141
  of section pages, 188
  content pages, 202
  task pages, 179
Page numbers
  impossible on Web sites, 78
  in books, 74, 75
Page weight
  definition, 300
Page width, 166–167
  content pages, 198, 202
  task pages, 179
Pages
  links to home page, 86
  must be searchable, 180

  navigation areas on, 87
  section, 175–176, 188, 189–190
  structure, 85
  task, 176–178
  templates. 172
  types, 175–176
Pageviews, 62, 132
  20% rule and, 87
  as site metric, 133, 204
  as site goals, 61
  definition, 300
  ensuring good, 262
  of home pages, 256
  of section pages, 256
  similar to newspaper pages, 78
  tracking to determine site
    navigation, 63
  size, 202
  using to determine site data, 256
Paging widgets, 198
Pareto's law, 80
PCs
  Optimal configurations for Web use,
    214–215
  Slower connections and, 215
.PDF files, 143, 197, 199
  use to preserve formatting, 278
Personal Web sites
  metrics for, 67
Personalizing Web sites
  Amazon.com as example, 60
Petroski, Henry, 296
Plug-ins
  must meet accessibility standards, 230
Polls. *See* Surveys
Pre-checks in usability walk-throughs,
    18–19
  of Dummies.com, 23–24
Press needs, 52, 53
Press releases, 232
Print widgets, 208

Printability, 163, 166
    of images, 205
    separate, downloadable pages, 207
Printing costs reduced, 57
Privacy, 30, 182, 186
    policies, 185
    services to ensure, 184
Product information on Web site
    reducing costs by supplying, 58
Products
    e-mailing descriptions from shopping
        site, 209
Products box, 207
Professionalism in design, 61
Project management
    and Web sites, 267
Proofreading, 199
Prototyping. *See also* Mockups
    clickable, 249–250
    definition, 300
    fat marker, 47, 249, 298
    fully interactive, 250
    rapid, 248
Public-facing sites, 223
Public relations, 232

Quality assurance, 184
QuickTime, 220
QuickTime VR, 221, 222

Random access, 83
Re-engineering page goals, 21
Readability, 154–156
Reading site data
    to analyze troublesome tasks, 262
    to maximize useful pageviews, 255–256

example of, 257
RealPlayer, 220
Reducing costs, 56
    by supplying product information, 58
    with online sales, 56–57
Registered users, 133
    as site metric, 63
Registration
    About.com example, 144
    as marketing metric, 132
    definition, 300
    example of good, 143–144
    for newsletters, 178
    limiting required information, 183
    pre-check definition, 19, 24
    privacy and, 193
    task pages, 178, 182–184
    testing, 184
    user benefits, 182
    walk-through identification, 21, 26
Related links box, 206–207
Releases
    and Usability Design Cycle, 174
Reporters, 232
Reports
    deliver final, 287
Redesign based on site data, 259–260
Research
    needed to use task pages, 177
Response time
    as a business goal, 61
Revenue generated
    as site metric, 63
Revenues, increasing, 58
Reverse engineering site goals, 21
Revision cycles
    limit size of, 279–280
Rokenbok Web site, 183
Rollover tabs, 115

Index 313

• S •

Sales. *See also* Online sales
  business to business, 31
  costs, 135
  customer satisfaction and, 60
  tieing to site content, 196
  to existing customers, 60
  working with to set site goals, 64
Sales channels
  comparing to online sales, 185–186
  task page, 178
  traditional, 59
  Web sites as low-cost, 50
Savings achieved
  as site metric, 63
Scannability, 81
Scanning Web sites
  user practices, 158–159
Schedules
  for single-page sites, 105
Schools
  Web sites metrics, 66
Scenarios
  developing for user testing, 241
Science of Web design, 11, 12
Scoring user tests, 244
Screen display targets, 35
Scrolling, 112, 120
  horizontally, 166
  in frames, 126
  on single-page sites, 106
Searchenginewatch.com, 180
Search engines, 104
Search capability, 88, 161
external Web searches, 91, 182
  on home page, 180
  user payoff, 160
Section 508 guidelines, 228

Section pages
  adding links from, 260
  advertising and, 188
  consistency critical in, 85
  content, 188
  complexity, 189
  design order, 172
  front pages, 176
  in newspapers, 79
  in Web sites, 80, 85
  look and feel of, 80
  page length, 188
  page templates, 188
  pageviews of, 256
Senior management. *See* Executives
Shopping. *See also* Online sales
  Amazon.com example
  design concerns, 185
  e-mailing product descriptions
    from, 209
  external services for, 184
  Extron example, 140–142
  Godiva example, 176, 177
  implementation planning services, 186
  pre-check definition, 19, 24
  walk-through identification, 21, 25
  Williams Sonoma example, 139–140
Shortcuts, 89
  in multi-level example, 141
  for power users, 231
Silicon Valley Confection Company Web
    site, 53–55
Simple sites, 53
  top navigation bars and, 116
Single-level sites, 108
  case for using, 119
  extensibility of left navigation, 121
  left navigation, 120–127
Single-page sites, 103, 104–107
  goals for, 104–105
  navigation, 106–107

Site engineering
  marketing, usability and, 266
  usability and, 268
  usability professionals working with, 269–270
Site goals
  achieving using navigation, 129–130, 132
  relating to navigation, 136
  must be written, agreed-on, and prioritized, 275–276
  setting, 61
  Williams Sonoma example, 142
Site logs, 245
Site maps, 77
  definition, 301
Site navigation. See Navigation
Site personalization
  task page, 178
Site Search functions, 77, 88, 161, 162
  acquiring externally, 180
  task pages, 178, 180–182
  testing, 180–181
  using feedback from, 181
Site speed. See Load time
Site traffic. See Traffic
SonoSite Web site, 233, 234
Spam concerns, 182
Spanish on the Web, 32, 33
Splash page, 190
Stakeholders, 52, 102
  definition, 301
  site content and, 96–98
Statistical significance
  of user tests, 245
Statistical validity
  of user tests, 238
Step wizard, 141
  definition, 301
Strips of links, 108, 109, 114
Structure. See also Sections
  conveying information, 82–83
  of books, 73–74
  of newspapers, 79–81
  of Web sites, 83–84
  page, 85
Suggestions from co-workers, 235
Style sheets, 280. See also Templates
  accessibility and, 229
Styles
  defining as part of a pre-check, 18, 23
  walk-through identification, 21, 25
Sun Microsystems, 294
  e-mail support, 209
  home page, 193
  multi-language support on, 224
  Web site, 181
Support costs reduced, 57
Survey research, 40
Surveys
  value in usability testing, 264

Tabs
  using to expand top nav bar, 117–118
Tables
  accessibility standards and, 229
Tables of contents
  as book organization tools, 73
  site maps as, 77
Targeted sites, 103
Task completion, 85, 162
  and Web users, 71
  as a business goal, 61, 65
  as marketing metric, 133
  encourages site reuse, 160
  evaluated in user tests, 241
  reading an article, 143
Task pages
  complete first, 172
  creating usable, 176–178
  drop-off, 263
  increasing completion rates, 263

pageviews of, 257
purpose, 178
reading site data to find problem, 262
worthy of research, 177
Technical support costs
and Web sites, 50, 57, 135
Technology used on sites, 211
Telephone costs reduced, 57
Templates, 172
for content pages, 202
for task page navigation, 179
Test scenarios developed for user
tests, 241
Testers
recruiting, 284
Testing. *See also* Usability testing, User
tests
critical to usability, 237
in development, 46–47
international site versions, 227
load time, 165
registration, 184, 243
Web pages, 13, 15
Testing consultants, 250
Testing room, 290
setting up, 286
Text
ALT descriptive tags providing
multimedia alternatives in, 229, 230
chunking, 143
links, 108–112
links and simplicity, 112
links and specificity, 92
loading first to increase speed, 54
multi-level example, 139
readability, 154–156
3D formats, 221
Titles
accessibility standards and, 229
as informational element, 73
definition, 301
on Web sites, 76

Thumbnails, 204
Top navigation bars, 113–118
advantages, 114
blending with links, 117
defined, 113
expanding using tabs, 117–118
expansion, 117–118
in multi-level example, 139–140, 142
minuses, 114–115
using frames with, 126
when to use, 116
Top navigation links, 108–112
advantages, 108–109
blending with bars, 117
defined, 108
expansion, 112
minuses, 110–111
on Bellingham multi-level, 137
user preferences affect, 110
using frames with, 126
when to use, 111
Trackability of advertising, 83
Trade paperbacks, 73, 74
Traffic, 65
do not balance site, 260
example of analyzing, 259
example of increasing, 260–261
monetizing, 62
Translated versions of sites, 224, 227
TRUSTe, 185
216-color palette, 157, 297
definition, 297

• U •

Under Construction announcements, 105
definition, 300
Unique visitors, 63, 133
as site goal, 61
United States
online population characteristics, 30

316 Web Usability For Dummies

Universities
  Web site metrics, 66
Unix workstations and Web access, 214
Uptime, 65
  definition, 301
Usability
  as good introduction to design, 3
  as process, 12
  as state of mind, 15
  challenge of on the Web, 16
  color and, 151
  customer satisfaction and, 60
  definition, 11
  expectations, 192
  goals, 64–65
  graphics and, 151–154
  history, 4, 16
  increasing revenues and, 57–59
  internationalization and, 226–228
  lack of perceived value. 267
  layout attractiveness and, 211
  multimedia and 156–157, 221–222
  multimedia tools and, 220
  online sales and, 185
  technology and, 211
  underemphasized until now, 14
  working with marketing and site
    engineering, 266
Usability Design Cycle, 3, 6, 12–15,
    173, 276
  provides design top-down
    framework, 17
  looping through, 174, 175
  steps in, 175
Usability engineering, 294
Usability professionals, 293–296
  credentialing, 268–269
  definition, 301
  education 293, 294–295
  emerging discipline, 265
  work experience, 294

Usability study
  clean up, 286
  deciding what to test, 283
  deliver reports, 287
  including team members, 285
  perform tests, 286
  prepare users, 285
  recruiting testers, 284
  request final thoughts, 286
  setting up testing room, 284
  write up results, 287
Usability testing, 237
  adapting existing tools for, 253
  analyzing click-through patterns, 255
  decreases negative feedback 238
  informal, 254, 255
  performing, 239
  saving time and money using, 238
  scheduling, 253
  statistical methods, 238
  surveys, 238, 264
  targeting informal, 254
Usability tools
  database program, 292
  graphics editing tool, 291
  laptop computer, 290
  listening, 289
  markers, 291
  prototyping tool, 292
  testing room, 290
  walkie-talkies, 292
  writing skills, 290
  video camera, 255, 291
Usability walk-throughs, 17, 19
  check-list for, 22
  checklist for pre-check, 20
  definition, 301
  example using Dummies.com, 22–26
  for own Web site, 27
  planning reasonable expectations
    before, 18

pre-check of Dummies.com, 23–24
pre-checks, 18–19
steps in, 20–21
User goals, 130–131
Bellingham example, 142
relating to navigation, 136
Useit.com, 294
User needs, 36, 50, 53
site requirements, 265
User preferences
can interfere with designer wishes, 110
User tests, 1, 2, 11, 14, 47, 237
benchmarking, 276
building scenarios for, 242
developers observing pre-release
tests, 247
focus groups and, 241
involving task completion, 241
justifying, 41
methodology, 244
never skip, 280–281
not statistically valid, 238
performing to define task problem, 262
pre-release, 246–247
precision possible, 16
problem solving by, 240
scoring, 244
Users
alleviating anxiety of, 178
constantly recheck with, 276
demographics, 30–33
design and, 175
disabled, 228–229
employees, 235
emulating during development, 46–47
engineers uncomfortable with, 270
executives, 235–236
gathering content input in, 99
high connectivity business, 215
investors, 233–234
non-American, 224–225
oriented by home page, 191, 192

power, 230–231
pre-check definition, 18, 23, 27
preparing, 285
repeat, 196
reporters, 231–232
require clear registration benefits, 182
studying, 13, 14
target, 18, 32–33, 34, 35
task completion and, 71
understanding key to design, 102
U.S. demographics, 30
visitors, 63, 301

• *V* •

Value
usability has little perceived, 267
Velosel Corporation, 85–86
Verisign.com, 184
Video
clips, 221
quality, 157
Video camera,
as usability tool, 255, 291

• *W* •

Walk-throughs. *See* Usability walk-
throughs
Wayfinding, 72
Web design. *See* Design
Web Design For Dummies, 4, 61, 107, 116,
151, 202, 217
Web navigation. *See* Navigation
Web pages. *See* Pages
Web-safe color palette, 151, 217
Web site metrics. *See* Metrics
Web sites. *See also* Alpha sites, Beta
sites, Single-page sites, Single level
sites, Multi-level sites
advantages, 83–84
bookmarks in, 75

Web sites *(continued)*
  bug fixing for, 174
  business role of, 50
  compared to books, 72–78
  compared to newspapers, 78–81
  creating one or many, 103
  definition, 301
  external searches on, 91, 182
  identifying individual pages in, 78
  live sites, 247
  making easily maintainable, 80
  minuses, 84
  multi-language, 224, 225
  multimedia tools, 219
  navigation levels, 65
  navigation models, 101
  non-business, 66–67
  personalized, 60
  pre-release, 246–247
  public-facing, 223
  role in business, 50
  scannability, 81
  selling-only, 261
  similar to newspapers, 78–81
  single-page sites, 104
  translated versions, 224, 227
  treat as real project, 277
  under construction, 105
  visit lengths, 87
  What's New areas, 88
Web search options, 91

Webtrends.com, 132
WebTV, 170
Where to buy links, 38, 59
What's New areas, 88
Wide Area Protocol, 34
Widgets
  definition, 302
  e-mail, 208–210
  paging, 198
  print, 207
Williams-Sonoma Web site, 139–140, 142
Within-level navigation, 102
Workstations and Web access, 214
Writing for the Web, 277–278

Xerox PARC, 72

Yahoo!, 32, 108, 109, 112
  partnering in online stores, 184

Zanzara.com, 8
  helping users on, 160
  old version of, 257–258
Zimiez.com, 196